KT-368-490

Understanding Social Science

A Philosophical Introduction to the Social Sciences

SECOND EDITION

Roger Trigg

BLACKWELL
Publishers

Copyright © Roger Trigg 1985, 2001

The right of Roger Trigg to be identified as author of this work has been asserted in accordance with the Copyright, Designs and Patents Act 1988.

First published 1985
Reprinted 1987, 1989, 1991, 1992, 1993, 1994, 1997 (twice), 1999

Second edition published 2001

2 4 6 8 10 9 7 5 3 1

Blackwell Publishers Ltd
108 Cowley Road
Oxford OX4 1JF
UK

Blackwell Publishers Inc.
350 Main Street
Malden, Massachusetts 02148
USA

All rights reserved. Except for the quotation of short passages for the purposes of criticism and review, no part of this publication may be reproduced, stored in a retrieval system, or transmitted, in any form or by any means, electronic, mechanical, photocopying, recording, or otherwise, without the prior permission of the publisher.

Except in the United States of America, this book is sold subject to the condition that it shall not, by way of trade or otherwise, be lent, resold, hired out, or otherwise circulated without the publisher's prior consent in any form of binding or cover other than that in which it is published and without a similar condition including this condition being imposed on the subsequent purchaser.

British Library Cataloguing in Publication Data
A CIP catalogue record for this book is available from the British Library.

Library of Congress Cataloging-in-Publication Data

Trigg, Roger.
    Understanding social science : a philosophical introduction to the social
    sciences / Roger Trigg—2nd ed.
        p. cm.
    Includes bibliographical references and index.
    ISBN 0–631–21871–8 (hc : alk. paper—ISBN 0–631–21872–6 (pbk. : alk.
    paper)
        1. Social sciences—Philosophy. I. Title.

    H61.T72 2000
    300′.1—dc21

                                                                00–025857

Typeset in 11 on 13pt Bembo
by Kolam Information Services Private Ltd., Pondicherry, India
Printed in Great Britain by TJ International Ltd, Padstow, Cornwall
This book is printed on acid-free paper.

024031

WEST SUFFOLK HOSPITALS
CLINICAL RESOURCE CENTRE
AND LIBRARY

DATE 28.2.02

VENDOR Tomlinson

CLASSMARK HM

PRICE £15.99

Contents

Preface to the Second Edition   viii
Acknowledgement   x

1 The Nature of Science
   Empiricism   1
   The Role of Theories   7
   The Views of Kuhn and Feyerabend   13

2 Objectivity and the Sociology of Knowledge
   The Social Character of Knowledge   23
   Wittgenstein and Rules   26
   The Sociology of Knowledge   30
   Objectivity and Reflexivity   33
   Truth and False Consciousness   38

3 Individuals and Society
   Consciousness and Behaviour   44
   The Goal of Social Science   48
   Social Reality and the Individual   52
   Constraints on Subjectivity   57

4 Understanding Other Societies
   Humans as Social Beings   64
   Public Practice and Private Understanding   69
   Understanding Alien Practices   75
   The Basis of Understanding Other Societies   80
   Samoa: An Example   83

5 Rationality
   Scientific Rationality and Ethnomethodology   89

Rationality as a Social Practice 93
'Expressive' and 'Symbolic' Practices 98
Belief and Rationality 102
The Explanation of Ritual 105

6 Facts and Values
'Value-free' Science 112
Scientific Values 115
Objectivity in Social Science 119
The Values of Social Science 123
Ideology 126

7 Economics and Society
Rationality and Desires 132
Economics and Egoism 136
Private Interest and Public Goods 142
Individualism 147
Rationality and Revolution 150

8 Culture: Function and Adaptation
Social Function 155
The Role of Consciousness 160
Biology and Social Science 163
Human Sociobiology 166
Biology and Altruism 170

9 Sociobiology and Determinism
The 'Leash' Principle 176
Opposition to Sociobiology 179
Determinism 183
Sociobiology and Freedom 187
Human Freedom 190

10 Markets and Social Institutions
Individuals and the Market 198
Religion and Rational Choice 201
The Social Context 205
The Nature of Social Institutions 208

11 Tradition and Reason
Tradition 216
Hermeneutics 219
The Reaction against the Enlightenment 221
A Middle Way? 227

Group Selection 230

12 The Philosophical Basis of Social Science
Critical Realism 235
Reason and Realism 240
Neo-positivism 243
Postmodernism 246
Conclusion 249

Glossary 254
Bibliography 261
Index 266

Preface to the Second Edition

In the fifteen years since this book was first published, the world has changed in significant ways. Social science has also developed, together with reflections on its nature, and it seemed appropriate for a new edition to take account of this. In order not to create confusion, I have left the first nine chapters untouched. I have, however, replaced the final chapter with three new chapters, retaining only some remarks about Gadamer and Foucault, who continue to be discussed. In particular, I have wished to take account of two contrasting modes of thought in contemporary philosophy of social science. They are critical realism, and the whole movement symbolised by the term 'postmodernism'. The former stresses the place of social science as a rational activity, reflecting on the nature of social reality. The latter attacks the whole idea of rationality, which we have inherited from the Enlightenment. It stresses the way we are each embedded in a historical situation. As a consequence, the role of social science becomes obscure, if not impossible.

Underlying all these controversies is the continuing debate about the relationship of individual and society. This has been affected by, and itself influences, changes in the political scene. Some of these have been profound, especially the cataclysmic changes in Eastern and Central Europe since 1989. As a result, debates about the role of markets, and the balance between individual and community, have become even more urgent. Many feel that Marxism as a philosophy has itself been discredited although some of its modes of explanation live on in other forms. It is clearer than ever that political arrangements themselves inevitably depend on philosophical assumptions about the role of society, and the place of the individual in it. The only question is how far these assumptions are made explicit. It is the task of the philosophy of social science to encourage this process.

I am grateful to many with whom I have discussed the topics of this book. In particular, however, I must mention the participants in the graduate seminar in Philosophy and Social Theory, which I have conducted, jointly with a colleague from the Department of Sociology, for over ten years at the University of Warwick. In particular, I must thank Professor Margaret Archer with whom I shared the seminar for many years. I am also grateful to Professor James Beckford for his more recent contribution. I have learnt a great deal from both, and much enjoyed the stimulating discussions in the seminar year by year.

As always, I owe more than I can say to my wife, Julia, and my daughter, Alison, for their unfailing help and encouragement.

Stratford-upon-Avon
May, 2000

Acknowledgement

The writing of this book was aided by a research grant from the British Academy. I am most grateful for this support.

Some of the material on sociobiology in chapters 8 and 9 is derived from two lectures given in 1983. I spoke on 'The social sciences and biology' at the 7th International Congress of Logic, Methodology and Philosophy of Science in Salzburg, Austria. I also lectured on 'Human sociobiology' to the Annual Meeting of the British Association for the Advancement of Science at the University of Sussex.

1

The Nature of Science

Empiricism

What is social science? This is a characteristically philosophical question, examining the assumptions and presuppositions of an area of human activity. It seems easy to give a list of would-be social sciences. Sociology and social anthropology would inevitably be on it, as would such subjects as politics and economics. History has a claim to be there too, although it is often not thought of as a social science. It certainly studies the interactions of humans in society. The main difference between it and the others is that it confines itself to the past. Psychology, even social psychology, should probably not be there as it concentrates on the individual rather than on his or her place in the wider group.

It is already obvious that the notion of social science is not as clear-cut as might be first imagined. Most people would accept psychology as a science, but would wonder about its qualifications as a *social* one. History deals with societies, as well as individuals, but perhaps it is often more like literature, and ought not to be classified as a science. Its imaginative reconstruction of individuals' motives may sometimes appear more like writing a novel than like the repeated experiments of a chemist in a laboratory.

All this assumes that 'social' qualifies 'science' in the same way that 'physical' or 'natural' do. A contrast is often drawn between physical and social sciences which takes it for granted that both sets of disciplines are sciences. Physicists study the natural world while sociologists study the social world. It would follow that social sciences are not different kinds of sciences from the physical ones. The same scientific method is being used in a different area. This could not be the case for, say, theology, if that were classified as a science. It has sometimes been described as one and has on occasions even claimed to be 'the queen of the sciences'. Yet no one has ever suggested that it proceeds in the way that a physicist does. It may attempt to study the nature of God in a systematic way, but it is not an empirical science. Much of its function lies in studying what, if anything, transcends human experience.

Social sciences claim to be empirical. The enormous success of modern physical science in manipulating the world has made it appear that its methods provide the key for the extension of human knowledge in all areas. Any intellectual discipline is thus put under immense pressure to appear 'scientific' in precisely the manner in which physics is; otherwise it may be deemed not to produce any contributions to genuine knowledge.

The question whether the social sciences are 'proper' sciences is not a terminological quibble. Given that modern governments provide money for scientific research, there is a political question whether social scientists should be treated on a par with physicists and engineers. Some social scientists are very eager to show scientific credentials, while governments intent on controlling public expenditure will query how far social science is 'real' science. In 1983 the Social Science Research Council in the United Kingdom decided to change its name to the Economic and Social Research Council. This was apparently after pressure from government ministers, and they were presumably not interested merely in the philosophical issues involved. The public view of the social 'sciences' will determine decisions about public spending.

Nevertheless the pressure to make all disciplines conform to the one model begins to lessen as cynicism increases about the ability of science to further human welfare. The bright hopes for human progress which were once pinned on science already seem childishly optimistic. It is now easier to re-examine the presuppositions of a scientific world-view. All science may not be like physics, and physics itself may not provide a very good example of an empirical science, at least as understood by empiricism. Empiricism in fact has been put on trial and in many philosophers' opinion has to be discarded.

There has already been considerable disagreement over whether the social sciences should follow the methods of the natural sciences and share their assumptions. Are they to uncover the laws governing human behaviour and explain its causes? This is to assume that the social world is indistinguishable from the natural world in important respects and may even be reducible to it. Many philosophers, particularly if they have been influenced by the European hermeneutical tradition, point out that the social world is constituted by the meanings and purposes of rational agents. The function of a social science is then to interpret and render intelligible rather than to invoke causes. People are different from physical objects and must be understood differently. This approach has been dubbed 'humanist', as opposed to the 'naturalist' approach of those taking natural science as a model. It has been alleged that each side focuses on part of the truth. For instance two writers about the social sciences say:

> These sciences are *social*, which is to say that the phenomena they study are intentional phenomena, and so must be identified in terms of their meanings. Secondly, these sciences are *sciences*, in the sense that they try to develop systematic theories to explain the underlying causal interactions among phenomena of a widely divergent sort. Because they each fasten on only one of these features, humanism and naturalism fail to provide an adequate account of social science.[1]

Naturalism, in various guises, has had the most influence on the social sciences. Its assumptions may be increasingly questioned, but any survey of the social sciences must start with them. The scientific character of the social sciences is emphasized, and anything that cannot be subsumed under scientific laws is excluded. This can be part of an empiricist outlook, according to which human experience provides the standard by which anything can be tested. What is beyond experience is discarded. Perhaps the most notable group of philosophers expressing this position in this century was the Vienna Circle. Meeting in Vienna in the 1920s and the 1930s, they championed what they termed the 'scientific world-conception'. They claimed this was empiricist and positivist and explained these terms in a pamphlet by claiming: 'There is knowledge only from experience, which rests on what is immediately given. This sets the limits for the content of legitimate science.' They were empiricists because they rested knowledge on human experience, and positivists because they considered that scientific method was the only path to truth. They continued:

> The aim of scientific effort is to reach the goal, unified science, by applying logical analysis to the empirical material. Since the meaning of

every statement of science must be statable by reduction to a statement about the given, likewise the meaning of any concept, whatever branch of science it may belong to, must be statable by step-wise reduction to other concepts, down to the concepts of the lowest level which refer directly to the given.[2]

The Vienna Circle explicitly dealt with the social sciences as branches of science and mentioned history and economics as examples.[3] They had a view of the unity of science, according to which all sciences fitted harmoniously together, and in which the social sciences were included. Science rested on the firm foundation of what was given in experience. 'Sense-data' is a term often used in this connection. Such data were supposed to be intersubjective, in that different people could grasp the same ones. This meant that science could apparently appeal to a fixed standard, and could repeat experiments to obtain the data according to which theories could be assessed. The data were independent of particular theories, since they were 'raw', in the sense that they contained no element of interpretation. Any theory had to fit them to be empirically adequate, and the meaning of observation terms was the same, whatever theory was adopted.

The details of this approach have been modified, but the shadow of the Vienna Circle still falls over the philosophy of science, even when philosophers are reacting against their views. The emphasis is often still on the empirical content of a theory. An empiricist will make no distinction between the empirical information it gives and its ability to explain. The description and prediction of observable facts becomes the aim of science. *Why* observed regularities should be as they are is not thought to be the most fundamental question. The reality of theoretical entities, unobservable but posited by the demands of theory, becomes a problem for the empiricist. A consistent empiricism must maintain that they are not really there but are a convenient fiction which helps in the prediction of what is observable. This problem becomes particularly acute when electrons and other sub-atomic particles are being dealt with. What is quantum mechanics about, if there can in principle be no unobservable entities? An empiricist can only conclude that it is attempting to describe and predict observations and measurements made on sub-atomic systems, rather than refer to any intrinsic properties of the systems. There can be no intrinsic properties beyond the scope of measurement, since what cannot be observed cannot be there. As a result the emphasis must move from the nature of reality to questions about scientists and their operations.[4] Sub-atomic particles can be talked of only in the terms of classical mechanics, and that means that the entity measured cannot in principle be separated from the act of measurement. The observation made provides the foundation for the theory, even though that involves a necessary reference to a human observer. What started by being a description of the basic constituents of matter apparently ends by being about an episode of human observation.

Its emphasis on experience lays empiricism open to the charge of being anthropocentric. It switches attention from what is or can be experienced to the mere fact of experience itself. By definition, what lies beyond human experience can be conveniently dismissed. The consistent empiricist cannot talk of the other side of the universe, the interior of a black hole, the position *and* the momentum of an electron, or a myriad other possible states of affairs which science may need to envisage. It is hardly surprising that realists who insist that what exists does so independently of human conceptions see idealist echoes in empiricism. Idealists make existence depend logically on its being perceived by a mind, usually a human one. Although empiricists may say that *what* is experienced does not depend on being experienced for its reality, they still limit reality to what can be experienced. Unobservable entities are thus contradictions in terms. This radically changes the character of scientific explanation. Theoretical entities cannot explain what we perceive. Perceptions themselves become the bedrock on which theory rests. Actual and possible observations become ends in themselves. Science may predict them but is left with no resources with which to explain them. Nothing else of a more fundamental nature can be invoked.

Many may object to a picture of the world in which reality is made to depend logically on the possibility of human observation. Another major criticism of empiricism has concentrated on the fact of observation. 'Raw' sense-data have been seen as the brute facts on which our knowledge of the world rested. For this reason empiricist epistemology is often termed a 'foundationalist' one. Such an epistemology is only as reliable as its foundations. Although much effort was expended by empiricists in showing how sense-data were experiences stripped of all interpretation, such as simple colour patches, there has been increasing scepticism about this. The view implied that the mind was a passive receptacle for experience, rather than an active searcher. Yet expectation can govern what we see. So far from experience governing how we interpret it, our interpretation can affect what we experience. If we are waiting for a red bus, the fluttering of reddish leaves can be mistaken for the approach of the bus. When we recognize the leaves for what they are, we may even find that we see the colour differently. The leaves may look more orange than before.

One of the most influential philosophers of this century, Ludwig Wittgenstein, was much exercised by questions about this kind of change of aspect.[5] One of the most famous examples is the 'duck-rabbit', the drawing that can be seen as a duck or a rabbit. One can see the beak of a duck, but one can also interpret the same lines as the ears of a rabbit. Wittgenstein could not finally decide whether the visual impression altered along with our interpretation.[6] Yet the very fact the question could intelligibly be raised spelt the end of the sense-data theory. Passive experience, according to that, would always be the grounding for the mind's interpretation, so that the latter could not alter the former. Any theory about the empirical foundations of knowledge was in jeopardy once it was accepted that what we thought we were seeing could influence what we saw. 'Sense-data' were supposed to be given to us and not created or altered by us. Our knowledge of them was supposed to be infallible, with any errors coming in our interpretation. Once it was accepted that our interpretation could govern the nature of the data, however, any error in interpretation was seen to be liable to infect the data. The 'rock-solid' foundations of empirical knowledge are revealed as being in as much a quagmire as other parts of human reasoning.

One major tenet of empiricist thought was the total separation of fact from value. Sense-data are what they are, and facts are just what we know is the case as a result of them. Human evaluation is a totally distinct matter. The empiricist philosopher, David Hume, had, in the eighteenth century, sternly forbade sliding from assertions about what *is* the case to some about what *ought* to be so.[7] Descriptions and evaluations are still distinguished, as for instance in the moral philosophy of the Oxford philosopher, R. M. Hare. The result is that a privileged status is accorded to facts, which are thought, in a typically empiricist manner, to be true or false in a way that evaluations cannot be. It has become something of a challenge to empiricists to rescue evaluations from the charge of arbitrariness, and to demonstrate how there can still be rational constraints on what we may value. Having suggested that values cannot be empirically verified in the way that facts can be, they are faced with the possibility that humans can logically value anything, without the possibility of error.

The importance of the idea of a 'value-free' science for the social sciences is clear. Social scientists want to be seen to establish 'facts' about society in the same way that they think that a physicist or a chemist uncovers 'facts'. They do not want to appear to be in the grip of an ideology or particular view of the world, which would make their results suspect to those who do not share it. The idea, for example, of a 'conservative' or 'liberal' social science seems to undermine the notion of a social science. Yet it is perhaps significant that Marxists find nothing surprising about the notion of Marxist social science. Most Marxists do not share the philosophical presuppositions of empiricists about the distinction between facts and values. This is a problem of major importance to which I shall return. For the moment, it is merely relevant to stress that any distinction between 'facts' and 'values' rests on empiricist assumptions, giving a privileged status to the idea of a scientifically verifiable fact.

The Role of Theories

Empiricism laid great emphasis on the possibility of testing through experience, and this constituted its conception of objectivity. Carl Hempel, the American philosopher of science, says of science that 'it is concerned to develop a conception of the world that has a clear logical bearing on our experience and is thus capable of objective test'.[8] We have already seen that this approach depends on a notion of 'neutral' experience, which does not already presuppose the holding of a particular theory. Hempel developed a notion of scientific explanation which involves fitting an isolated phenomenon into an overall pattern. Scientific laws are then to be understood as mere observable regularities under which we can subsume whatever we wish to explain. This view is derived from Hume's analysis of causation as constant conjunction. Perceived regularities thus form the basis of our idea of cause, and explanation involves fitting our experiences into a pattern of such regularities. Hempel says: 'The explanation fits the phenomenon to be explained into a pattern of uniformities and shows that its occurrence was to be expected, given the specified laws and the pertinent particular circumstances.'[9]

Hempel proposes as a model what he terms 'deductive-nomological' explanation. This takes the form of a deductive argument, whose premisses include general laws as well as statements about particular observations. One example of a deductively valid inference which he gives is the following:

> Any sodium salt, when put into the flame of a Bunsen burner, turns the flame yellow.
>   This piece of rock salt is a sodium salt.
>   Therefore, this piece of rock salt, when put into the flame of a Bunsen burner, will turn the flame yellow.[10]

One acknowledged difficulty of this form of explanation is that not all generalizations can have the status of general causal laws. It may well be true that the barometer falls when it gets windier, but it would not be right to say that the wind makes the barometer fall. The wind and the fall of the barometer each have the same underlying cause. In other cases there is no genuine connection at all. The sounding of a factory hooter in one city has no effect on workers in a factory a hundred miles away, even if the latter always stop work when the former sounds. The importation of counterfactuals (concerning what would happen if certain facts were different) can help to distinguish between accidental generalizations and causal laws. The issue is then whether the same apparent connection continues if one of the factories changes its hours of work.

Sometimes it is far from clear whether something is a coincidence or whether there is a causal connection. It used to be a joke in one English city afflicted with particularly bad traffic congestion that there was always a policeman on point duty in the middle of the worst traffic jams. It was a joke because everyone assumed that the situation would be worse if the police were not there. Yet, when they were withdrawn as an experiment, the traffic flowed more freely and there was less congestion. There proved to be a causal link in what appeared to be a mere empirical regularity.

Fitting particular instances into a network of regularities which are established empirically conforms to some ideal of explanation. Yet problems remain. The difficulty of sifting out 'real' empirical regularities from the coincidences arises only because empiricists wish to stop at the level of observation. Their ideal of explanation is the association of different experiences on different occasions. Yet *why* should these be associated? Even the appeal to counterfactuals so as to discover genuine causal connections merely pushes the question back a stage. What makes a connection a genuine causal one? Many philosophers still follow the eighteenth-century philosopher, Hume, in wishing to deny the existence of hidden powers and necessary connections. It is impossible to *experience* the way two events are causally related. One can merely observe that one typically follows the other. Anything more requires a theory which may need to posit unobservable entities as the source of the relevant causal power. That seems irredeemably metaphysical, and therefore bad to genuine empiricists. They would not see the point of postulating mysterious causes behind observable effects but would be content to be successful in predicting observations. Yet this is done at a cost. Explanation becomes merely a summary of actual and possible observations, and the reason why events are linked as they are can never be given.

Another source of worry for empiricism is shown in the example given by Hempel of a deductive inference. How can one observe that 'this piece of rock salt is a sodium salt'? We are already a long way from the level of simple sense-data. If the simplest colour patches cannot be disentangled from interpretation, the making of complicated observations in a scientific laboratory is certainly going to be 'theory-laden'. The recognition of a substance as 'rock salt', let alone its classification as a 'sodium salt', is in no sense a 'raw' experience, uncomplicated by interpretation. A trained chemist may well see at a glance what the substance is, but it is naïve to imagine that a schoolboy could immediately see a substance as 'rock salt' without being told. Reference to a 'sodium salt' goes further and presupposes a scientific theory.

Classification is the outcome of theory, even at fairly simple levels. It is not a question of neutral observations forming the basis for theory. The observations we make, the way we classify them, and even what counts as a relevant observation, may be governed by the theory we hold. Once this was understood, the emphasis inevitably swung away from sense-data to the role of theory or, more generally, of our conceptual scheme in making sense of the world around us. Of course, much depends on what is meant by 'theory', and it may be that, within our overall scheme, different theories will still compete with each other. Nevertheless, a theory seen as a whole claims priority, instead of each level in it being ultimately reducible to statements about what the Vienna Circle saw as the given. This means that at every level, whether at that of the observation of colour or of the study of complex social phenomena, the 'facts' become secondary. They cannot be read off without a theory to guide classification and selection.

One writer on Marxism says, in a manner reminiscent of those attacking sense-data:

> There are no 'brute' facts, descriptions which describe facts but independ-
> ently of any interest in terms of which they are relevant. . . . The objects of
> knowledge are objects only in relation to some knowledge-generating
> inquiry. For 'objects', being 'facts *for*' some inquiry, are classes of events or
> states of affairs *under some description*, the descriptions in question being
> determined by the controlling interest of the inquiry.[11]

He mentions for illustration that there are many possible descriptions of the kind of society which Marx classified as capitalist:

> Any society which is capitalist is also, necessarily, an 'industrial' society,
> and any modern industrial society which is capitalist is modelled, at any
> rate fundamentally, on market relations, and so can be called a 'market'
> society. Most market societies are politically 'liberal-democratic'.[12]

It appears that, instead of facts being discovered in the world, our descriptions are governed as much by our interests and purposes as by what is there. Human knowledge is then not just the passive reflection of reality but is itself partly constituted by human interests. This move in the social sciences was inevitable once the physical sciences were partially detached from empirical phenomena. Contemporary philosophers of science have themselves emphasized the crucial role of theories more and more, dismissing the notion that experience can be neutral. It seems that everything is 'theory-laden'. Even the contemporary American philosopher, W. V. Quine, who attended meetings of the Vienna Circle, and still stresses the importance of sensory stimuli as a starting-point for theory, shows how our most ordinary experiences already include an element of interpretation. To take one of his most famous examples, a linguist in a foreign country confronted by a native saying 'Gavagai' when a rabbit scurried by would have difficulties translating this unknown word.[13] Quine would assume that the native and the linguist had the same 'ocular irradiations', but these are physical states, far removed from sense-data, which were supposed to be mental ones. On this sensory base, Quine thinks, we have to build our theories, but there can be no guarantee that the native and the linguist possess exactly the same theory. When we see a rabbit, the native may see 'rabbit stages' or 'rabbit parts'. Quine insists that there will always be a certain indeterminacy of translation, even given the same sensory input. Interpretations of the most basic experience may differ, and indeed the very notion of a basic experience is exposed as an empiricist prejudice. What we say about the world always goes beyond available data, so that all theories are underdetermined. Quine writes:

> The truths that can be said even in common-sense terms about ordinary things are themselves, in turn, far in excess of any available data. The incompleteness of determination of molecular behavior of ordinary things is hence only incidental to this more basic indeterminacy: *both* sorts of events are less than determined by our surface irritations.[14]

The ghost of empiricism lives on in Quine, with his insistence on 'surface irritations'. They still provide the starting-point for all theory. Yet the very fact that even our ordinary experience of the world is itself the result of theory places, he says, ordinary physical objects on a par with the most theoretical of entities. Tables and chairs have no privileged status over electrons and protons. They are all posits of a theory. Quine says: 'Everything to which we concede existence is a posit from the standpoint of a description of the theory-building process.'[15] Yet, if theories are underdetermined by data, alternative theories can in their own terms be equally valid. One example he has given is seeing a procession of three lumps moving along at the surface of the water. We may posit a school of dolphins or a single Loch Ness monster. We choose our theory in such cases, he thinks, by preferring the simpler or more familiar explanation. Further observations may sometimes settle the matter, but, even if all possible observations have been made, Quine holds that alternative theories are always possible. Empirically equivalent theories may still be significantly different. In this and in his whole-hearted acceptance of theoretical entities, he shows himself as no empiricist.

Quine's acceptance of theoretical entities as posits does not raise them to the level of familiar objects. Rather, he appears to question the objective reality of the latter. He would insist that 'to call a posit a posit is not to patronize it'.[16] He says that 'we can never do better than occupy the standpoint of some theory or other, the best we can muster at the time'. It is perhaps fruitless to complain that theoretical entities are 'only' theoretical if all entities are. Insisting, though, on the complete priority of theory like this is bound to raise some misgivings. According to Quine, we can only talk about what our theory counts as real. He would deny that there is any sense in which we can further refer to reality. We can only conceive of what we can conceive.[17] The notion of objective reality thus becomes what our current theory says is real. Quine's view demands that 'world', 'reality' and all such concepts are theoretical, and that theories cannot be simply understood as attempts to describe an independently existing world. The world becomes the reflection of theory, rather than theories mirroring the world, more or less well. This is why translation becomes such a problem for him, since he cannot assume that different theories are *about* the same world. He has to attempt to correlate the words of one theory with those of another without assuming that each refers to the same entities. He cannot assume that the native sees a rabbit and he certainly cannot dogmatically assert that there just are rabbits and the native is wrong if he does not recognize the fact. That is only so from the standpoint of *our* current theory. For Quine the fundamental relationship has to be between word and word, and not between word and object. There are no such things as objects viewed outside the mediation of any particular theory. There is no possibility, therefore of a unique description of the world. Alternatives are always possible, because theories are underdetermined by data.

If theories are not merely means of predicting phenomena, nor are deducible from them, the importance of the empirical content of a theory has somehow been downgraded. It is not just that we are now free to posit unobservable entities to explain experience. The loosening of experience as a constraint on our choice of theory raises the question of what other influences there might be. The foundationalist epistemo-logy of empiricism provided a curb on what could be rationally adopted. If the possibility of such an epistemology is an illusion, the status of rationality itself must be queried. There may seem something highly suspicious about asking for reasons for being rational, but we have to ask where our theories come from and on what they are based. Just how desperate the situation could be is illustrated by the way in which Richard Rorty can talk of 'the cultural space left by the demise of epistemology'.[18]

The same problem arises at a multiplicity of levels. Epistemology as a discipline flounders once the tight constraints of empiricism are loosened. It seems that we do not know where to look for justification, whether it is of our most general theory about the external world, for the practice of science, for the holding of particular theories within science, or for social theory. The same applies to the myriad other forms of belief which we may fondly imagine constitute knowledge.

The practice of physical science has come under particular scrutiny, because empiricism laid such store by observation, and modern science has appeared to be built on the results of observation and experiment. It was part of the received doctrine about science that the history of science was logically distinct from the philosophy of science. The rational justification of a theory may not coincide with the way the theory was actually arrived at. Philosophy laid bare the philosophical foundations of science, while history showed what actually happened. Such an outlook presupposed that science *had* epistemological foundations. Once, however, scientific theory is cut loose from its empirical base, it becomes unclear whether the philosopher can any longer stand aloof from history. Maybe there is no way of distinguishing between what ought to have happened in the development of science from what actually did happen. Insistent questions, however, remain to be answered. What is the purpose of science if it is no longer understood as the search for greater accuracy in empirical observation and prediction? Why should scientists ever change their theories? What, in fact, constitutes scientific progress?

The Views of Kuhn and Feyerabend

One of the major influences in the cataclysmic changes that have affected modern philosophy of science has been the work of T. S. Kuhn. Significantly, he was a historian of science. He introduced the notion of a scientific 'paradigm' which governs a scientist's view of the world. A major change in scientific thinking involves a change in paradigm and the switch from classical to quantum mechanics would provide one example. Kuhn's thesis is that, when scientists work under a paradigm, they take part in what he calls 'normal science', trying to solve the problems thrown up by the theory they hold. Every so often, however, a scientific revolution occurs when the existing paradigm proves unable to cope with what appear to be anomalous situations. Kuhn's views are particularly interesting as regards what happens when a scientific community shifts from one paradigm to another:

> The historian of science may be tempted to exclaim that when paradigms change, the world itself changes with them. Led by a new paradigm, scientists adopt new instruments and look in new places. Even more important, during revolutions scientists see new and different things when looking with familiar instruments in places they have looked before.[19]

The inversion of the empiricist scheme of things is clear. The theory determines the observations, according to Kuhn, instead of observations determining the theory. Indeed, he seems to be going further than saying that a new theory shows us how to notice what we did not notice before. He appears to be asserting that the world is actually different for different theories. What counts as real under one paradigm does not under another. Scientists once believed there was a substance called phlogiston and now do not. They once believed the atom could not be split, whereas now they continue to search for new sub-atomic particles. There is a continuing ambiguity, though, in illustrations like this. Everyone accepts that scientific theories change our conceptions of reality, but the question is whether there is a sense in which they actually change reality. Perhaps the way the issue is posed begs the question, since it presupposes that we can sensibly talk of a reality which is independent of our conceptions of it. Yet this is what Quine denied, and Kuhn seems merely to be taking this a step further by saying that the world might itself change. The world as conceived by scientists does change, but does that mean the world itself changes? The distinction between these two positions is of major philosophical importance. Arguments rage over whether such a distinction can be made. Kuhn poses the question of what scientific theories are about. Can they be measured against anything external to themselves, and therefore at least in principle be judged correct or mistaken, true or false? The alternative is that we are left with a succession of different theories, or conceptions of the world, with no means of determining which is better than the others.

Kuhn uses the 'duck-rabbit' drawing as an analogy to illustrate the way in which a scientist's vision can change after a switch of paradigms. He draws attention to the way in which theories can govern what we see. A student, he says, may only see confused and broken lines when looking at a bubble-chamber photograph, whereas a trained physicist will actually *see* a record of sub-nuclear events. He says:

> It is as elementary prototypes for these transformations of the scientist's world that the familar demonstrations of a switch in visual gestalt prove so suggestive. What were ducks in the scientific world before the revolution are rabbits afterwards.[20]

One consequence of these radical shifts in a scientist's vision is that scientists working under different paradigms possess different concepts and make different observations. They cannot appeal to any theory-neutral observation, and Kuhn removes the possibility of referring to the same objective world underpinning all paradigms. Since 'the world' is seen only through a paradigm, there is a problem as to how those with allegiance to different paradigms can discuss their theories with each other. Empiricists could argue with those they disagreed with, by appealing to the experience they all shared. Kuhn cannot do that and considers the introduction of a neutral language of observation 'hopeless'.[21] He has to talk instead of the 'incommensurability' of different scientific theories. At a time of revolution a scientist will find the world of his research here and there 'incommensurable with the one he had inhabited before'.[22] This has an important and worrying consequence. Since scientists will each see a world constituted by their own paradigm, those with allegiance to different paradigms will be talking at cross-purposes to each other. They will actually be referring to different entities and their theories will not rest on a common base, nor apparently even be about the same world. Kuhn does not even use the physical impact of the world on our senses as a starting-point, as Quine does. There is instead a competition between different visions of the world, some of which may overlap, but which cannot formulate their disagreements in any common language.

Why, then, should scientists change their paradigms? The history of science shows that this has often happened and Kuhn attempts to describe that process. At what point do the strains of an existing theory become unbearable? Kuhn has left himself with few resources to answer that. It cannot be because of an appeal to experience, since that is governed by a paradigm. It cannot be because we discover basic errors, since the paradigm controls what is to count as correct. Discovering basic 'errors' is, in fact, tantamount to changing the way we choose to see the world. Kuhn points out that individual scientists embrace a new paradigm 'for all sorts of reasons and usually for several at once'. He continues:

> Some of these reasons – for example the sun worship that helped make Kepler a Copernican – lie outside the apparent sphere of science entirely. Others must depend upon idiosyncrasies of autobiography and personality. Even the nationality or the prior reputation of the innovator and his teachers can sometimes play a significant role.[23]

This is not a very encouraging summary of the rational processes of scientists, and Kuhn goes on to stress that his interest is mainly in the sort of community that re-emerges after a time of scientific crisis. He mentions that those who resist the new paradigm cannot be said to be wrong, and indeed he could have no criterion by which they could be judged wrong. He says of the historian: 'At most he may wish to say that the man who continues to resist after his whole profession has been converted has *ipso facto* ceased to be a scientist.'[24]

The philosophy of science can thus no longer provide a rational reconstruction of the way theories logically depend on each other and can justify each other. There is nothing left but the question how science has actually developed. The philosophy of science has to become the history of science, since there is no way left in which what has happened can be rationally criticized. Science is what particular communities happen to do, rather than being an impressive rational creation of the human mind. It is hardly surprising that Kuhn's views have paved the way to a growing interest in the sociology of science. The account he gives of paradigm shifts cries out for a sociological explanation for them. Sociologists must feel confident that they can contribute to our understanding of a sudden change in the behaviour of a community, particularly if there is no possibility of its having occurred on rational grounds. By talking of the interaction of scientists with each other, Kuhn focuses on the idea of a community, and he explores the idea of standards enforced by the community. The very fact that a particular social group can accept one solution to a problem but not another, or can see one argument as a justification but not another, cries out for sociological analysis. So at least a sociologist of science would argue. The conventional character of scientific judgement has seemingly been exposed, and it is the sociologist's concern to show us how the conventions operate and change. One such sociologist writes:

Scientific standards themselves are a part of a specific form of culture; authority and control are essential to maintain a sense of the reasonableness of the specific form. Thus, if Kuhn is correct, science should be amenable to sociological study in fundamentally the same way as any other form of knowledge or culture.[25]

Kuhn's attack on the rational foundations of science (for that is in effect what it is) has not been a solitary one. Its anti-empiricism has been in tune with the mood of the times and has found a ready following. There is no doubt, though, that at times the reaction from the idea that knowledge has firm foundations in experience has been very extreme. It is one thing to say that theories can govern how we see and experience the world, but quite another to make it impossible any longer to refer to the world. It is one thing to question whether experience is the only source of human knowledge, but quite another to say that knowledge is conventional. The latter is to say that societies or traditions determine what we count as knowledge. Our grasp on reality becomes exceedingly tenuous, if that is so. What we believe or claim to know is merely the product of social forces of which we may be utterly ignorant.

The philosopher of science, P. Feyerabend makes it explicit that reality in some sense actually depends on our choice. He says flatly: 'We decide to regard those things as real which play an important role in the kind of life we prefer.'[26] He considers that there is no more ultimate way of referring to reality than through the particular tradition we belong to. Instead of reality controlling our beliefs, at least to some extent, it seems as if the beliefs of a tradition determine what is to count as real. There are countless traditions, each of which has firm teaching on what is real. Within any one of them, we can gain the illusion that knowledge can be and has been attained. Yet, once we see that many conflicting traditions have the same conceit, we realize, it is alleged, that judgements of truth only have relative validity. They hold for our colleagues in the tradition to which we are attached, but not for those outside.

Feyerabend's unsettling view is that this kind of argument can be applied in any sphere. The practice of science, and even the exercise of reason, can be revealed as themselves historical traditions. He says:

> Scientific practice, even the practice of the natural sciences, is a tightly woven net of historical traditions. . . . This means that general statements

about science, statements of logic included, cannot without further ado be taken to agree with scientific practice.[27]

The notion of a philosophy of science with an ideal of rational justification is again under attack. What is left is merely what scientists happened to have done, or are doing, and that forms suitable material for sociological study. Scientific standards are 'not imposed upon science from the outside'.[28] Instead Feyerabend insists that they are produced by scientists in the course of their research. He particularly stresses the importance of being able to choose between competing alternatives, and advocates the principle (or anti-principle) of 'anything goes' as a basis for scientific method. Because he sees Western science as one tradition among many, he wants freedom of choice between that and its alternatives. He also talks of the exercise of reason itself (or 'rationalism', as he puts it) as a tradition:

> Each tradition, each form of life, has its own standards of judging human behaviour and these standards change in accordance with the problems that the tradition is constrained to solve. Rationalism is not a boundary condition for traditions: it is itself a tradition, and not always a successful one. There exists, therefore, a plurality of standards just as there is a plurality of individuals. In a free society, however, a citizen will use the standards to which (s)he belongs: Hopi standards, if he is a Hopi: fundamentalist Protestant standards, if he is a fundamentalist.[29]

This is a classic statement of relativism. There are different, self-contained traditions and ways of life. Each generates its own standards. None can be understood, let alone judged, by means of criteria rooted in a different tradition. Many have found this an attractive doctrine when applied to human customs or even morality. It is perhaps a philosophical version of the saying, 'When in Rome, do as the Romans do'. Different societies have different ways of doing things, and sometimes at least there is mere difference, without one set of practices being better or worse than another. An obvious example is which side of the road we drive on. No one can say that driving on the left is better than driving on the right, or vice versa. We naturally tend to prefer what we are used to, but as long as everyone in one country conforms to the same convention that is enough. There is a story of a newly independent nation which decided to change from driving on the left to driving on the right, but to do so gradually. That is clearly the speedy route to chaos. So it is with many social conventions. Conformity to particular ones in a given society is necessary for the functioning of that society, but a different society can conform to totally different ones.

Questions about this kind of relativity in the case of moral standards become much more controversial. Feyerabend, however, goes even further. So far from accepting scientific method as the very model of rationality, or indeed considering rationality itself as a universal ideal, he belittles each as being one tradition among many. He says of scientists that they are 'salesmen of ideas and gadgets, they are not judges of truth and falsehood'.[30] This is not the raving of a crank but is the inevitable outcome of the attacks on empiricism which removed the foundations of our empirical knowledge without putting anything in its place. As a result, questions of knowledge, truth, reality and reason are all discarded. We step back from knowledge to belief, from what is true to what is held true, from reality to people's beliefs about it, and from questions of rational standards to all the peculiar ways in which humans do actually purport to reason. We step from justification to description, and from philosophy, or, at least, epistemology, to sociology. The emphasis laid on the incommensurability of theories by Feyerabend, as well as Kuhn, develops into a position where theories or traditions set their own standards of rationality and are immune to criticism from outside.

Feyerabend eagerly seizes on Wittgenstein's view that the meaning of concepts is given by their use in a practice.[31] Concepts are not labels for things but are grounded in ways of acting. I shall return to this later, but Feyerabend draws out one very important consequence. If we understand what a word means by using it in connection with a particular activity, the only way to learn it is by participating in that activity. Instead of words referring to an objective world or an experience which can be shared intersubjectively, they are rooted in what Wittgenstein refers to as a 'language-game' or a 'form of life'. The purpose of both expressions is to drawn attention to the fact that language is intimately connected with activities. It cannot, it is suggested, be peeled off and understood apart from the life of which it is a part. Yet this means that non–participants cannot understand what is being said in any practice. This doctrine, if true, has tremendous consequences for the social sciences, and the problem of *Verstehen* (understanding) is indeed one of the most venerable topics for the philosophy of social science. Clearly, though, on Feyerabend's view, all the sciences face the same difficulty.

So far from the social sciences finding it difficult to live up to the exacting standards of the natural sciences, the latter seem to be dissolving into social groupings posing problems of understanding and interpretation for the social scientist.

This might seem an argument against Feyerabend's position, but unfortunately it is a consequence that he embraces. He has rejected the idea that philosophy can uncover basic rational principles according to which science proceeds. He rejects the idea of an objective, extra-theoretical reality, so that as a result everything is valid only within the confines of a particular theory. The practices of a science are valid only for the practitioners of the science. Feyerabend explicitly mentions the position of traditional methodologists of science who have held 'that a historian studies a distant culture by trying to "understand" it while a physicist who deals with explicit abstract notions "explains"'.[32]

He will have none of this dichotomy between the interpretation of a social scientist and the explanation of a natural scientist. In fact, he has left the latter without any materials with which to explain in a manner that can be either intelligible or relevant to a non-physicist. Explanation can only satisfy those who are physicists. By insisting that physics is itself a social practice or tradition, Feyerabend has removed its claims to have any ultimate answers, or to be in a privileged position compared with other disciplines. He explicitly follows in Kuhn's footsteps and says with approval: 'Kuhn makes the highly interesting and revolutionary suggestion that *physics is a historical tradition and therefore as much in need of Verstehen as history proper.*'[33] The theories of a contemporary physicist, therefore, may stand in as much need of interpretation and understanding as those of an ancient Greek. Physics is no longer seen as the base to which other sciences can be reduced, but as one tradition out of many; it can be investigated only by means of the methods of the social sciences.

We have arrived at a bewildering conclusion. According to a dominant trend in contemporary philosophy of science, science is not a path to truth at all, let alone the only one. It sometimes looks as if some philosophers are saying that there is no such thing as truth. The incoherence of that is revealed if we realize that they are asserting *as true* the proposition that there is no such thing as truth. Feyerabend himself realizes that he may appear to be giving reasons for his view that reason 'is a tradition in its own right with as much (or as little) claim to the centre of the stage as any other tradition.'[34] There are times when it looks as if he views the opportunity of choice between different traditions and theories as a good stratagem in the pursuit of truth. Refusal to be bound by a rigid methodology may itself be the last of all methodologies. At other times, it seems as if his advocacy of relativism is leading us perilously close to denying that any view is better than any other, or any reason more valid than any other. The problem that remains is whether it is possible to dethrone the natural sciences without undermining the possibility of human reason. Can the social sciences step in with new modes of explanation?

Notes

1 B. Fay and J. D. Moon, 'What Would an Adequate Philosophy of Social Science Look Like?', *Philosophy of the Social Sciences*, 7, 1977, p. 227.
2 'The Scientific Conception of the World: The Vienna Circle', in M. Neurath and R. S. Cohen (eds), *Otto Neurath: Empiricism and Sociology*, 1973, p. 309.
3 Ibid., p. 315.
4 For a further discussion of quantum mechanics and reality, see my *Reality at Risk*, 1980, ch. 6.
5 Ludwig Wittgenstein, *Philosophical Investigations*, 1958, II, xi.
6 See my *Pain and Emotion*, 1970, pp. 81ff.
7 David Hume, *A Treatise of Human Nature*, Book III, reprinted in *Hume's Ethical Writings*, ed. A. MacIntyre, 1965, p. 196.
8 Carl Hempel, *Philosophy of Natural Science*, 1968, p. 47.
9 Ibid., p. 50.
10 Ibid., p. 10.
11 D. Turner, *Marxism and Christianity*, 1983, p. 104.
12 Ibid., p. 104.
13 W. V. Quine, *Word and Object*, 1964, p. 29.
14 Ibid., p. 22.
15 Ibid.
16 Ibid.
17 For a longer discussion of Quine, see my *Reality at Risk*.
18 Richard Rorty, *Philosophy and the Mirror of Nature*, 1980, p. 315.
19 T. S. Kuhn, *The Structure of Scientific Revolutions*, 1962, p. 110.
20 Ibid., p. 110.
21 Ibid., p. 125.
22 Ibid., p. 111.
23 Ibid., p. 151.
24 Ibid., p. 150.

25 Barry Barnes, *T. S. Kuhn and Social Science*, 1982, p. 10.
26 P. Feyerabend, *Philosophical Papers*, vol. I, *Realism, Rationalism and Scientific Method*, 1981, p. xiii.
27 Ibid., p. 4.
28 Feyerabend, *Philosophical Papers*, vol. II, *Problems of Empiricism*, 1981, p. 27.
29 Ibid.
30 Feyerabend, *Philosophical Papers*, vol. II, p. 31.
31 Ibid., p. 129.
32 Ibid., p. 237.
33 Ibid.
34 Feyerabend, *Science in a Free Society*, 1978, p. 8.

2

Objectivity and the Sociology of Knowledge

The Social Character of Knowledge

Traditional philosophy of science has always made a firm distinction between what it termed 'internal' and 'external' reasons for holding theories. The success of a relevant experiment would be an internal reason, while the rejection, say, of evolutionary theory because of a fundamentalist belief that the book of Genesis was true would count as an external one. In other words, some reasons would be properly grounded in scientific method, in the building of theories on repeated observations, while others would cut across it. The presumption has been that scientific method set the standard for the pursuit of knowledge, and indeed positivism has insisted that it is the only standard.

Once the possibility of scientific method is challenged, and it is suggested that we can only study what scientists actually do, any distinction between internal and external reasons is removed. We can no longer assume that the Protestant fundamentalist is wrong in rejecting one of the theories of modern science. As Feyerabend pointed out, the fundamentalist just belongs to a different tradition from the scientist, with different standards.

There are some very odd consequences of putting different outlooks into self-contained compartments like this. Things are more complicated in real life; the distinctions between the compartments are blurred. One can be both a scientist and a fundamentalist, and it would be curious to have one set of beliefs on Sunday and another in the laboratory in the week. One will inevitably have to face the question which set of standards are right. Relativists would have us believe that such a question cannot arise. They claim that the whole edifice of Western science is a mere sociological fact, which cannot be judged better or worse than astrology, witchcraft, or any other set of practices. It is significant how the adjective 'Western' can easily be attached to the word 'science'. That already locates it in a particular time and place and suggests that it is merely a particular kind of social practice.

Science has often been extolled as the basic source of knowledge, and scientific method has been held up as an example of objectivity, detached from the interests and prejudices of its practitioners. As a result scientists have perhaps gained an inflated reputation for wisdom. They appear to be good at manipulating the world, and giving us such things as non-stick frying pans and colour television. Yet now we are told their activities are to be investigated on a par with, say, the rain-dances of a primitive tribe. Are we then to conclude that scientists do not make discoveries about the world or extend our knowledge of it? The genuine relativist would always say, at this point, that notions such as those of 'the world' are already theoretic. They can only be under-stood in the context of someone holding beliefs. 'Reality' has no mean-ing apart from what is believed real by some group. The very concept of an objective world, independent of all points of view, is dissipated. It may be a convenient idea *within* science, but it cannot be used to adjudicate between science and other activities. Ontology has thus to become dependent on epistemology. What there is is seen as the product of our strategies for finding things out. If our epistemology changes, as when we move from one world-view to another, so do our beliefs about what is real.

Feyerabend sums up his advocacy of this position when he says:

> We no longer assume an objective world that remains unaffected by our epistemic activities, except when moving within the confines of a par-ticular point of view. We concede that our epistemic activities may have a decisive influence even upon the most sordid piece of cosmological furniture – they may make gods disappear and replace them by heaps of atoms in empty space.[1]

This view may be an affront to common sense. It is also an explicit denial of the philosophical doctrine of realism which insists on the objectivity of reality in the sense that it is independent of all beliefs about it. For the realist there is, at least in principle, a standard by which all human societies and their beliefs can be judged: they can all have beliefs about the world which turn out to be mistaken.

The denial of realism makes us turn our attention to the fact of belief and away from what is believed. It invites us to replace the traditional attempts of epistemology to show *the* path to reality with the empirical descriptions of the sociologist of knowledge. Instead of trying to find out timeless, abstract principles, we look at the strategies that are actually adopted in different times and places. Philosophy and the natural sciences themselves become objects of study for the social scientist. The social sciences no longer need to appear respectable through being 'scientific', but instead seem to be putting the natural sciences in their place.

One of the major reasons for this is the increasing emphasis on the *social* character of knowledge in general, and science in particular. The very fact that science has been seen as a social institution, in which the notion of objectivity is determined by the structure of the institution, means that it is a fit object of study for the social scientist. It is in this context that the attacks on empiricism have been so important. If knowledge was obtained through the senses, it was clearly an individual matter. Each person could obtain knowledge in isolation. If, on the other hand, it is a product of a community, it is by definition attainable only through education in the ways of that community. Similarly, empiricism seemed to suggest that knowledge came in bits and pieces. Its approach was atomistic, in contrast to the view of knowledge which suggests that it is deeply embedded in the way of life of which it is a part. Thus particular strands cannot be torn away from the wider whole. Marjorie Grene expresses this type of view when she writes:

> Science is a family of practices.... And practices are by their nature rooted in community, and permit communication only on that ground. Each science requires from its initiates a long and arduous apprenticeship.... Thus it is only a philosophical approach which accepts the sociality of human nature from the very beginning that can begin to deal adequately with the cognitive claims of science, let alone its relation to other commitments of the culture to which it belongs.[2]

Wittgenstein and Rules

Wittgenstein provides an example of this kind of philosophical approach, at least in his later work. He emphasized the rule-governed nature of our practices. Human activity is not to be understood as the isolated actions of individuals, and we cannot make sense of what anyone does except in the context of a wider whole. For this reason, this kind of view has sometimes been dubbed 'contextualist', particularly in, say, social anthropology. It stems naturally from Wittgenstein's equation of meaning and use. Words mean what they do because of the context in which they are used. Meaning cannot be privately conferred, and is not, for instance, to be correlated with internal sense-impressions. Wittgenstein's arguments against the possibility of a 'private language' are well known,[3] although much of the discussion about them has occurred in the philosophy of mind. How do we learn the word 'pain'? We can all communicate with each other about pain and teach the word, but it apparently refers to a private sensation. Wittgenstein was concerned to show how the meaning of such a word can only be rooted in a public language, with public checks that it is being used correctly. He was looking for a 'criterion of correctness',[4] and argued that one cannot have a private rule for using a word. In that case there would be no distinction between my having a rule which I kept, and my having a rule which I thought I was keeping even when I was not. The rules of the private language could not be *impressions* of rules.[5]

This apparently applies merely to problems about communicating the nature of our sensations, but Wittgenstein is making a point which concerns *all* concepts and the way they are used. The discussion about private language comes after a long discussion about following rules, in which he stresses how all rules have to be rooted in public practices. He asks at one point: 'Is what we call "obeying a rule" something that it would be possible for only *one* man to do, and to do only *once* in his life?'[6] His answer is that it would not be, since all practices, whether linguistic or not, are rooted in ways of life and cannot be understood in isolation. They gain their meaning from their context and are passed on by means of shared, public criteria. He says: 'To obey a rule, to make a report, to give an order, to play a game of chess, are *customs*.'[7] He makes a logical link between the use of a word, the custom of a people and the institution of a society. Words cannot be understood apart from the practices in which they are embedded, and these practices are social institutions.

In a paragraph which clearly anticipates the 'private language' argument, he says:

> And hence also 'obeying a rule' is a practice. And to *think* one is obeying a rule is not to obey a rule. Hence it is not possible to obey a rule 'privately': otherwise thinking one was obeying a rule would be the same thing as obeying it.[8]

I cannot be said to be obeying a rule if there is no way any mistake I made could be uncovered. I may even be changing the rules unconsciously as I go on. If there is no distinction between doing that and accurately keeping to the rule I set myself, we cannot talk of rules.

Wittgenstein is very fond of analogies with games, as his famous phrase 'language-games' indicates. A group of boys are not playing cricket if each plays according to his own personal rules. Someone who decides to play 'hit and run' and then refuses to run even though he has hit the ball cannot defend himself by saying that he has changed his rule for that ball. There would then be no distinction between his having a rule and playing in a totally arbitrary fashion. What is the difference between his changing the rule without telling anyone, and forgetting to keep to the rule? Rules are of their very nature public, or so Wittgenstein would argue. One may wonder how far Wittgenstein was himself still influenced by the strictures of the Vienna Circle on the importance of verifiability. Even though he himself had abandoned any trust in experience as a source of knowledge, his stress on the importance of public checking apparently has its roots in the verification theory of meaning. According to that theory the ascription of meaning depends on the possibility of public checking, so that what is unverifiable is meaningless. It could be argued from this that the private mental processes of individuals are themselves unverifiable and that language purporting to be about 'them' must be rooted in public criteria. Private processes are, then, irrelevant for meaning.

This seems to be precisely Wittgenstein's conclusion, although it is somewhat ironic that his argument against private languages itself has appeared to be a challenge to the empiricism of the Vienna Circle. The latter relied heavily on the incorrigibility of private experience, and Wittgenstein replaces that with the public rules of social practices. His quest for public criteria as a basis for meaningfulness leads him to stress the social origins of thought and experience. We are what we are largely because of the practices and institutions in which we are immersed. Knowledge does not come from the atomistic experience of individuals but is the product of rule-governed activities, which must be public and social. A game of cricket cannot be understood in terms of the private intentions of individual players. What they are doing can gain its sense from the rules of the game in which they are participating. Boys banging a ball around a field with a bat are not necessarily playing cricket. Unless their activities are governed by rules, they are just banging a ball with a bat.

Where, then, do rules come from? They are embedded in society and indeed constitute a society. Rules make a society what it is. Different rules and institutions will by definition produce a different society. Wittgenstein's views provide an invitation to the sociologist to describe the practices and rules of a society. Once again, it looks as if epistemological foundations have been repudiated and only sociological investigation will throw light on the nature of society.

It is hardly surprising that Wittgenstein's views have provided inspiration for sociologists of knowledge wishing to emphasize the social character of knowledge. Although of very different origin, his notions fit very easily with those of Kuhn. What is at stake, however, is not just a question about epistemology or sociology of knowledge. Wittgenstein's opinions can apparently give support to all who stress the priority of the society over the individual. If the activities of individuals only gain sense through participation in social practices, we have to look at the latter as sources of explanation.

Embedding rules in societies does not finally answer questions about their origin. Much controversy has raged over whether Wittgenstein's later views lead to relativism. If rules can be justified only in the context of a particular society, what happens when we come to the question whether societies as a whole can be judged right or wrong, correct or mistaken? A genuine relativism ensues when everything is 'contextual', with consequences I shall later investigate.

In saying that the individual does not choose a rule but obeys it 'blindly',[9] Wittgenstein shows how rules are a starting-point. We have no resources with which to choose or discard rules, since the rules themselves provide the context for choice. This leads Wittgenstein to conclude that asking for justification is impossible: 'If I have exhausted the justifications, I have reached bedrock, and my spade is turned. Then I am inclined to say: "This is simply what I do".'[10] This leaves un-answered what constitutes the bedrock. It is easy to find instances where Wittgenstein seems to be suggesting that the bedrock will be different in different societies or systems of thought.[11] He seems to think, for example, that it is impossible for a physicist to give any rational justifica-tion for physics to people who trust in oracles rather than science.[12] Yet in the course of his discussion of rules he also asks a question of funda-mental difficulty to the relativist, and gives an answer that is apparently totally at odds with relativism:

> Suppose you came as an explorer into an unknown country with a language quite strange to you. In what circumstances would you say that the people there gave orders, understood them, obeyed them, rebelled against them, and so on?
>
> The common behaviour of mankind is the system of reference by means of which we interpret an unknown language.[13]

Wittgenstein is intent on showing the way in which language is rooted in activities, so that there must be a regular connection between the sounds people make and what they do. The striking point he raises, at least in this passage, is that, despite their multiplicity, language-games have a common base in the 'common behaviour of mankind'. The problem of understanding other societies is acute, without some such reference point. Elsewhere he talks of 'the correspondence between concepts and very general facts of nature', and seems to be tracing human ways of acting back to the most general facts about human nature.[14] This is markedly different from stressing the ultimate nature of language-games or forms of life, so that everything has to be under-stood only in its social context, which may itself vary radically. What is at issue is whether the social context is itself rooted in anything more fundamental. When Wittgenstein says that what has to be accepted – the given – is forms of life,[15] this looks like a charter for relativism. Indeed it must be if the phrase 'forms of life' is taken to refer to different social institutions. At times, though, it looks as if he may regard such forms of life as grounded in human nature. They are what they are, not because of any social context, but because of what he terms 'the natural history of human beings'.[16] Certainly what he says about pain, for example, would seem to be linked to the most general features of human behaviour, rather than to the particular facts about particular institutions.

Whatever Wittgenstein's own position, he has been interpreted in many different ways. The issue is clear enough. Are human institutions to be studied in their own terms or traced back to a common base? Wittgenstein's emphasis on the priority of the social has certainly been a spur to many who consider that sociological understanding is of prime importance.

The Sociology of Knowledge

Science can be regarded as a rule-governed social practice, and so its institutions are obvious candidates for sociological investigation and explanation. Because scientists work in groups and enforce communal standards, the sociologist may have much of interest to tell us. Yet how much can be explained in this manner? Perhaps science can be regarded merely as a social institution. It is significant that Peter Winch specifically refers to science as a 'mode of social life' in contrast to religion, which he considers to be a different mode. He says that 'each has criteria of intelligibility peculiar to itself'.[17] This has obvious echoes of Wittgenstein, but it raises an important problem. A clear corollary of this view is that the rules of a particular practice determine what is to count as real. Science may be concerned with electrons, while religion deals with God. The reality of each is an internal matter for the mode of social life concerned. There is no neutral language in which the respective claims of each can be discussed, and neither can ever contradict the other. Yet this means that reality is not what belief-systems are about, but is what is expressed in them. There is not one reality against which all putative knowledge can be measured, even if only in principle: there are as many realities as there are different institutions of belief. Kuhn's readiness to admit of different worlds for different paradigms involves a similar position. It tends to lapse into incoherence since it is difficult to talk of there *being* different realities, without inviting the charge that one is still in some sense talking about reality. It seems that any statement about reality can only be made from the standpoint of a particular social practice. It is an illusion on this view that there is any way of transcending all practices and talking about them meaningfully.

The conclusion can easily follow that 'reality' is given sense only by the rules of a particular social institution. Science forms one such institution, and its notions of reality can be studied, it seems, from a sociological standpoint, as can all human conceptions of reality. The sociology of knowledge tells us that knowledge is a human construct, grounded in the facts of our social life. It denies traditional definitions of knowledge which insist that knowledge must involve *true* belief, and reflect reality. For the sociologist of knowledge, reality is what is reflected by the beliefs of a society. Some have suggested that the sociology of knowledge is misnamed, since it is in fact concerned with explaining the social context of *beliefs*. This trades on a distinction between knowledge and belief which depends on the assumption that reality is independent of human conceptions. The sociology of knowledge often appears to attack this view head-on. One of its exponents, David Bloor, says:

> Knowledge for the sociologist is whatever men take to be knowledge. It consists of the beliefs which men confidently hold to and live by. In particular, the sociologist will be concerned with beliefs which are taken for granted or institutionalized or invested with authority by groups of men.[18]

Far from looking at the content of knowledge and trying to assess its worth through reason, the sociologist of knowledge will refuse to abstract what is known from its social setting. Any remaining contrast between knowledge and belief would have to be between what is socially accepted and what is individually held. The sociologist will wish to investigate the 'agreement in judgements' which Wittgenstein held to constitute a social practice. Individual deviations from this would not affect the general social setting. The social sources of authority and the institutional basis for what is counted knowledge are the focus of sociological concern. Implicit, of course, is the assumption that social rules and public practices are not merely the product of individual decisions. The sociologist of knowledge needs the priority of the social as a starting-point. The judgements of the individual gain their sense from a public framework. Reality is the product of social agreement.

The sociologist of knowledge can locate objectivity in the public practices of an institution. Individual deviations from this standard provide the possibility for error. It is, however, an odd kind of error, since it is error within a context. Any Christian who denied the divinity of Christ would appear to be making an error according to the rules of the institutional Church. In this sense, he or she is objectively wrong, but it is tempting to raise the further question whether the Church is right. Was Christ really the son of God? This type of question is forbidden us by the sociologist of knowledge. To ask it, let alone answer it, we have to step outside all institutional frameworks and social practices, and try to discover the truth without their aid.

Yet even this example shows that any sociological idea of rigid practices is misleading, since many theologians do wish to debate the divinity of Christ and the meaning of the 'Incarnation'. Some who would claim to be Christians and have an influence within the Church seem to be suggesting that Christ was not uniquely divine, as traditional orthodoxy insisted. How can they do this when they are challenging the 'objective' or at least public standards of their institution? It seems as if they should acknowledge those standards or leave the institution. There are doubtless many orthodox believers in the Christian Church who would say precisely that. Yet if what is claimed is objective truth, in a non-contextual sense, belief must be susceptible to justification and be subject to criticism. The possibility of justification is, of course, normally ignored in the sociological account, where the mere fact that beliefs are held is taken to be sufficient. Without that possibility, the question must arise why the standards of any institution should ever be challenged from within. Institutions do, of course, change through time, but the socio-logical account has to rule out any justification for change or for questioning existing standards. At the most, it can map the causes of change. However, if it follows that all practices can only be judged in accordance with their own existing standards, sociologists of knowledge lay them-selves open to the charge of conservatism: each practice must be accepted as it is, and no reasons can be given for changing it.

Bloor contrasts the belief in progress championed by spokesmen of the Enlightenment with the appeal a conservative makes to history: 'In opposition to the appeal to the individual reason, conservatives appealed to the wisdom of tradition. In opposition to the rights of the individual, conservatives stressed our dependence on culture, nation and institu-tion.'[19] Given the way in which Wittgenstein stresses the importance of 'forms of life', it is not surprising that Bloor classifies him as a 'con-servative thinker'. This is perhaps paradoxical, since Marxists also tend to find affinities with him, particularly because of his emphasis on the priority of society over the individual. Yet, whereas conservatives will take custom and tradition as their authority, Marxists will be eager for radical social change. Wittgenstein himself certainly accepted that social practices can alter through time. Language-games could change or lose their point. If rational justification for such change had been ruled out, the sociologist will look to other influences. In fact, since rational justification is simply whatever a particular community takes it to be, sociologists may argue that they alone are in a position to chart the currents of social change. Questions about the divinity of Christ cease to be questions about a purported fact, or even merely questions about the existing rules of an institution. They are transposed by the sociologist of knowledge into questions about the character of the institution which produces such beliefs. Reason becomes merely the product of social arrangements, and, as they are put under pressure by alterations in their environment, so standards of rationality themselves change.

In the example given about arguments concerning the divinity of Christ, a sociologist of knowledge would find it easy to point to the impact of other religions on Christians. Immigration into England, for instance, by Muslims and others, has meant that the problem of living side by side with adherents of other religions has literally been brought home to English theologians. As social pressures increase, pressures on the institutional Church to moderate its claims to absolute truth also grow. The roots of an apparently theological argument lie, the socio-logist might claim, not so much in eternal truth, but in the changing social patterns of a particular place and time. Reason is thus the product of social arrangements.

Objectivity and Reflexivity

The views implicit in the sociology of knowledge are gaining increasing currency within and beyond the social sciences. They affect every intellectual discipline from theology to physics and even mathematics. The views of such diverse thinkers as Wittgenstein and Kuhn are applied in a manner which seems to undermine traditional conceptions of knowledge. The writings of David Bloor provide one illustration of this approach. For example, he argues that objectivity is social. He holds that the impersonal and stable character of some of our beliefs has its origins in the existence of social institutions. The emphasis must be

moved from the reality we believe in to the social causes which incline
us to accept that (whatever it may be) as real. Echoing Wittgenstein, he
holds that 'what counts as obeying a rule is a matter of convention'.
Different societies may then have different 'objective' beliefs:

> Suppose the tribe on this side of the river worship one god, and the tribe
> on the other side of the river worship another god. If the worship of the
> gods is a stable feature of tribal practice, if they are spoken of routinely, if
> courses of action are justified by reference to them, then I would say both
> beliefs are objective.[20]

This is a far cry from notions of objectivity linked with truth. At least
one tribe must be mistaken in its beliefs, if an 'objectivist' view of truth is
invoked. That is ruled out by Bloor. 'Reality' is not the focus of his
interest, but he holds instead that 'variations in objectivity ought to be
locatable as variations in the institutions that embody knowledge.' He
tells us that 'we know reality *with* our conventions, not in spite of them'.
This suggests that he himself still wishes to retain some idea of a reality
independent of our conceptions of it. His brand of sociology of knowledge, however, pushes any such reality for ever beyond our reach.
Whatever we 'know' is socially conditioned, and is apparently explicable
wholly in terms of the social institutions in which we find ourselves. The
only interesting question remaining can be why we trust something as
real. Whether it is real is a question that can never be answered, since any
answer is itself the product of social convention. Claims to knowledge
will be the outcome of group interests rather than the way the world is.

An example of Bloor's approach is his treatment of the increasing
professionalization of science over the years in Britain. He argues that, in
order to claim a special expertise, independent of, say, the authority of
the Church, scientists were led to champion the idea that knowledge
gained by experiment comprised the whole of knowledge: 'One way of
ensuring that it was to be all was to deny any reality over and above that
revealed by "experience" – where experience was defined to mean just
those things one which the scientific expert can pronounce.'[21] Thus, he
says, 'empiricism functioned as the ideology of scientific professional-
ism'.

Bloor has put forward what he terms 'the strong programme' of the
sociology of knowledge.[22] He sketches its main characteristics by saying
that it is causal, and concerned with the conditions bringing about

knowledge. It is also impartial and symmetrical in its style of explanation. In other words, it treats true and false beliefs in identical fashion, and in so doing ultimately removes all distinction between truth and falsity. Bloor also hopes that it will be reflexive, so that, 'in principle, its patterns of explanation would have to be applicable to sociology itself'.

Just how strong a programme is envisaged can be judged by the fact that Bloor thinks that even the 'truths' of logic and mathematics are susceptible to sociological explanation. Since he is interested in the social origins of belief, he is immediately suspicious of appeals to self-evidence or to authority of any kind. What makes us treat certain statements as self-evident? What is the social grounding even of intellectual authority? Writing with Barry Barnes, he says:

> As a body of conventions and esoteric conditions the compelling char-acter of logic, such as it is, derives from certain narrowly defined purposes and from custom and institutionalized usage. Its authority is moral and social, and as such it is admirable material for sociological investigation and explanation. In particular, the credibility of logical conventions, just like the everyday practices which deviate from them, will be of an entirely local character.[23]

Far from logic being an indispensable presupposition of all thought, it is thus demoted to being a custom or convention. The result is that the fact of contradiction matters less than that one should feel it wrong to contradict oneself. Yet, although society enforces this kind of norm, we are still left wondering why its authority should be used in this way. The answer to this might appear to lie in the province of sociology, but at this point the sociology of knowledge overreaches itself. It cannot be a matter of purely local convention that it is undesirable for someone both to assert and to deny the same thing, since the speaker is then saying absolutely nothing. He is withdrawing what he is also putting forward. It is not an accident the societies disapprove of contradiction. The law of non-contradiction is an example of a logical law providing an indispensable framework for rational thought and for language. The alternative is not a different kind of society. It is silence.

Bloor accepts that there will be 'other types of causes apart from social ones which will cooperate in bringing about belief'.[24] This is an inter-esting admission which raises a question about the scope of the sociology of knowledge. It can be a very imperialistic discipline. Not content with disposing of epistemology, it aspires to explain the whole of science too. Presumably it would wish to explain the practice of psychology or of neurophysiology in sociological terms. Yet these disciplines themselves have ambitions of explaining the origins of human belief. Psychological causes might be very potent in inclining an individual to one set of beliefs rather than another. Research into the workings of the brain has barely begun. The sociology of knowledge has to decide whether such causes are genuine. Bloor's admission seems to accept this. On the other hand, why should we not say that social influences incline psychologists to accept psychological causes as genuine? If we do, the sociology of knowledge apparently becomes a crucial discipline, able to interpret the functioning of all other intellectual disciplines. If we do not, its significance depends on how important a role we ascribe to society and its influences. The impact of Wittgenstein's views, together with those of Kuhn, have led some to consider that the role of society is predominant, and perhaps all-pervasive.

The sociology of knowledge appears to be locked in a battle for supremacy with other intellectual disciplines. Looked at from a sociological point of view, such a battle itself provides plenty of material for study. That very fact, however, raises an insoluble problem. Bloor mentioned the requirement of reflexivity. The sociology of knowledge is itself a social practice with its own rules. Sociologists are themselves subject to the influences of the influences of the society to which they belong. The idea, therefore, of a sociology of the sociology of knowledge is not ludicrous: it is essential. Yet an infinite regress beckons at this point. Sociological explanations may be given for the sociology of knowledge. There may be something about the conditions of our society at this time which gives rise to such a discipline. The ease with which it can attack the previously revered portals of physical science itself invites sociological explanation. Why should sociologists find it plausible to suggest that science is not the discovery of truth but merely one rule-governed social activity among others? Sensible answers can no doubt be given to these questions, but if they are given we face the next one. Why do they seem sensible to us now, when they may not have to intellectuals fifty years ago? Thus we get sucked into a sociology of the sociology of the sociology of knowledge.

This process is not an interesting curiosity like the Cotswold village which includes a model village portraying itself. In the model, at the appropriate place there is a model of the model and in that a model of the model of the model. The regress in sociology is a vicious one, since the sociology of knowledge purports to offer *explanations* of why beliefs are held. Yet each explanation turns out not to be valid at all, but only what a particular group holds valid. The reason they do can itself be 'explained', but that, it turns out, is itself only an explanation held by a particular group. In each case, the explanation may be accepted because of social conditions and group interests which have nothing to do with the explanation. There can be no reason why any such sociology should be accepted by other groups who may have their own interests. Psychologists, or even philosophers, can reject the grandiose claims of the sociology of knowledge if they choose, and on the premisses of the latter they will inevitably do so. Each group can only operate according to its own rules.

Unless sociologists are prepared to assert certain things as *true* and to maintain that certain types of social conditions *are* causes, there is no reason why non-sociologists should accept anything they say. The trouble is that, if sociologists of knowledge do this, they undermine their own thesis. If the strong programme of the sociology of knowledge is true, it is thereby shown to be false. Its whole purpose is to shift attention from what is the case to what people hold is the case. Since this appears to involve the denial of objective truth, the basic distinction between what is and what is not the case is removed. Without it the linguistic acts of assertion and denial seem pointless. It is hard to avoid the conclusion that anyone presenting rational arguments for the sociology of knowledge to those beyond the discipline cannot in consistency believe what he or she is saying.

No one would deny that social influences on belief can be very powerful, but the question is whether they tell the *whole* story. Reflexivity only becomes a logical problem if they are held to do so. Otherwise we still appear to have access to whatever the beliefs are about. We are on the verge of unutterable bewilderment when *any* reality is repudiated. It seems then that we have beliefs, which are the product of our society, but that they are not really *about* anything. Language then floats free and science becomes pointless. Indeed, even an assertion that we have beliefs seems a claim about part of the reality that is prescribed.

Barnes and Bloor realize the incongruity of all this. Apparently they do not wish to deny the existence of objective reality so much as to question its relevance: 'Reality is a common factor in all the vastly different cognitive responses that men produce to it. Being a common factor it is not a promising candidate to field as an explanation of that variation.'[25] This, they think, gives them *carte blanche* to investigate the social causes operating locally which enable many different beliefs to seem credible. There is undoubtedly a problem why mankind has produced so many different systems of belief if confronted by the same objective reality. It seems inescapable that many have been mistaken. Perhaps even many of our own most firmly held beliefs may be wrong. Saying, though, that there is no such thing as a mistake, or even that questions of truth and falsity are irrelevant, not only removes the motive for any further intellectual effort on our part. More important, it fundamentally distorts many of the activities which sociologists may wish to study.

Truth and False Consciousness

Viewing a body of belief as a social practice may be illuminating, since it enables us to see social influences which we may have previously ignored. Suggesting, though, that we have then given an adequate explanation for the belief misrepresents the belief. I touched on this when remarking how sociologists can concentrate on the fact of belief rather than the content. The sociology of science may have interesting discoveries to make about the conduct of science, but that cannot be all there is to science. Scientists themselves are presumably often unaware of the social influences on their work. Yet someone cannot play cricket without having some idea of the rules, and similarly the rules of science cannot be totally hidden from the participants. This is the beginning of a major issue concerning the relationship between sociological explanation and the understanding of participants which I shall pursue later. Suffice it to say at the moment that scientists obviously think that they are acquiring knowledge of the world. Even the empiricist stress on observations carried with it the assumption that the world was being observed. Being told by sociologists that they are not really doing what they think they are doing is bound to be unsettling. Instead of discovering truth, scientists are, they will be told, merely engaging in a complex social activity. It does not matter that sociologists only need to be listened to if they are claiming the kind of truth for their theories that they are denying to branches of the physical sciences. The fact remains that, if any group of people are told that they are not doing what they imagine they are, this may itself influence their actions. They may even stop what they are doing.

This comes out more clearly if we examine the sociology of religion. Religious institutions, such as denominations of the Christian Church, are prime targets for sociological investigation. Their organizations and their impact on society, not to mention the secularizing influences of Western society on them, will be of consuming interest. Even the impact of different beliefs on societies can be studied. One can, for example, examine the respective impact of Catholic and Protestant versions of Christianity on different countries. Does Protestantism really encourage greater self-reliance and enterprise so that the 'Protestant work ethic' contributes to the prosperity of nations? Does Catholicism, with its opposition to contraception and its traditional emphasis on large families, contribute to the poverty of others? These are hotly debated issues which are of legitimate sociological concern.

The impact of society on belief can also be studied. There has been a marked tendency for some theologians to revise Christian belief to make it more acceptable to those around them. They themselves may have been influenced by complex currents in society which a sociologist can chart. Yet this does not face the underlying question: is Christianity true? Sociologists would immediately say that it was illegitimate for them to deal with such a question. Some of them would reject the idea of objective truth, with the consequences we have already sketched. Others would say that they wished to 'bracket off' the question of truth, and merely look at the fact of belief, together with its causes and influences. This position may seem more acceptable, but it too has its dangers. By trying to ignore questions about the content of a belief, it fails to take seriously the fact that to the person holding it the most important aspect is that *it is true*. The religious believer, rightly or wrongly, considers that he or she possesses knowledge. Any sociological interpretation which undercuts this falsifies what it is interpreting. 'Bracketing off' questions of truth may be the inevitable function of the sociologist, but it must not result in the view that questions of truth are of no importance.

The central feature of religious belief, as of theories in science, may well lie in its claim to be about an objective reality. It has this feature, even if it is mistaken. It is not a mere body of practices or rituals, because these are themselves based on assumptions about the kind of reality that confronts mankind. As a result, religious believers may quite justifiably feel threatened by sociological attempts to 'explain' their religion.

Accepting the sociology may mean that they can no longer retain their beliefs. That is a curious state of affairs, since sociology should not undermine any such beliefs unless it is willing to proclaim the falsity of religion. What has happened is that the essential nature of religious belief has been ignored. By side-stepping issues of truth and falsity, sociology has often forgotten the importance of claims to truth. Ignoring that can appear tantamount to assuming their falsity.

Since any denial of objective reality as such must be self-defeating, it is prudent for sociologists of knowledge to take seriously the fact that those they are studying do make claims about reality. Their own discipline thereby becomes less important, because they cannot adjudicate between different claims about reality. That is irrelevant. The very fact that they are willing to participate in an intellectual discipline in a rational manner shows that they are committed to the rational pursuit of truth. Whatever the social influences at work, we do have access to the real world, and can uncover real social influences at work. Sociologists are themselves in the business of studying reality and must accept that others do the same. Sociology has to claim objectivity so as to be taken seriously, and must note the similar claims of others.

Two sociologists, writing about the problem of reflexivity which haunts the sociologist, say the following:

> It is important to re-iterate that the sociologist does not interpret 'reality' but rather interprets various interpretations of 'reality' (or 'reality definition'). 'False consciousness' as a concept implies 'correct consciousness', which in turn implies a direct access to reality which the sociologist cannot supply.[26]

The term 'false consciousness' is in fact often used in sociology. Must sociology be neutral towards different world-views and does that suggest that the term is illegitimate? I have warned against the dangers of sociological scepticism about the possibility of objectivity, understood as the grasping of objective reality. That view can produce the conclusion that no beliefs could be true because truth is unattainable. Another approach, however, could start from the assumption that it already possesses knowledge, and attack beliefs it considered false. If it not only proclaimed the possibility of objective truth but said that it possessed it, is this a coherent position? Since I have already implied that the striving for truth is an important feature of scientific disciplines, there would seem to be nothing in principle wrong with it. We might, though, be suspicious of such arrogance, given the fallibility of mankind. An important consequence of stressing the objectivity of truth and denying that it is context-dependent is the realization that we may ourselves always be mistaken.

Berger and Kellner imply that sociologists have no access to reality. That is certainly so if it means that sociologists have no privileged position from which to judge which of several rival interpretations of reality is correct. They cannot properly use the prestige of sociology to tell us that Christianity is or is not true. They have strayed beyond their professional competence if they do so. What, though, is the position if a sociologist does not assess the worth of beliefs, but refers to the functioning of 'social reality'. If sociology cannot tell us anything about that and has no direct access to it, we might well wonder what is the supposed scientific value of the subject. It is at least plausible that, just as physics can investigate one level of reality, sociology and the other social sciences can discover laws about the functioning of a different level.

If there is such a thing as social reality, over and above the reality perceived by the individuals participating in a society, then participants may perhaps not properly understand it. Sociology may be able to uncover facts about societies of which their members may be totally unaware. It may even show why participants persistently misunderstand what is occurring in that society at the social level. It could, for instance, show how the class structure of a society has a pervasive and misleading influence on the way its members see themselves and their roles in society. On the other hand, it might be able to assert that some groups are in a favoured position to see society as it is. Georg Lukács thought that the proletariat was able to do this: 'It was necessary for the proletariat to be born for social reality to become fully conscious.'[27] We might wonder how Lukács himself was in a position to assert this. How had he obtained knowledge of social reality so as to endorse the beliefs of the proletariat? He seems to be saying that all beliefs are conditioned by the social background, and yet that means that his own views are bound merely to be the product of *his* background. Sociologists must be wary of claiming knowledge unless they can show some basis for it. If there is no independent way of establishing the truth of a belief, the mere fact that they endorse it themselves is irrelevant. Yet we must be careful that this does not immediately drive us to the conclusion that sociology is not concerned with reality but only interpretations of it.

Berger and Kellner are well aware that they hold a controversial position about the function of the social sciences. Sociology, they believe, does not discover laws about social reality, but investigates the different ways humans give meaning to the world. In their view, the sociologist 'presents a spectrum of meanings and values' but 'cannot tell people whether they should or should not adopt these meanings and values as their own.'[28] In other words, the main object of sociology is the understanding of meaning, or the different ways in which people can construct social reality. The focus of attention is the making of social reality and not the nature of social reality. Different forms of consciousness have to be accepted at face value, since there is no sociological standard by which they can be assessed. Any belief in reality is the product of consciousness, and sociologists must recognize that, if, like Lukács, they try to set up a standard of truth, they are merely setting up the constructs of their own consciousness over those of other people.

There is some force in this view, but it is a position which can undercut itself. Anyone claiming knowledge has to give reasons to justify the claim. The retort that 'that is just your opinion' can make all truth unattainable and induces the very paralysis which the strong programme of the sociology of knowledge brings on. We cannot always reduce the notion of a reason to 'what someone thinks is a reason'. Sociology and the other social sciences may claim that social reality is distinctive and cannot be adequately understood by those immersed in it. Such a belief is not just the product of the consciousness of sociologists. It may have much to commend it, but this has to be shown. Its truth depends on whether there is such a thing as social reality.

Notes

1   P. Feyerabend, *Science in a Free Society*, 1978, p. 70.
2   M. Grene, 'Dogmas of Empiricism', in R. S. Cohen and M. W. Wartofsky (eds), *Epistemology, Methodology and the Social Sciences*, 1983, p. 104.
3   See L. Wittgenstein, *Philosophical Investigations*, 1958 I, § 243ff.
4   Ibid., § 258.
5   Ibid., § 259.
6   Ibid., § 199.
7   Ibid., § 199.
8   Ibid., § 202.

9   Ibid., § 219.

10   Ibid., § 217.

11   See my *Reason and Commitment*, 1973, p. 94ff.

12   L. Wittgenstein, *On Certainty*, 1969, § 609ff.

13   Wittgenstein, *Philosophical Investigations*, I, § 206.

14   Ibid., II, xii, p. 230.

15   Ibid., II, xi, p. 226.

16   Ibid., I, § 415.

17   Peter Winch, *The Idea of a Social Science*, 1958, p. 100.

18   David Bloor, *Knowledge and Social Imagery*, 1976, II, p. 2.

19   Bloor, *Wittgenstein: a Social Theory of Knowledge*, 1983, p. 160.

20   Bloor, 'A Sociological Theory of Objectivity', in S. C. Brown (ed.), *Objectivity and Cultural Divergence*, 1984, p. 236.

21   Ibid., p. 243.

22   Bloor, *Knowledge and Social Imagery*, pp. 4–5.

23   D. Bloor and B. Barnes, 'Relativism, Rationalism and the Sociology of Knowledge', in M. Hollis and S. Lukes (eds), *Rationality and Relativism*, 1982, p. 45.

24   Bloor, *Knowledge and Social Imagery*, p. 5.

25   Bloor and Barnes, 'Relativism, Rationalism and the Sociology of Knowledge', p. 34.

26   P. Berger and H. Kellner, *Sociology Reinterpreted*, 1982, p. 74.

27   G. Lukács, *History and Class Consciousness*, 1971, p. 19.

28   Berger and Kellner, *Sociology Reinterpreted*, p. 74.

3

Individuals and Society

Consciousness and Behaviour

The idea that all standards are embedded in particular social practices and that 'objective' claims only have validity against a particular social background is self-defeating. It destroys itself, since it can no longer claim the kind of truth it needs if others are to take notice of it. It also seems to undermine the possibility of comparing different societies. There would be nothing in common to facilitate comparison, if each could only be understood in its own terms. Social scientists would be immersed in their own society and would inevitably judge other societies in the terms of their own. Their views would be ethnocentric and parochial, merely assuming the concepts of their own background, although we might well wonder what else they could do.

Social science is distinct from physical science in that it studies human society rather than inanimate objects. Positivism may well have inclined some social scientists to treat social interactions as if they were the colliding of physical objects. The emphasis on obtaining neutral observations and measurements as the basis for theory led to the exclusion of whatever could not be conveniently observed or measured. Behaviourism in psychology, for example, led to the systematic exclusion of whatever could not be scientifically tested in a laboratory. Pain behaviour, rather than the feeling of pain, would be the focus of attention. The same approach could lead to the exclusion of all questions concerning human consciousness. The important question would be what actually happened rather than how it was viewed by the participants. The latter was not testable from a scientific point of view.

This all begs a basic question, since it is assumed that we can distinguish what happened from what the participants thought. One of the issues, indeed, is just how important human consciousness is. Does it constitute human social activity by the meaning it bestows on it, or is it irrelevant? One of the problems of dismissing consciousness and its products as perhaps an interesting, but irrelevant, appendage to human activity, is that this must be done through arguments emanating from human consciousness. The extreme materialist who says that ideas are unimportant is, in fact, in the grip of an idea. Those who believe that society functions at a level untouched by human understanding have to come to terms with the irrelevance of their own understanding of this fact. Yet those who believe that society is constituted by human consciousness also have their problems. Since the repudiation of empiricism has removed the possibility of 'raw data', the problem of understanding different societies becomes acute, if all that is left is the different ways the world is perceived in them. Interpretation becomes the sole aim of the social sciences, although it is sometimes unclear on what basis this can be achieved.

Even before the demise of positivism, there were strong voices in the social sciences urging concentration on human consciousness rather than human behaviour. The very vigour of the positivist approach created a reaction away from it. Instead of looking to the natural sciences as models for a social-scientific methodology, many have urged that the social sciences must be distinct. The reasons for this are not hard to find. Any would-be science of human behaviour, modelled on a positivist conception of the natural sciences, is not just appealing to neutral observations to provide the raw data on which theories can be based. It is restricting its attention to what can be observed, or better still, measured. Its prejudice for what is public and verifiable means that anything which is apparently subjective can be ignored. What is subjective is denigrated precisely because it is out of reach of controlled scientific observation. The viewpoint of an individual is left out of account, since science, according to the positivist, can only take hold of what is viewed intersubjectively. The objectivity of science sometimes appears to consist precisely in this abstraction from all points of view. The scientist believes that an experiment can be repeated by anyone else and still give the same results; the fact that a particular person is conducting it must be irrelevant. Yet that means that scientists abstract from the objects of their study all traces of anyone's point of view and conception of the situation. This is quite proper when they are experimenting on physical objects. What is measured is distinct from the person measuring, and what is observed is distinct from the observer. There are difficulties in quantum mechanics, but the basic view that reality is logically independent of anyone investigating it is crucial.

Problems arise when the reality to be investigated includes human beings. They can be studied as if they are mere physical objects; their movements can be charted and their behaviour noted. Studies of animal behaviour can do this without any speculation about how far animals understand what they are doing. That is a further question. They may be acting intentionally, but it is still possible to question how far they are conscious of what they are doing and why they are doing it, or how far they have been programmed by evolution to act *as if* they know what they are about. Animals can certainly learn through imitation, so that patterns of behaviour are passed on from generation to generation. One of the most famous examples is that of a group of Japanese macaques.[1] One female monkey began washing the sand off potatoes with which she was fed on a beach. Others followed her example, and most of the monkeys there now wash them in the sea. The tradition is passed on to infants, who imitate their mothers. Apart from cleaning the potatoes, the sea-water presumably leaves a salty taste. All this can be observed without taking into account how the monkeys conceive of the situation. Their behaviour can be recorded even if we leave aside questions about such subjective aspects. My reference to a salty taste is itself perhaps a piece of needless speculation, by positivist standards. Even talk of 'tradition' is perhaps unnecessary. Baby monkeys imitate their elders, and we need only refer to the way individuals behave, apparently copying others. Suggesting that teaching occurs is unnecessary, since that could imply the deliberate transmission of conscious knowledge. Richard Passingham says: 'We have little evidence that any animal does teach. In almost all instances there is a more parsimonious description of what the animal is doing.'[2] He points out that young lions certainly learn to hunt by being taken on expeditions with their mothers. He considers it likely that the mothers happen to allow the infants to go on the hunt, rather than set out with the deliberate intention of training them. They do not appear, for instance, to make any effort to demonstrate the relevant techniques.

Whether cases of animals intentionally teaching others can be produced or not, animal behaviour can be adequately studied without assumptions being made about animal culture, tradition or consciousness. Even here there is a danger. Because the mental states of animals are inaccessible to scientists, it is easy to conclude that they do not have any. It would not be surprising to discover that empiricist prejudice had led us to underrate the abilities of animals to feel or even to think. Nevertheless their mental life can only be rudimentary, and there is no way it could be reasonably suggested that an animal's understanding of what it was doing actually changed the character of its behaviour. The monkeys washing potatoes could do so whether they have any views about the matter or not. Questions about the interpretation of actions do not arise. It may be suggested that 'washing potatoes' is itself a human classification of an action. This, however, merely demonstrates that animal behaviour is understood by reference to human categories and not animal ones.

It is not as easy to discount the concepts which human agents possess. Human beings do not just *behave*. They *act*, and their actions occur with an understanding of their significance in a wider social context. Human actions are endowed with meaning, and it may appear that they cannot be properly understood unless that meaning is grasped. Human behaviour, viewed as a mere succession of bodily movements, and human actions performed with definite motives and intentions may not be the same. The bodily movements involved in signing a cheque, for instance, can never by themselves explain what is occurring. We would have in addition to understand the agent's reasons for wishing to transfer money – to buy a house, give a present, pay a bribe, or perform countless other actions. All these actions presuppose a wider social setting; indeed the whole notion of paying by cheque itself presupposes an elaborate background of banking institutions.

Once we venture on explaining human action, we cannot treat humans as physical objects. The abstraction of what is occurring from all points of view, including those of the agent and of the observer, does not allow for any consideration of the individual's, or other people's, understanding of what he or she is doing. All psychological and social aspects of behaviour are excluded. Founding the social sciences on a positivist methodology will inevitably draw criticism from those who see human action in terms of the meaning given to it, whether by the agent, the whole society, or even the observer trying to make sense of what is observed.

The Goal of Social Science

Any attempt to exclude from the study of society whatever the positivist might view as unscientific 'subjective' elements would appear to many to evacuate human society of all that is essential to it. The very term 'subjective' means something different to positivists and to their opponents. Positivists might use it to refer to what should be excluded because it is private and unverifiable. Others do not use it in the pejorative sense. Alfred Schutz, who was influenced in his work on social science by the phenomenology of Edmund Husserl, puts the matter in this way:

> The critics of understanding call it subjective, because they hold that understanding the motives of another man's action depends upon the private, uncontrollable and unverifiable intuition of the observer or refers to his private value system. The social scientists, such as Max Weber, however, call *Verstehen* subjective because its goal is to find out what the actor 'means' in his action, in contrast to the meaning which this action has for the actor's partner or a neutral observer.[3]

We are at the point of a major divide in the understanding of the social sciences. There are several strands to the argument. At the root is the question whether the natural and social sciences should have the same methodology, if that methodology stems from positivism. The stand taken on that issue also has implications for other arguments. For instance, if the goal of social science is to discover 'meanings', the direct conclusion must be that it is not concerned with causal explanation but has a different aim. Social reality would then appear to be different from physical reality, and the question must arise about its relationship with the individual. The controversy over whether there is such a thing as social reality is a recurring one. A positivist view of human behaviour denies it.

Schutz referred to Weber, whose concept of *Verstehen* provided an alternative to the positivist ideal of causal explanation. By *Verstehen* is meant something like interpretive understanding. Weber insisted that what we had to understand was the subjective meaning attached by an individual to his or her behaviour. There was, then, no question of imposing any framework of explanation which the agent would not accept. One had to get into his mind and look at his actions through his eyes. Weber defined sociology as a 'science which attempts the inter-pretive understanding of social action'.[4] Behaviour is action in so far as 'the acting individual attaches a subjective meaning to it' and social in so far as the individual takes account of the behaviour of others.

Both Weber and Schutz were anxious to differentiate the kind of explanation they were seeking in the social sciences from the 'external observation' which they believed characterized explanation in the na-tural sciences. While accepting that this kind of subjective understanding delivered results which possessed a 'mere hypothetical and fragmentary character', Weber emphasized that 'subjective understanding is the spe-cific characteristic of social knowledge.' Schutz, whose views have also been highly influential, puts the matter this way:

> We cannot deal with phenomena in the social world as we do with phenomena belonging to the natural sphere. . . . We want to understand social phenomena, and we cannot understand them apart from their placement within the scheme of human motives, human means and ends, human planning – in short – within the categories of human action. The social scientist must therefore ask . . . what happens in the mind of an individual actor whose act has led to the phenomena in question.[5]

Ethologists do not have to ask what is going on in the minds of monkeys washing potatoes; the monkeys' behaviour requires no further interpretation. Human action, however, can only be understood, it is suggested, in terms of human concepts. This inevitably raises the ques-tion of interpretation, since, if the nature of an action is determined by the consciousness of an agent, there is a difficult question how far an observer can become attuned to that consciousness. Similar problems arise when we wonder about any aspect of the private mental life of another. Positivism was naturally accompanied by behaviourist views, which would, for example, countenance motives only in so far as they were understood as dispositions to behave in particular ways. Social theories which emphasize the importance of the contents of individual minds are also often linked to philosophical presuppositions about the status of mind – for example, the dualist position, which distinguishes between bodily movements and mental activity. Mind and body are regarded as distinct, the mind giving meaning to bodily behaviour. In that way, reflex actions, such as the involuntary jerk of one's knee, can be distinguished from meaningful activity. The notorious problem then arising is how to gain access to the contents of another's mind. The argument from analogy is normally invoked here: I know the kind of pain you are feeling because I know what I feel in similar circumstances. Nevertheless philosophers are always aware of the dangers of scepticism. We find it easy enough to imagine that animals do not have minds, and perhaps conclude that too easily. Why should we not assume that because other minds are inaccessible 'they' are non-existent? In essence, this is the verificationist or 'anti-realist' position. Because we cannot verify the existence of other minds, we just have to deal with public ways of behaving. Yet one curious feature of some versions of empiricism, defending doctrines about sense-data, is that they stress the importance of what is publicly accessible through the concept of intersubjective experience. The sense-data themselves, however, which form the foundations of empirical knowledge, are archetypal instances of what is private and subjective. Wittgenstein's emphasis on the public and social led him to repudiate any such basis for knowledge.

The dualist conception of mind makes it private and subjective in the sense that it is accessible only to the subject of the experiences and thoughts. In another sense, it is not subjective at all, since the contents of mind are real enough if dualists are right. It is objectively true that someone is, or is not, in pain. There is sometimes an unfortunate slide from the notion of what is accessible only to a particular subject, to what is subjectively valid or true only for that person. The positivist attack on the subjectivity of experience makes what is private and hence not susceptible to scientific investigation not an objective matter in any sense. The objectively true becomes synonymous with the scientifically accessible.

Phenomenological views of social action explicitly challenge positivism in matters of this kind. Far from considering it a virtue to be bound by the standards of physical science, they consider that this empties society of all that is distinctively human. By basing society on the products of individual minds, they are not merely taking a position on the privacy of the mental, they also stress the primacy of the individual as the source of society. The social is thus created by the individual thoughts of individuals. Society is not a 'thing' coercing individuals, and social explanation is not at a different level from that of the explanation of the understanding of individuals. *Verstehen*, in Weber's sense, is not groping for the concepts of one society from the standpoint of an alien system. It is one individual trying to understand another.

The argument about the relationship between individuals and society is of basic importance for social science, and the significance of the social sciences as a whole is tied up with this question. Sociology, for example, is going to be of much greater interest and relevance if it uncovers structures in society to which no other discipline has access. If, however, society can be adequately explained in terms of the individual contents of individual minds, psychology might perhaps seem of more vital importance for the understanding of society. Sociology would then have to become a branch of social psychology which concentrates on the small-scale interactions of individuals. A basic issue is whether it is possible to gain insights into politics or economics, say, through concentration on individuals. Can individual actions throw light on social currents flowing through whole societies? According to one sociologist, David Rubinstein,

> The belief that the intentional actions of concrete individuals are the exclusive concern of social science produces a seriously limited kind of sociology, a sociology that is programmatically unable to deal with issues encompassing entire societies.[6]

The question is well illustrated by economics. Is economics to be concerned with the cumulative effects of individuals interacting with each other, or are there economic laws operating beyond the consciousness of any individual agent? This is one more instance where a social science might wish to give explanations of behaviour which would not have been conscious to an agent and which indeed that agent may vehemently reject. Any position locating the origin of the social world in the individual consciousness may be restricted to explanations that individuals would accept. Otherwise the social world is treated as if it were independent of its origin in the individual mind.

A complication in all this is that the actions of individuals very often have unintended social consequences. The combined effect of these may itself be worthy of study, even when the individual agent is unaware of them. Even if the working of the market depends on many individual decisions, it might itself function in a way that seems independent of them. If everyone decides simultaneously to buy the same kinds of goods, shortages will develop, even though no one deliberately tried to create them. It might appear that, once created by individuals, social reality has a life of its own. Those who emphasize the role of individual consciousness are not saying that, but insist that any social-scientific understanding has to be in accord with the agents' commonsense understanding of their society. The everyday world of agents cannot then differ from the social world as studied by social scientists. There is no other reality for them to investigate. They may bring their own categories to bear on it, but they must remember that social reality is dependent on the minds of the agents.

This theory thereby betrays its idealist origins. For idealists, reality is dependent on mind: what exists does so because it is being perceived by a mind. Such a theory goes against common sense when applied to physical reality. However much we may debate the reality of the 'external' world, we know that tables and chairs are there, whether they are perceived or not. Perhaps slightly more dubiously we assume that a clock goes on ticking even when there is no one in the room to hear it. The theory, however, does seem more congenial when applied to social reality. Is society an abstract force that goes on working regardless of the thought process of its members? Perhaps this is another way of asking whether a whole is more than the sum of its parts. A jigsaw puzzle may form a striking picture when put together, but it is still merely a collection of different pieces. It is more plausible to think of a car as more than that, since when assembled it seems to form a new entity able to function as one complex piece of machinery. The question is whether society is a collection of individuals or whether it is a new kind of entity, depending for its existence on its parts but not reducible to them.

Social Reality and the Individual

The notion that society or particular social patterns are entities with an existence independent of human minds has often been attacked. It is said to be *reification*, a process which treats essential human characteristics as if they were non-human *things*. Berger and Luckmann give as an example the ways in which human marriage can be reified:

> Marriage may be reified as an imitation of divine acts of creativity, as a universal mandate of natural laws, as the necessary consequence of bio-logical or psychological forces, or for that matter, as a functional imperative of the social system. What all these reifications have in common is their obfuscation of marriage as a human production.[7]

Stress on individual consciousness as the source of society certainly reminds us that society is a human creation, and that the way humans live together is the result of human decisions. It is possible to go too far, however, since a completely idealist emphasis on consciousness inevitably removes any notion of an objective, or independently existing, reality. The only way, then, of understanding a society is to look into the minds of its members. It will not help to look at the reality confronting those minds. From holding that social reality is a human creation, some theorists can easily get drawn into treating all reality in the same way.

Berger and Luckmann say: 'All symbolic universes and all legitimations are human products: their existence has its base in the lives of concrete individuals, and has no empirical status apart from those lives.'[8] This is a reiteration of the importance of the individual as the source of society. Yet it can lead not just to a view of social reality as a human creation, but also to an undue extension of what is regarded as within the scope of human creation. It may seem obvious that, if all social arrangements are the product of human minds, everything social must be the result of mental categories. This in turn leads to the impression that they might have been created otherwise. Indeed, different societies seem actually to possess different categories. Yet all this precludes the possibility that some arrangements might have been imposed on society, and on the minds creating it, by external contingencies.

Berger and Luckmann show how an institutional world can be experienced as an objective reality by an individual. We feel that we are placed in something that constrains us. It seems objective, because it has been created by other minds. Yet they say: 'Despite the objectivity that marks the social world in human experience, it does not thereby acquire an ontological status apart from the human activity that produced it.'[9] A university, for example, may seem to be as objectively there as its buildings. Different participants in the life of the institution come and go, but it remains recognizably the same institution. It is possible to look at an ancient college and see the way its life continues through many generations of students. Similarly the Christian Church, even if viewed merely as a social institution, without any supernatural overtones, continues through history. Popes, bishops and clergy all change, yet the same Church lives on into new generations. It is, of course, possible to identify such institutions with the buildings they inhabit, but that would be an obvious mistake. The question is whether they have an ontological status apart from the activity of those producing them. They appear to influence their members, and that might indicate that they do, despite the danger of reification. It is easy to see why some are tempted to insist that an institution does have an existence of a different order from that of the individuals participating in it.

It may nevertheless seem plausible to deny that what is created by humans can exist apart from them. The more, though, that we focus our attention on the active role of the human mind in the creation of such institutions, the more we are in danger of ignoring the way in which the mind might itself be constrained by external factors. For example, taboos are rules enforced by societies, sometimes with great ferocity. They are in one sense the creation of minds, and yet that leaves open the question why they were created. Berger and Luckmann refer to the incest taboo and say that it is 'nothing but the negative side of an assemblage of typifications, which define in the first place which sexual conduct is incestuous and which is not.'[10] This could suggest that such definitions are merely products of the human mind, and are arbitrary ways of categorizing social behaviour. Yet *why* have minds produced just those definitions? The incest taboo appears to be universal. Why is this so? A phenomenological approach concentrates on minds as the source of society. Even if we accept the individualist emphasis, there remains the question: what makes them produce the kinds of society that they do?

One answer would refer to human nature, however that is to be explained. It is significant, however, that the more that individual consciousness is asserted to be the source of conceptual schemes and of society, the less room is left for any such general notion. Indeed, the concept of human nature, like all concepts, could itself be portrayed as a product of consciousness. Stress on the active role of consciousness seems to leave little beyond the scope of its creation. Luckmann explicitly denies that human life possesses any 'elementary structures' which could constitute 'anything like an immutable human nature'. He sweepingly asserts: 'Modern philosophical and social anthropology cured us of this illusion.'[11] His position is explained more fully as follows:

> No doubt both human consciousness and social organization have a phylogeny which goes far back into our primate and even mammal ancestry. Yet human society structures have become historical; in part they have become emancipated from simple phylogenetic determination.

They are the result of purposive as well as blind, of individual as well as collective, human *action*.[12]

This is the edge of a major controversy to which I shall return. The strength of this type of approach is its recognition of the distinctiveness of *human* society as a *human* creation. This may paradoxically also be a weakness, but emphasizing the role of consciousness certainly distinguishes humans from animals, or mere physical objects. Understanding the significance of what is being done distinguishes human action from animal behaviour or the movements of objects.

Writers such as Weber and Schutz do not so much concentrate on the significance of the human as deal with the priority of the individual. Yet the social sciences do not merely need to differentiate themselves from the physical sciences. It is not sufficient for them to show that social reality cannot be studied by the physicist or biologist. Unless society possesses 'emergent properties' the social sciences will tell us little more than we can understand through the study of individuals. An emphasis on human consciousness in an idealist manner can easily be combined with beliefs about society as a 'thing'. Combinations of individuals may, for instance, form a collectivity with its own forms of consciousness which transcend the individual. References to the 'spirit of a nation' or the 'spirit of an age' perhaps suggest something like this.

Weber would have none of that kind of theory. He is very emphatic that apparent collectivities are merely combinations of individuals, and reducible to them. It is easy to talk about all kinds of human social units as agents. We may say about a mother that the family were concerned about her health. This means nothing more than that the individual members were severally concerned about it. Matters are perhaps less clear-cut if we talk of vast multinational business corporations or even states. They can certainly be party to legal agreements, and there is often a definite distinction between the liabilities of a corporation and those of its employees. Weber grants that the law may see things differently but insists that sociology cannot make this kind of distinction. He says of such social institutions as states and corporations:

> For the subjective interpretation of action in sociological work these collectivities must be treated as solely the resultants and modes of organization of the particular acts of individual persons, since these alone can be treated as agents in a course of subjectively understandable action.[13]

This approach must lead to the search for an empathy with individual members of a society, so that sociology involves the understanding of people's motives. It does not then uncover laws of human behaviour or of the functioning of social structures. There would thus appear to be little room for any misunderstanding by agents of the social significance of what they were doing (although even many opposed to holism might accept that the unintended social consequences of individual action were a proper subject for study). The concept of false consciousness would have no application. Individual self-deception may be possible, but the social analogue of this is ruled out. Whole groups cannot misunderstand the nature of their actions, and one class could not, it seems, exploit another, while being unaware of the fact. Since, on this view, groups are combinations of individuals, reference to the agency of classes as such, rather than merely of their members, is prohibited.

Weber gives as an example the working of a socialist economy, the members of which may perhaps have a belief in the importance of 'society' and the 'social'. He says that any sociological understanding would have to proceed in terms of the actions of individuals. It could, for example, refer to the types of officials found in it. He continues:

> The real empirical sociological investigation begins with the question: What motives determine and lead the individual members and participants in this socialistic community to behave in such a way that the community came into being in the first place and that it continues to exist?[14]

Sociology, on this understanding, is built on what Schutz calls 'the thought objects constructed by the common-sense thinking of men',[15] and it is in no position to repudiate its foundation. It elucidates the ways ordinary individuals see themselves as interacting in society. These cannot be contrasted with what is actually going on. Because individual consciousness is regarded as the source of society, it cannot be detached from it and be judged by it. Social reality is as it is seen by common sense, since that is what made it. Schutz made this very clear when he wrote:

> By the term 'social reality', I wish to be understood the sum total of objects and occurrences within the social, cultural world as experienced by the common-sense thinking of men living their daily lives among their fellow-men, connected with them in manifold relations of interaction.[16]

Once it is suggested that social reality goes beyond what individuals conceive, the whole function of the social sciences has to change. It always seemed implausible that they were only concerned with understanding individual motives, since this left out of account the sheer complexity of society. Individualist accounts are atomistic. The meaning of actions becomes the meaning given separately to them by individuals acting in isolation from each other. Each separate social happening can then be understood even when it is wrenched from its social setting. This, though, is an impossible view for anyone to take to extremes, since human beings are born into societies and are made by them, as well as making them. Berger and Luckmann themselves can admit, in the same breath as saying that society is a human product, that man is a social product.[17] They argue that we can participate in a social world by playing 'roles'.[18] Just as we expect certain behaviour of a waiter in a restaurant, and a good waiter will fulfil these expectations, all of us fill roles expected of us by others. This is still consonant with individualism, but a strong feeling that society is exerting pressures on us can easily lead to the view that the social cannot be reduced to the individual. The complex reality of society might appear visible only in its entirety. This approach is termed 'holistic', and would be connected with the contextualist view which demands that proper understanding must see the part played by agents in a wider social pattern. Social explanation is then made irreducible to psychological explanation, so that what happens at the one level cannot be understood merely in terms of what happens at another.

Constraints on Subjectivity

Durkheim provides a good example of someone putting forward a view of society which does indeed explicitly reify it, treating it as totally separate from the minds of its members. He takes as his starting-point the feeling that each of us is confronted by something apart from ourselves when we are immersed in society. We are faced with demands and claims that are created by social conditions and are not of our own making. As individuals we are introduced to traditions and ways of living which are seemingly 'there', confronting us as much as the physical world does. The complexity of individual interactions entails that any individual has to cope with a system of demands and expectations. The problem is whether the system can ultimately be understood in terms of the choices and ways of acting of countless individuals, or whether social phenomena can be explained in other terms without changing the subject.

Many dualists vehemently object to individual actions being explained totally in neurophysiological terms. While recognizing that brains are indispensable, they refuse to accept that as the whole story: reference to the brain is necessary but not sufficient for the explanation of human action. Dualists would argue that the mental is irreducible to the physical, and an understanding of, say, the intentions of someone getting married could not be explained in terms of electrical activity in the brain. This is analogous to the argument about society and individuals. Indeed, it is a continuation of it, since there are those (as we shall see) who would like to explain the complex arrangements of society in terms of the activity of individual brains. To do so they have to ignore both the protests of the dualists, and the arguments of those who do not in the first place wish to reduce the social level to that of the individual. The latter would argue that questions about the significance of marriage are not simply questions about the attitude of individuals to marriage, because marriage is a social institution with its own rules and functions and, as such, cannot be fully explained in terms of the motives and thoughts of individuals.

Indeed, the role played by an institution in society may be so complex that it is not fully understood by any individual. Individuals are introduced to the institution, rather than perpetually re-creating it through their own thoughts and understanding. Berger and Luckmann's view of marriage as an ongoing human production would be seen by some as woefully inadequate. Just as we need brains to think, social institutions cannot exist without members. The individual provides a necessary condition for the existence of society. That may not mean, however, that a proper understanding of society can be gained through studying individuals, even if we take into account the effects of their interaction with each other. Society may provide a distinct level of explanation.

One illustration of this is the family. Is that constituted by society or by the motives and wishes of individuals? An answer to this by some is linked to the understanding of social rules which we have encountered in Wittgenstein. It is holistic in emphasis, explaining the family in social terms. David Rubinstein puts it this way:

The family is constituted by the rules that obtain in a given society. The biological uncle may be the social father if societal rules establish him to be. The social scientific definition of the father must therefore be tied to the rules of the society under study. . . . As there is no game of chess apart from its rules, there is no family, in the social sense, apart from the rules that constitute it.[19]

The rules are grounded in ways of life, and they may be imperfectly understood by some individuals. The existence of the institution with its public rules gives meaning to actions, whatever the inward thoughts of participants may be. The argument would be that it is the existence of institutions, like marriage, that gives individual actions their social significance. Indeed, they give actions the only significance they can have. Two people are not married just because they regard themselves as being so. Saying 'I do' in accepting marriage vows means nothing outside the proper institutional setting. Even a wedding rehearsal is not a wedding. Abstracting such an institution from its social background is, in fact, to destroy it. The proponents of this position could argue that the casual arrangements often made whereby a couple live together with regard only to their own private wishes does not so much modify previous understandings of marriage; rather, it begins to undermine the social institution, and hence eventually the nature of our society itself.

This approach appears to break sharply with emphases on the role of individual consciousness, but both share an important feature. If the source of meaning is the individual, this reduces the significance of external contingencies. Human nature seems irrelevant. The same conclusion can be drawn when society is made the focus of meaning. No greater scope is given to human nature, and society seems as unconstrained as the individual. A constant danger for a phenomenological approach is that, in stressing the importance of the individual subject, it lapses into a position which makes all judgements valid for the person making them. It finds itself embroiled in a rampant subjectivism which could easily turn into solipsism, according to which I am trapped in my own world. It is difficult even to state such a position clearly, since it is almost impossible consistently to assume that other people exist only in so far as I believe that they do. If 'my world' and 'the world' are coextensive, I can never be mistaken, since there is nothing objective with which my judgements can be compared. Other people do not then really exist. It is all too easy to lapse into the position of the old lady who wrote to a famous philosopher saying that she was so convinced of the truth of solipsism that she could not understand why other people did not agree with her.

In view of this, the step from individual to society as the source of meaning might seem a natural one to take. Whether it solves the under-lying problem is another matter. Many positions try to mediate between the apparently stark alternatives of individual or society. Some stress the importance of 'symbolic interaction' between minds and the meanings found in human societies. The individual consciousness is thus not completely isolated, but interacts with others to form society, while being itself a product of society. One account of this position says that 'society is to be understood in terms of the individuals making it up and individuals are to be understood in terms of the societies of which they are members'.[20] A drawback of this type of compromise is that it is very easy for it to favour one or other of the alternatives. Symbolic inter-actionism does try to avoid the dilemma that behaviour is caused either by forces internal to an individual, such as instincts, or by social forces impinging from outside. Yet we are told that it emphasizes 'the social origins of the self and human nature'. Thus in the end it appears to devalue the position of the individual and ignore the possible contribu-tion of human nature.

Once this step has been taken, and due note made of the way in which society moulds us, it is easy to locate meaning in the rules of a society and to deny that an individual can be abstracted from the context. Every-thing that makes us what we are and gives sense to our lives, it will be said, comes from our society. A baby chimpanzee does not need to be initiated into a society in the way that a human baby does. It seems to follow that an individual even gains his or her own identity in the context of society. A strong emphasis on the social will suggest that the self is created by society, so that society cannot be made by individuals. Individuals are created by society. Even our concept of an individual, it will be emphasized, is created by our society, and may indeed have emerged in particular historical conditions. The same arguments apply to our concept of human nature. The very notion might seem to have been produced in society. Human nature cannot therefore have created society, because society would have formed our ideas of human nature.

Only if it is accepted that society is much more than a conglomeration of individuals can the category of the social be given prominence. Emile Durkheim certainly accepted this and says firmly: 'Social phenomena must be considered in themselves, detached from the conscious beings who form their own mental representations of them.'[21] He explicitly contradicts those who locate the origins of society in the consciousness of the individual, and stresses the priority of the social with an emphasis on 'social facts'. He says that they are 'like moulds into which we are forced to cast our actions'.[22] He talks of 'external coercion' and takes as an example what happens in a gathering when there is an outburst of collective emotion.[23] This is a well-known phenomenon. We may be gripped by the fervour of an election rally or of a football match. Representatives may be swayed by a feeling of common purpose when a difficult matter is discussed in a parliament or a synod. Many know that being caught up in a crowd can produce startling results, and individuals behave collectively as they would not if they were each on their own. Sometimes the mood can become ugly, and the crowd demands what the decent individuals composing it would not normally tolerate. At other times, a collective purpose can extort nobler behaviour than any of the individuals involved thought themselves capable of. Yet the problem remains the same, whatever the occasion. Durkheim maintains: 'The group thinks, feels and acts differently from the way its members would if they were isolated.'[24] This illustrates his belief that 'society is not the mere sum of individuals' but instead forms a specific reality.

Once this position is adopted, the consciousness of the individual becomes merely the reflection of society. Human nature cannot be considered of primary importance, since that could only operate in the first instance through individuals. Explanations in terms of human nature are invariably rivals to those which invoke society. Durkheim not surprisingly rejects the idea that psychical states can be the causes of social phenomena. In asserting the 'given' nature of society, he not only discards the idea of the priority of the individual consciousness but also criticizes all accounts rooting society in human nature.

Although the social epitomizes the human for many thinkers, the idea of human nature is often anathema to them. It seems fixed and unalterable and, as such, appears irrelevant as an explanation for the many different forms of human society. Faced with a wealth of human differences, appeals to one human nature seem irrelevant. Yet the differences may be more apparent than real, since we may too easily take for granted our similarities and become obsessed with our differences. However that may be, cultural differences are a fact, and any theory in the social sciences has to take account of them. Whether the differences can be explained is controversial, and the easy way out will be to accept them as ultimate, so that each society has to be seen in its own terms. Wittgenstein maintains that we ought not to look for explanations but ought merely to say that 'this language-game is played'.[25]

Durkheim is impressed by cultural differences and resists the temptation to explain them in terms of human nature. He may accept that human nature helps to set the scene for human social life, but it will not be relevant, he considers, in explaining even fairly constant phenomena in human social life. For example, religion seems well-nigh universal in human societies, or so it is claimed. Family relationships often seem of fundamental importance to human life. Is marriage really a mere product of particular societies and not related to basic pre-social needs? Questions concerning religion, marriage and the nature of the family constantly recur in accounts of what constitutes human social life. Durkheim explicitly rejects any suggestion that they are the product of innate tendencies in individuals:

> It has been held that a certain religiosity is innate in man, as is a certain minimum of sexual jealousy, filial piety, or fatherly affection etc., and it is in these that explanations have been sought for religion, marriage and the family. But history shows that these inclinations, so far from being inherent in human nature, are either completely absent under certain social conditions, or vary so much from one society to another that the residue left after eliminating all these differences . . . is reduced to something vague and schematic. Thus these sentiments result from the collective organization and are far from being at the basis of it.[26]

It may seem that Durkheim is at least partly making an empirical point. Perhaps some societies do not possess religious belief, and perhaps their family arrangements are so utterly different from ours as to be virtually non-existent. Yet at this juncture we must begin to wonder at what point a society is so different from ours that our concepts cannot apply. At some point cultural divergence must be so complete that talking of 'religion' or 'families' or 'fathers' as we understand these terms becomes totally inappropriate. Societies that are so utterly different from each other would not have enough in common to enable the beginnings of mutual understanding. Indeed, because of their differences from us, it would just be true by definition that they do not possess 'religion' or 'families' as we understand these terms. It seems that, once the concept of human nature is abandoned, the task of understanding other societies becomes enormous.

Notes

1   Case quoted in Richard Passingham, *The Human Primate*, 1982, p. 181.
2   Ibid., p. 188.
3   Alfred Schutz, *Collected Papers*, vol. I, *The Problem of Social Reality*, 1962, p. 56.
4   Max Weber, *Theory of Social and Economic Organization*, 1947, p. 80.
5   Schutz, *Collected Papers*, vol. II, *Studies in Social Theory*, p. 85.
6   David Rubinstein, *Marx and Wittgenstein*, 1981, p. 70.
7   P. Berger and T. Luckmann, *The Social Construction of Reality*, 1967, p. 107.
8   Ibid., p. 146.
9   Ibid., p. 78.
10 Ibid., p. 73.
11 T. Luckmann, *Life-World and Social Realities*, 1983, p. 179.
12 Ibid., p. 162.
13 Weber, *Theory of Social and Economic Organization*, p. 92.
14 Ibid., p. 97.
15 Schutz, *Collected Papers*, vol. I, p. 59.
16 Ibid., p. 53.
17 Berger and Luckmann, *Social Construction of Reality*, p. 79.
18 Ibid., p. 91.
19 Rubinstein, *Marx and Wittgenstein*, p. 37.
20 See B. N. Meltzer, J. W. Petras, L. T. Reynolds, *Symbolic Interactionism, Genesis, Varieties, Criticism*, 1975, p. 2.
21 Emile Durkheim, *The Rules of Sociological Method*, 1982, p. 70.
22 Ibid., p. 70.
23 Ibid., p. 56.
24 Ibid., p. 129.
25 L. Wittgenstein, *Philosophical Investigations*, 1958, I, § 654.
26 Durkheim, *Rules of Sociological Method*, p. 131.

4

Understanding Other Societies

Humans as Social Beings

Philosophical views which demand that we start with the products of the individual consciousness raise questions about how we can understand each other. A dualist view of mind and matter naturally gives rise to the so-called 'problem of other minds'. Holistic views starting with some idea of society as prior meet an analogous problem. How can we understand the members of societies which are very different from our own? Both positions stress the distinctiveness of the human, and in so doing are paradoxically quick to dismiss appeals to human nature. Those who stress the importance of consciousness do not wish it to be constrained by anything extraneous, while those who emphasize the priority of the social feel that appeals to human nature explain little. It seems as though consciousness is not to be explained further, whether it produces society or is produced by it. This is not surprising, since neither position would welcome any reductionist programme. Those wishing to stress the importance of the individual mind, and those who stress the significance of the society into which we are born, are both united in resisting explanations in naturalist terms. They do not want the social sciences to become a branch of physics or of biology; they agree that the social sciences are radically different from the physical sciences. Social reality is utterly distinct from physical reality, so that, whether it is constituted by the thoughts of individuals or has a life of its own, it is bound up with meanings and human consciousness. Humans are thus more than animals.

This comes out very clearly in the early writings of Karl Marx, which, it is sometimes alleged, are more 'humanistic' than his later work. He inveighs against workers becoming mere commodities. In talking about 'alienation' he protests against the way in which the products of labour can seem to confront the worker as a 'power independent of the producer'.[1] People can become slaves to what they have produced. We are told that 'the more the worker externalizes himself in his work, the more powerful becomes the alien, objective world that he creates opposite himself, the poorer he becomes himself in his inner life and the less he can call his own.' The workers' products exist outside them in a way that even becomes a threat. Human work is alienated from humans and free activity, which, Marx considers, is what distinguishes us from animals, is distorted so that 'man makes his vital activity and essence a mere means to his existence'. The significant feature is that Marx has a definite view of human consciousness as what makes the distinction between human beings and animals. He says that 'free conscious activity is the species-characteristic of man'. Alienation means that we can no longer express our true nature as free and active producers.

This emphasis on the importance of consciousness perhaps reveals the influence of idealist theories of Marx. However that may be, he makes human consciousness the mark of the species. However much we are forced to live in a way that is not true to our 'species-being', the fact remains that we should be free. Work, Marx believes, should be our own free expression and not be torn from us as a mere means towards our physical existence. My work no longer belongs to me when I am forced into an alien activity. Only free production as an end in itself can confirm humanity as a 'conscious species-being'.

Nevertheless this Marxian emphasis on consciousness should not be interpreted as a covert emphasis on the individual. Marx tries to abolish the dichotomy between individual and society. He denies that society is a 'fixed abstraction opposed to the individual', because he believes that individuals are social beings.[2] He refers to a particular individual as 'the subjective existence of society as something thought and felt'.[3] Thus society and individuals cannot be separated from one another in any futile argument about which comes first: 'as society produces man as man, so it is produced by man'.[4] The outcome is that the dependence of society on us is stressed at the same time as it is recognized that we are our true selves only in a social context. Even when we are not engaged in communal enterprises, all that we do is, as Marx put it, 'a manifestation and confirmation of social life'.[5]

Once it is accepted that we are social beings who cannot be understood apart from our social context, understanding individuals entails understanding the society of which they are a part. We have seen how Wittgenstein's view of rules involves an emphasis on the public and the social. Like Marx, he does not oppose the individual to society, arguing that one or the other is prior. He brings the two together by suggesting that an individual can only be understood in a social context. Despite their manifest differences, Marx and Wittgenstein have sometimes been compared in this respect. Both appear to stress that social practices provide the essential context for understanding ideas. One writer comments that for both 'the social level of explanation is irreducible'.[6] Such a remark highlights the fact that this kind of position is inevitably opposed to an atomistic understanding of the individual as source of meaning. Its stress on the social nature of the individual ensures that meaning can only be found at the level of social practice.

In the case of Wittgenstein, the comparison of the rules of society with those of games gives rise to the question of understanding. When we are embedded in the rules of one society, how can we hope to grasp those of another? Wittgenstein's coupling of meaning and use implies that if we are not able to use a word in a particular context ourselves we cannot hope to understand its meaning. Understanding seems to entail participation in a society. The great danger is that we encounter an unfamiliar society and assume it is just like our own. We then proceed to interpret its practices in our terms and assume they will fit exactly.

Marriage is a good example, since this is certainly something which anthropologists look for in strange societies. I have already remarked that marriage is a social institution, and that two people cannot be married just because they see themselves as married: the society has to recognize the fact. Nevertheless it is important that individuals have some idea of what is taking place. Social institutions do not normally exist when no one in the society is aware of them. Whatever room we may wish to leave for the phenomenon of false consciousness, it cannot be easily applied to something like marriage. Animals may mate and can stay together for life, but we should hesitate to call that marriage. They do not understand the significance of what they are doing, and in fact it has no social significance. Human marriage is embedded in society, but this does not mean that the marriage partners can be oblivious of the institution. The rules may be public rather than private but participants must understand *what* they are doing. Just as the players of a game do not do so blindly and accidentally but must have some grasp of the rules, the same applies to participants in a social practice.

Peter Winch has argued for the distinctiveness of social science from natural science by emphasizing these points. He contends that a historian or sociologist of religion 'must himself have some religious feeling if he is to make sense of the religious movement he is studying and understand the considerations which govern the lives of its participants'.[7] He refers to this as a 'common-sense consideration', but it is in fact highly controversial. It suggests that atheists and agnostics cannot study religion because they cannot make sense of it. However that may be, Winch insists that any reflective understanding of a society depends on an understanding of how participants understand what is occurring. The one is built on the other.

The argument that meaningful behaviour is rule-governed and that rules are rooted in social life leaves out the question whether the participants understand the rules. The temptation will be to say that, if they follow the rules, they understand them. Yet is there a difference between a couple marrying in accordance with the practice in their society and marrying because of an understanding of that practice? Behaviourist philosophers would say nothing more needs to be added. Dualists will distinguish between private understanding and public practice, even if the latter must ultimately be defined in terms of other people's private understanding.

These reflections are important when we examine what it means to understand another society. Even if this involves understanding that society's rules, the question arises whether this is achieved by observing behaviour or by understanding what the rules mean to the participants. Wittgenstein's strictures against private languages would make many hesitate to adapt Weber's notion of *Verstehen*, since that would seem to suggest that each individual's consciousness is private. Winch insists that 'the concepts in terms of which we understand our own mental processes and behaviour have to be learned, and must, therefore, be *socially* established'.[8] This means that 'private' understanding of social rules is, in fact, dependent on public criteria. Thus reference to the understanding of a participant does not undermine the emphasis on the social. Admitting that individuals differ from animals in having understanding need not entail a dualist approach. The public world still has priority, and 'private understanding' need not involve reference to private mental processes.

The dualist is unlikely to be satisfied by this. The emphasis on public criteria for understanding a rule forces us back to the position that consistently acting in accordance with the rule *is* understanding it. We would refuse to accept that those who went against the rule understood it, or, at least, their breaking of the rule would have to be *prima facie* evidence that they did not understand it. Yet it seems plausible that rule-breakers know whether they are acting intentionally or not.

To return to the example of marriage, the mere fact that a couple marries in accordance with the rules of their society leaves some questions unanswered. Do they themselves make sense of the rule, or just blindly act in accordance with it because of the coercion of society? No doubt in a very settled society there would be one institution of marriage and one understanding of it. In a very complex society, like those comprising modern industrial nations, there may be many different understandings of the one institution. Some will have a Christian view of marriage, as vows for life made in the sight of God. Others will regard it as a purely legal contract to be terminated if either of the partners wishes. Some will have little reflective understanding of what they are doing, and merely do what is conventional. Those who are more reflective may well disagree. Some will see marriage as particularly designed for the protection of women, while others will regard it as a method, designed by men, for enslaving women. It seems implausible to suggest that there are different institutions for each of these groups. Indeed, one of the troubles is that a single institution is being given different, and incompatible, functions. There may be different views of marriage, but there are not different marriage practices in Western society.

Some may question this and wonder whether those who enter into a series of marriages, divorcing their partners at regular intervals, are not changing the nature of marriage. If enough members of a society begin to treat marriage as a temporary legal arrangement rather than a solemn undertaking broken only by death, it may well be that the institution of marriage will change. Saying this, though, suggests that institutions do depend on the understanding of their participants to such an extent that, if the latter changes, then eventually so will the former. The rules will be changed to take account of the changed understanding and thus cannot be thought logically prior to that understanding.

Public Practice and Private Understanding

Discussion of institutions such as marriage may be complicated by the suggestion that, despite appearances, there is more than one society in a country such as England. The mere existence of one set of legal rules may cloak the fact that there are many different forms of life coexisting. Each may have its own rules for, and its own understanding of, the institution of marriage. In other words, there may be several different institutions of marriage within the same nation. This only serves to raise the question how different ways of life, or cultures, with different social practices, can be identified. For an anthropologist visiting a geographically isolated tribe, it may be reasonable to see the tribe as a unit. A modern state which comprises citizens of many different backgrounds and beliefs provides more of a problem. Is it one society or many? Sometimes reference is made to a pluralist society. According to some definitions of a society, that is bound to be a contradiction in terms. One society cannot encompass practitioners of many different religions and of none. In Wittgenstein's sense of the term, they would belong to different forms of life, basing their lives on different sets of agreed judgements and possessing different concepts. Yet they all live together under one legal system and, perhaps not surprisingly, experience tensions.

The problem confronting us, however, is a strictly conceptual one. What counts as a society? Tension between black and white, Muslim and Hindu, or Protestant and Catholic may be a symptom of different societies clashing. It may equally be an example of groups of like-minded individuals clashing with other groups in the same society. What criteria can we appeal to in order to settle this? The concept of a society is complex, but Wittgenstein's emphasis on agreement in judgements would mean that basic disagreements are an indication of clashes between societies. The scientist will belong to one society with one set of assumptions; the believer in oracles to another. The Christian has one society, the atheist another. Once we begin to identify societies in this way, it is obvious that many overlap. Some scientists will be Christian and others atheist. Every time a new basic disagreement appears, we can go on multiplying societies, assuming that we can identify 'basic' disagreements, which presumably involve a clash of conceptual schemes. Some atheist scientists will believe in marriage as a lifelong bond, and others will not. Some Christians may countenance divorce, and others will not. It is difficult to know where to stop once this process is started. Every issue on which different groups cannot reach agreement seems to raise the question whether we are encountering a fresh form of life.

Is a disagreement a matter of two groups sharing the same concepts but contradicting each other, or does something occur analogous to the incommensurability of scientific theories? In the latter case, different concepts are applied and the parties to the dispute do not so much disagree as talk past each other, because they are members of different societies, each of which has its own standards of truth and falsity. In fact, if we accept that apparently insoluble disagreement is a criterion of different forms of life, we shall eventually arrive at a situation where forms of life contain only one person. Everyone disagrees with everyone else on something. The class of Christian, conservative scientists who are against divorce can no doubt be distinguished from atheist, radical non-scientists who see nothing wrong in it. Such classes can easily be further subdivided, with Christian non-scientists, and conservative atheists, not to mention new issues arising to complicate things still further.

If we refuse to start on this slippery slope down to subjectivism and even solipsism, we have to accept that one society can comprise individuals who disagree very firmly with others in the same society. The definition of a society will not, then, include the condition that there be agreement on basic issues. The sharing of concepts will not depend on a unanimity of view. Judgements about what is true will be separated from the social background against which they are made. Personal understanding of social institutions cannot then be identified with the way they work. People may even follow the rules while disagreeing with them. They can marry while not really believing in marriage as an institution. When this happens, however, a society is in trouble. If private understanding and belief begin to diverge from public practice, the practices themselves will eventually be changed.

Wittgenstein's emphasis on the public and the social is more plausible as a description of a settled society, and is not so well designed to explain how societies can develop and change. Like Kuhn's account of scientific theories, it runs into trouble at precisely the point at which one theory is superseded by another or a society is fundamentally changed. The stress on holism ensures that all fundamental change has to be revolutionary. There has to be a massive upheaval when one system is superseded by another, with gradual transactions ruled out. All such change must be catastrophic, one way of living being replaced by another. There may be a period in which an earlier way of life comes to mean less and less to its participants. For instance, strongly held religious beliefs become watered down, yet the form of the religion remains after the content has gone. In the same way Kuhn believes that anomalies in a theory will begin to pile up. In the end, however, the change is a revolutionary one and the previous system is destroyed. This is inevitable if all explanation is in terms of societies or systems of one kind or another, since the only way of changing a whole system is by putting another in its place.

Issues about the definition of a society or a community are not of mere academic importance, because there are times when that can have marked social consequences. It is no doubt implausible to pretend that scientists really form a homogeneous community in any sense, whatever some philosophers of science might say. Yet those concerned with race relations often talk of 'community relations' and run the risk of reifying communities which are in fact far from internally homogeneous. An example is provided by the position of Pakistanis in Britain, who are sometimes grouped together in the minds even of well-meaning promoters of good race relations. Pakistan is a young country and its population spans five main ethnic groups. One commentator suggests:

> Those who speak of a Pakistani ethnicity are misinterpreting their experience of individual contexts and specific situations by stressing cultural differences between the British and Pakistani populations. They ignore the internal differentiation of the Pakistani population.[9]

Pakistanis can, in fact, be classified together only on the basis of religion or of a nationality which many of them only acquired when they were already adults. To term them a community or to imagine them constituting an identifiable society is highly misleading. What is happening is that the resident English population fairly arbitrarily imagine a group of immigrants to form the 'Pakistani community', and even hope that they can deal with 'community leaders'. The classification is made more on the basis of their difference from English people than similarity among themselves. Saifullah Kahn writes that 'although Pakistanis in Britain do not perceive the population of their fellow nationals as a community (in the sense of a group of people with common identification, values and perspective, who interact with each other and have common associations and leaders) they become aware over time of how outsiders see them'. External pressures may eventually force them to see themselves as a distinct community, even though that was originally far from the truth. The way other people see us will affect the way we see ourselves, and our own self-understanding will govern our behaviour. The paradox is that, although sociological definitions may be inaccurate, they may none the less have real consequences in society through their influence on how individuals see themselves. If individuals are made to feel members of a separate community, they will act accordingly.

Once it is accepted that communities, institutions and social practices do not provide the sole context of social explanation, we see that individual understanding is also important. Changes will not come at the level of systems without operating through individuals. If enough people's understanding of an institution like marriage is changed, the institution itself will be changed. Conversely, the change of an institution will be pointless unless the attitudes of the individuals who participate in it also change. Even if the institution of marriage were abolished by political action, people might still want to commit themselves publicly to each other, if they continued to believe in it. Political revolutions often do not achieve all they are intended to for precisely this kind of reason. The system may have been apparently changed but the individuals involved in it may not have.

Winch tries to make several different distinctions simultaneously. One example he gives is the following:

> A historian of art must have some aesthetic sense if he is to understand the problems confronting the artists of his period; and without this he will have left out of his account precisely what would have made it a history of *art*, as opposed to a rather puzzling external account of certain motions which certain people have been perceived to go through.[10]

He thus wishes to distinguish the understanding of human activity from 'the natural scientist's understanding of his scientific data'. This puts him squarely on the side of someone like Weber criticizing positivism. Human action cannot merely be observed in a detached, scientific way. To understand its significance we have to see the situation from the point of view of a participant. We cannot conflate the reasons a participant has for an action with the causes as seen by a scientist. The 'internal' and 'external' perspectives should not be confused, and genuine social explanations, according to Winch, lie with the internal one.

However, Winch also wishes to combine the *Verstehen* approach with a Wittgensteinian account of concepts. The 'internal' perspective turns out to be irreducibly social, rooted in modes of social life. It appears to follow that this kind of perspective does not so much involve seeing a situation from the point of view of an individual as participating in a society. The emphasis has swung from the individual to society, and *Verstehen* is turned into the need to participate in whatever society is being studied. Yet all Winch said about the need for an aesthetic sense seemed to demand not participation in social practices but the kind of empathy which a more individualist theory would demand.

Much of the attraction of Winch's theory lies in his insistence that knowledge of society is nothing like knowledge of physical regularities. The latter leaves out of account the meaning agents give to their activities. Yet once the emphasis drifts away from individuals to societies, and from the subjective to the publicly verifiable, a similar gap threatens to open again. The scientist may study observable behaviour and leave out of account what Winch himself refers to as 'the participant's un-reflective understanding'.[11] The study of social rules in a form of life still leaves precisely this out of account. Despite his apparent endorsement of *Verstehen*, he seems to have removed its very possibility.

Winch would reply that this is to ignore the importance of Wittgen-stein's argument concerning a private language, according to which private meanings have to be excluded. This is to rule out by definition the point of view of a participant in a practice, except in so far as it merely reflects the practice. Such a conclusion follows from the verifica-tionist bias built into the position, favouring the publicly accessible over the private. The shadow of positivism lingers even in the work of the later Wittgenstein. The exclusion of the private, or at least its dismissal as irrelevant for the formation of concepts, is arbitrary, and fails to do justice to the basic features of human experience. The concept of pain, for example, which Wittgenstein uses as an example, may certainly depend on public criteria if it is to be properly taught.[12] We can learn that pain is the kind of reaction we normally feel in particular situations. Nevertheless what that feels like depends on personal experience, and the phenomenal quality of the private sensation of pain is fundamental for understanding the concept. We cannot apply the concept properly unless we recognize what the sensation is like. For this reason, those who are congenitally insensitive to pain and have never felt it are unable to grasp the meaning of the concept. It is no use their concluding from the fact that they are in the same circumstances as normal people that they must be feeling pain. They are not if they do not feel a definite kind of sensation, just as a colour-blind person does not see red.

Shared public concepts may need public criteria for their application, but we should not ignore the reality and importance of private mental events. The association of concepts and language has been particularly pernicious. Private mental experiences seem otiose if concepts are identified with the use of words. Yet this involves the identification of thought and language which even suggests that animals and infants can have no determinate experience merely because they lack linguistic competence.[13] It assumes that they cannot recognize what they cannot talk about. This leaves unexplained how language is learnt in the first place, since, without some prior ability to perceive objects as the same again, we would not be able to learn when the use of words is appropriate and when it is not. Being taught the use of words by means of public criteria itself presupposes an ability to recognize things in the world in the same way as our teachers. Learning language becomes very problematic without this. Because people totally blind from birth cannot see colours, for example, their grasp of colour terms is bound to be somewhat tenuous. They may understand that green is the colour of grass, but will not be able to grasp *what* colour that is or even understand the nature of colour. Private experience cannot be ignored in the teaching of language, since language presupposes it.

Winch's attack on the view that the scientific observation of behaviour can give a proper understanding of human action is a distinct issue from the argument about public and private languages. It deals with a problem which remains even if we are reluctant to treat social explanation as irreducible to the explanation of individual behaviour. The dichotomy between public and private, and the associated distinction between social and individual, must not be confused with that between a scientific view of a society and the viewpoint of its participants. The problem of interpretation still arises, whether one is trying to understand an alien society as a whole or its individual members. Doctrines of forms of life set up self-contained societies with their own conceptual schemes which are distinct from those of the outsider. They thus preach conceptual relativism, and such schemes are apparently made unintelligible to non-participants by definition. Yet a problem remains if we see our task as one of understanding individuals with strange beliefs. How do we avoid the charge of ethnocentricity or parochialism, of judging others in terms of our own concepts? It is always a great temptation to do so. Some would say that we can do nothing else. The snag is that there is a suspicion that in doing so we must actually falsify what we are studying.

Understanding Alien Practices

An anthropologist may wish to study different forms of marriage in human societies. It should be obvious that there are different forms of association between men and women in different places. Lifelong monogamy is not the only pattern. One may take a series of husbands or wives, and in some non-Western societies one husband can take several wives. In some circumstances, a woman could have more than one husband. The question is whether it is right to talk of 'marriage' or even of 'husbands' and 'wives' in contexts which may be so radically different from our own. Can our concepts be used to refer to other societies without taking into account the participants' understanding of what they are doing? We may seem to be restricting the term 'marriage' unduly, if we apply it only to monogamous relationships. Why cannot a man be married to more than one woman? If we deny that is genuine marriage, we may be presupposing one particular understanding of marriage which may not be universally shared. Yet all bonds between men and women may not count as marriage even if they are sanctioned by a group or society. Some societies make distinctions between wives and official concubines. An alternative danger is that an anthropologist may decide that marriage is universal before examining particular societies, and may assume that in each society it is merely a question of deciding which relations between the sexes are to be termed 'marriage'. It is hardly surprising if the consequence is that anthropological investigation appears to establish that marriage occurs in every society.

If we concentrate on the beliefs of the participants in a society, we may find, assuming that we are able to interpret them, that the participants have a concept for a bond between a man and a woman blessed by the ancestral spirits. How would we settle whether that is equivalent to marriage or not? Let us assume they call this bond 'gamage'. Is 'gamage' to be translated 'marriage'? One obvious difficulty is the question of the ancestral spirits. The anthropological report of 'gamage' cannot involve any ontological claims about spirits, and saying that a ceremony of 'gamage' took place cannot mean that the ancestral spirits did bless a particular union. The participants may believe that, but the anthropologist presumably does not. Yet, if 'gamage' does mean to participants that spirits blessed the union, are we to conclude that 'gamage' never actually takes place in the society, even though the participants thought it did? At this point the attraction should be obvious of a form of conceptual relativism, which relates concepts to their social background and refuses to allow external standards of truth and falsity. Anthropologists are reluctant to march into a society, quickly expose the ignorance and superstition supposedly to be found there, and march out again, their job done. There seems a lack of any real understanding of what is actually going on, and it looks as if all that has been shown is that the natives do not think like the anthropologists. There is too, it must be admitted, something of a post-imperialist reaction in all this. Anthropologists are very reluctant to make adverse judgements about societies different from our own, in the commendable belief that it shows a misplaced arrogance and intolerance.

One example of this is the following:

> Religions re-state and then reveal to people the 'true' nature of Nature. By 'true' here is meant 'culturally true'. Thus religion may tell a person that a certain kind of animal is sacred and must not be killed or eaten; or in parts of South America, it may insist that good crops occur only when the spirits of the ancestors so wish it, and the spirits have to be approached with reverence and ritual before planting seeds.[14]

By restricting the notion of truth to a culture in this way, we are not involved in making embarrassing judgements about the value of some beliefs. Yet it is clear that by 'culturally true' is meant nothing more than that the members of that particular culture believe certain things to be true. The concept of truth is again being reduced to what is held true. This can only be done by repudiating a realist notion of truth, since the question of objective truth cannot be brushed aside if things are either the case or they are not, whatever people happen to believe. It is not surprising that anthropologists can easily start talking of how the members of different cultures inhabit different worlds. A relativist view of truth inevitably leads to a view of reality being created by people's conception of it. Different systems of belief then inevitably entail different realities.

We might well wonder how social anthropologists can do their work if there are so many different realities. The reality of professional anthropologists would clearly be different from the realities of the various cultures they wish to study. This is another instance of the problem which arose in connection with the sociology of knowledge, namely that of reflexivity. If all societies create their own realities, this applies to anthropologists too, or to the wider society to which they belong. In any case, the scientific character of their discipline is in jeopardy, since it becomes merely the reflection of their own construction of reality. It certainly becomes impossible to compare societies. One may compare beliefs, but if these are all trapped in different realities, with different 'cultural truths', access to them and all cross-cultural comparison must be ruled out. Perhaps there is one inclusive reality encompassing the others. This suggestion, though, gives the game away because it allows that there is after all an extra-cultural background against which cultures can be examined and even judged. There has to be, or we could not talk of 'different realities' in the first place. If talking like that was merely a result of the culture of anthropologists and is not meant to tell us about what is actually the case, there is no point in listening to what anthropologists say if we are not already one. Their beliefs are irrelevant and can tell us nothing about 'the world' because *ex hypothesi* there is no such thing.

Real issues are connected with such questions. For example, in nineteenth-century India there was a deliberate practice of killing female babies. This was connected with the Hindu caste system, whereby parents endeavoured to arrange marriages for their daughters which would improve their social position. Unfortunately, though, high-born women could not easily be married to men of lower castes, while Hindu society has little room for unmarried women. As a result many women found themselves in difficulties, needing to marry but not being able to acquire a husband of a suitable social background. Parents, therefore, would prefer sons, and some villages produced twice as many as girls, who were killed at birth.

Reynolds and Tanner, writing from the standpoint of anthropology, say the following about the situation:

> The British administration waged a long campaign against these practices based on the Christian premise that they were no less than murder, without really understanding the Hindu preference for sons, let alone the overpopulation problem.[15]

The implication of this is that the campaign was a Christian one against Hindus, undertaken without due regard for the way an alien society worked and viewed things. Indirectly the British were attacking the caste system, and even the Hindu religion, probably without having any clear perception of what they were doing. They simply saw what was wrong in Christian terms and tried to stop it, with some success. The problem is whether they had the right, as opposed to the power, to interfere with another culture in this way. It is easy to produce cases like this from the history of the British empire. It is perhaps no coincidence that its passing has coincided with a growth in the feeling that such interference is misplaced. The confidence of imperialism is replaced by something tantamount to loss of nerve. This is far from being a philosophical point and is precisely the kind of issue likely to be raised by sociologists of knowledge. It may certainly help to explain why philosophical arguments for relativism are readily accepted.

Was the Hindu practice murder, and should it have been stopped? The morality of infanticide from a contemporary standpoint is a separate issue which I shall not discuss. The question is whether, given the belief of the British that infanticide was murder, they were justified in classifying the Hindu practice in that way. Were they justified in treating the killing of an infant girl in a village in Mysore in the same way as an apparently similar killing in a Glasgow slum? Can an action be torn out of its cultural context and treated as if it is in fact very different from the way the agent conceived it? Few would consider it an adequate defence against a charge of infanticide in Western society that the person killing the infant did not see it as murder. There are sad cases of mercy-killing where our sympathies may be aroused, but even there the relevant considerations would be the facts of the case and not just how the agent saw the situation. Why should the fact that it takes place in a different cultural context make a significant difference? This is a genuine question, but suggesting that the social context does matter elevates the notion of a society or a culture to an important position in social explanation. Viewing one culture through the assumptions, or concepts, of another will seem to create major problems of understanding. Reynolds and Tanner imply just this, that the British did not understand, and perhaps because of their Christian background could not. The awkward fact, though, is that Reynolds and Tanner themselves are British and do claim to understand. They are able to give a plausible account of the working of Hindu society. Their reference to the problem of overpopulation in giving reasons for infanticide show that they are willing to give explanations for what occurred which may not have been the ones given by Hindus. It is not clear how far a Hindu would have realized that a preference for sons arose from the working of the caste system. Quite possibly he just did not want daughters without ever fully understanding why.

Anthropological accounts have themselves to depend on an understanding of alien societies, and very often give accounts of the working of those societies in terms which would be unintelligible to the participants. The discipline of anthropology depends on the falsity of cultural relativism. The post-imperialist squeamishness of anthropologists is just that. The problem of how far it is right to interfere with other societies is a moral and not a conceptual question. If, indeed, we are all locked up in our separate societies, unable to see the world in terms other than our own, anthropologists are the very last people to warn us of this. If they do so, they admit that their discipline is engaged in a hopeless enterprise.

Understanding other societies depends on the simple assumption that there are not different realities. Each society confronts the same reality, but may try to deal with it in different ways. The British in India went to considerable pains to work through native rulers and forms of society. They intervened when basic questions about the worth of human life were at stake. Another famous example is that of suttee, a practice in which widows sacrificed themselves on their husband's funeral pyre. Wifely devotion was, and is, venerated by Hindus, and there was no provision, at least in higher castes, for the remarriage of widows. The British attempted to stop the custom by an Act in 1829. The question is whether they were importing the concepts and standards of the England of George IV to an alien and inappropriate context. The fact that it is impossible to translate 'suttee' into English might suggest this. Yet there is something odd about a position which would hold that 'to us it is a suicide which is barely voluntary because forced by social pressure, but to them it is a noble and admirable sacrifice'. There is some truth in that, because of the difference in background belief, but it is impossible to leave it at that. Who sees correctly what is happening? Once anyone starts saying that to us it is the murder of a child but to them it is a religious sacrifice, or to us it is despicable cannibalism but to them a sacred meal, they are treading a dangerous path.

Such people opt out of the need to make moral judgements about what is occurring, but they might consider that as gain. However, they also involve themselves in deep incoherence. They stress the radical nature of cultural differences by spelling them out in an intelligible way. However abhorrent female infanticide might seem, it is perfectly possible to understand why there should be a preference for sons. Even in Western society a wish for a son to carry on a family business is not unknown. Hindus were not acting without an intelligible reason. Similarly the emphasis on wifely devotion might seem somewhat excessive, particularly to modern 'liberated' women, but the idea that a wife should be devoted to her husband is also one that has been found in Western society.

The Basis of Understanding Other Societies

Understanding the practice of other societies does very often come down to realizing that there is a common base which they share with us. Humans have similar wants and needs, and strange behaviour can become intelligible when we realize that people like ourselves are reacting to a very different environment. There is also the complication that they may have different beliefs from us about that environment. The key question is whether we are in fact dealing with people like ourselves, or whether society shapes people in such radically different ways that we cannot assume a common human nature.[16] Without any chance of using human nature as a basis for interpreting an alien society, the possibility of understanding and comparing the activities of the members of different societies seems remote. They would be as difficult to understand as those of the alien life forms beloved of modern science fiction. In fact, it is significant that the latter often turn out to be very human after all, even to the extent of mysteriously being able to speak English. Otherwise they would be so far beyond our understanding that it would be impossible to include them in any intelligible story.

Winch recognizes this and takes up with approval Vico's idea of natural law as basis for understanding human history. He quotes Vico as saying that all nations 'keep these three human customs: all have some religion, all contract solemn marriages, all bury their dead'.[17] Thus Winch takes birth, death and sexual relations as what he calls 'limiting notions'. He says:

The specific forms which those concepts take, the particular institutions in which they are expressed, vary very considerably from one society to another; but their central position within a society's institutions is and must be a constant factor. In trying to understand the life of an alien society, then, it will be of the utmost importance to be clear about the way in which these notions enter into it. The actual practice of social anthropologists bears this out.[18]

Certain typical human desires and tendencies are taken as basic, and we are then entitled to look for points of contact between alien societies and our own. Undoubtedly Winch is right in saying that this is how many anthropologists proceed. Yet my earlier point that those intent on finding forms of marriage in every human society will be certain to find them remains. How can we be sure that in our eagerness to establish points of contact we do not arbitrarily treat as similar institutions that are very different? Must the assumption that humans always 'marry' be a necessary presupposition for the understanding of relations between the sexes in different societies? Winch was perhaps wise to talk of sex rather than marriage. The assumption that the members of another society are like ourselves need not involve the assumption that the institutions of their society correspond to those of our own. They may, but they may not. It is an empirical question whether what we call 'marriage' is to be found in all societies. Nevertheless there will always be some basic human needs and interests which will have to be expressed in one way or another. Men and women will have sexual relations, and these will be regulated in a society.

One distinction between a society and individuals randomly mating with each other is that there will be settled procedures governing contact between the sexes. This is particularly important because of the question of the status of children. Modern methods of birth control may have broken to some extent the correlation between sexual relations and the birth of children, and this has had profound repercussions in some societies. The fact remains that relations between the sexes and the rearing of children both provide a set of constraints which human societies cannot ignore. A society must provide a framework in which such basic needs are met, if it is to be distinguished from a set of individuals arbitrarily interacting with each other. The important point, however, is that because of the basic features of human life, all human societies have to possess a similar framework. Societies can respond to basic human needs in many different ways, but, if they fail to respond, they will not flourish and probably cannot even survive. A society banning sexual intercourse, or killing all its children, is unlikely to last long.

What constitutes a basic human need depends on our view of human nature. Whatever that may be, understanding other societies presupposes an assumption about the universality of human nature. Too much emphasis on the strangeness of alien societies and their inhabitants can result in an inability to interpret what is occurring in them. Kuhn's notion of the incommensurability of scientific theories is not a good model for societies. Saying that each society can only be judged by its own criteria removes the point of studying other societies. We may become dissatisfied with our own society and go to join another, but that should not be the position of an anthropologist doing fieldwork.

It is often used as an argument against conceptual relativism that it makes understanding other societies impossible unless we become participants. We are either members of a society, seeing everything through the eyes of a participant, or we fail to find it intelligible. This is a telling criticism. Such relativism makes any scientific understanding of cultures impossible, since detached study and comparison of different cultures becomes impossible. Sometimes the stress on fieldwork might almost result in this position, so that absorption in an alien culture could become an end in itself. Yet this criticism may already concede too much, since it assumes that it is possible for a member of one culture to join another and acquire its concepts. Even if it is not thought possible to compare different conceptual schemes, it is taken for granted that one can acquire a fresh scheme. The problem is whether conceptual relativism explains how this is possible. Presumably the way in which we can learn the concepts of our own culture is a model. We are taught them, so why should we not also be taught another set later? We simply adopt a different form of life and learn how to use the appropriate words in an appropriate setting, just as children are taught how to speak their native language. Even this, however, stands in need of explanation. Children may latch on to what is said, but this is precisely because they see what their teacher sees. The child and teacher see the same world in the same way. When people enter an alien culture they must assume that they and the natives also see the same world in the same way. This requirement remains, even if they have abandoned any hope of translating from the native language to their own. Even while consciously trying to learn as a child might who does not already possess a language, they must assume that they are able in some pre-linguistic manner to grasp what the natives are talking about. For example, the visitor can see a cat, without knowing what the natives call it. Thus conceptual relativists may try to undermine all possibility of translation, but they are still forced to rely on the fact that they and the natives share common human reactions to a common, objective world. Otherwise teaching and learning become impossible. Paradoxically, however, this then means that translation is possible after all, since different languages must after all refer to the same world.

A thoroughgoing relativist may wish to resist this argument by denying any basic similarity with the members of another society, whose culture may have conditioned them to see things differently, to act differently, and to divide up the world differently. People within a culture would be similar enough to communicate, but there would be a great divergence between cultures. This is a possibility, but such radical differences would surely not just undermine the possibility of translation between the language of one society and that of the other; it would prohibit participation by anyone in a society that was not their own. If I have been moulded by my society to live in a world constricted by that society, I cannot unmake myself. I am what my society has made me. Although it might appear as if another society could then mould me in another pattern, I could never truly free myself of the influence of my own society. The only conclusion could be that if indeed the conceptual relativists are correct (and that notion of correctness is not a relativist one) we are locked in the culture into which we are born. If it *is* possible to leave one society and to join another, then membership of a society is not the most important fact about people. Their conceptual schemes are not totally conditioned by a society but depend at least in part on their membership of the human race and on the same objective world in which they all find themselves.

Samoa: An Example

In 1925–6 Margaret Mead spent some months in Samoa, and as a result of researches there into the life of adolescent girls she published *Coming of Age in Samoa*.[19] This proved to be a work of enormous influence within social anthropology and beyond the confines of the discipline, and is still widely read. It purports to be an account of a society in which the stresses of adolescence are avoided. Because these have occurred in Western societies, but not, it is alleged, in the very different environment of the South Pacific, they appear to be induced by culture rather than by biology. This is not only significant for those confronting the specific problem of how to educate young people, but seems to add further support to those who are convinced that culture or 'civilization' rather than biology determines how people behave.

The book was explicitly used to disprove the arguments of those who were at that time emphasizing the importance of biological inheritance in moulding human character. Much attention was then being devoted to the study of 'eugenics', a discipline finally discredited by its association with the racist theories of Nazi Germany. Franz Boas was bitterly opposed to eugenics and set about showing with the resources of cultural anthropology how misguided such views were. He was the major figure in American cultural anthropology when Margaret Mead began her career, and he exercised considerable influence on her. He wrote a foreword to *Coming of Age in Samoa*, concluding with the resounding sentence:

> The results of her painstaking investigation confirm the suspicion long held by anthropologists, that much of what we ascribe to human nature is no more than a reaction of the restraints put upon us by our civilization.[20]

In fact, Margaret Mead went to Samoa in order to demonstrate this as a fact, although we may wonder how she hoped fully to understand a culture she regarded as utterly different from her own, without assuming that she and the natives had something in common. The more different she assumed the teenage girls she met were from herself in their emotional reactions and their view of the world, the more impenetrable their life would be likely to be. She manages to give a confident account of life in American Samoa, while showing it to be radically different from anything experienced in America. There is little doubt that she wanted Samoan life to be different because of philosophical preconceptions about the importance of culture. It is ironic that an ability to understand native girls sufficiently to show how different they were could only depend on an actual underlying similarity. Otherwise understanding and interpretation would have to be ruled out from the beginning. In fact, Margaret Mead appears to have been thoroughly misled about the nature of Samoan life in general and adolescent life in particular. Her account of it certainly paints a picture of an exotic society, as she intended, but at crucial points it seems highly implausible.

Derek Freeman, whose experience in Samoa as an anthropologist far exceeds the few months spent there by Margaret Mead, has presented a devastating attack revealing the deep misconceptions which she acquired about Samoan society.[21] Mead wrote of carefree South Sea Islanders who indulged in promiscuous sexual activity without incurring any harm. Her account seems to owe more to Western fantasies about tropical islands than to actual conditions in Samoa. For instance, she implies that Samoans avoid stress by not becoming too committed to any individual. The life she portrays is one of careless ease, where the anxieties and tensions of civilized society do not arise: 'From the first months of its life, when the child is handed carelessly from one woman's hands to another, the lesson is learned of not caring for one person greatly, not setting high hopes on any relationship.'[22] Freeman, on the other hand, presents evidence which enables him to conclude: 'The primary bond between mother and child is very much a part of the biology of Samoans, as it is of all humans.'[23]

Mead's account of promiscuity among teenagers runs into trouble when it is contrasted with the Samoan cult of virginity. She says that adolescent ambition is 'to live as a girl with many lovers as long as possible and then to marry in one's own village'.[24] Yet virginity was highly prized in pagan Samoa, and the acquiring of a virgin wife was especially desired. This was reinforced by the conversion of Samoans to Christianity in the early nineteenth century. It seems that that the girls' alleged ambitions were likely to be mutually incompatible. No man would readily marry a girl with a reputation for promiscuity. The predominantly Congregationalist London Missionary Society was very active in Samoa. As had happened to Fiji and Tonga, where the missionaries had been Methodist, the conversion of the islanders had made a profound difference to their lives, in some cases making fierce warriors into men of peace. Cannibalism was eradicated. Mead, however, hardly mentions Christianity. Were she to admit its influence, the whole point of her fieldwork would be lost. She wanted to show the differences between a simple, primitive paradise and complicated, civilized society. Were she to admit, even to herself, the fact that Samoans were as strict and sincere in their application of Protestant Christianity to their lives as any American, the whole point of her researches would be lost. She preferred to imagine that pagan Samoa had been left virtually untouched by the missionaries.

Mead was far too sanguine about how easy it was to get to grips with an alien society. She claimed that 'a trained student can master the fundamental structure of a primitive society in a few months'.[25] She believed that it was possible in that time to learn the native language sufficiently to enable her to use it to extract the most intimate details of their private lives from teenage girls who were likely anyway to be shy with foreigners. She did not even live in a Samoan household. When these disadvantages were coupled with the fact that, as a methodological assumption, she was looking for differences from, and not similarities with, American girls, it is hardly surprising that her conclusions must be regarded as dubious. Freeman says: 'I have yet to meet a Samoan who agrees with Mead's assertion that adolescence in Samoan society is smooth, untroubled and unstressed.'[26] This itself is of great importance, since Mead is allegedly depicting the experience of individuals in Samoa. It is scarcely surprising that Freeman maintains that her main conclusions 'are, in reality the figments of an anthropological myth, which is deeply at variance with the facts of Samoan ethnography and history.'[27]

Mead's misreading of Samoan society was undoubtedly encouraged by her belief in what she termed 'the tremendous role played in an individual's life by the social environment'.[28] She placed little reliance on human nature as a basis for understanding, and her researches were used as empirical evidence to show the radical differences that are alleged to exist in humans placed in different cultures. Cultural anthropology was established as a discipline in its own right, freed of the need to be dependent on biology. Freeman explicitly links the final establishment of anthropology as an independent discipline with the results of Mead's researches. He suggests that her findings were a major influence in the exclusion of biology and the acceptance of the absolute priority of culture as a force in the moulding of society. Referring to such 'cultural determinism' as a myth, he says:

> On the basis of Mead's writings, Samoa came to be recognized in intellectual circles and in the social sciences as providing conclusive proof of the cultural determinism central to the Boasian paradigm. . . . So enthusiastically was Mead's vision of Samoa accepted that her conclusions, as they were elaborated by herself and others, gave rise to what has

become the most widely promulgated myth of twentieth-century anthro-pology.[29]

The disproving of Mead's account of Samoan life does not disprove her views about the primacy of culture over nature. Nevertheless her conclusions cannot any longer be used as an example of the magnitude of cultural variations. Her refusal to assume the existence of any universal human nature not only led her into notable errors. It gave the discipline of anthropology an exceedingly precarious basis. Without the assump-tion of some similarities between humans, any account of their beha-viour becomes speculative, and there is no standard by which it can be judged whether people are likely to be telling the truth or not. It seems highly likely that the teenage girls to whom Margaret Mead spoke gave a highly coloured view of their life which was largely untrue. Mead's adherence to what Freeman calls 'cultural determinism' left her defence-less against this treatment. A believer in the universality of human nature might have been more aware that this is just how such girls might react to a stranger who asked about their sexual activities.

Notes

1   Karl Marx, *Early Texts*, 1971, p. 135.
2   Ibid., p. 150.
3   Ibid., p. 151.
4   Ibid., p. 149.
5   Ibid., p. 150.
6   D. Rubinstein, *Marx and Wittgenstein*, 1981, p. 180.
7   P. Winch, *The Idea of a Social Science*, 1958, p. 88.
8   Ibid., p. 119.
9   V. Saifullah Kahn, 'Pakistanis in Britain: Perceptions of a Population', 1976, p. 228.
10   Winch, *Idea of a Social Science*, p. 88.
11   Ibid., p. 89.
12   See my *Pain and Emotion*, 1970.
13   See my 'Thought and Language', *Proceedings of the Aristotelian Society*, 79, 1978–9.
14   V. Reynolds and R. Tanner, *The Biology of Religion*, 1983, p. 5.
15   Ibid., p. 55.
16   See my *The Shaping of Man*, 1982.

17 P. Winch, 'Understanding a Primitive Society', reprinted in his *Ethics and Action*, 1972, p. 47.

18 Ibid., p. 43.

19 Margaret Mead, *Coming of Age in Samoa*, 1928, reprinted 1943.

20 Ibid., p. 6.

21 Derek Freeman, *Margaret Mead and Samoa*, 1983.

22 Mead, *Coming of Age in Samoa*, p. 160.

23 Freeman, *Margaret Mead and Samoa*, p. 201.

24 Mead, *Coming of Age in Samoa*, p. 129.

25 Ibid., p. 14.

26 Freeman, *Margaret Mead and Samoa*, p. 259.

27 Ibid., p. 107.

28 Mead, *Coming of Age in Samoa*, p. 11.

29 Freeman, *Margaret Mead and Samoa*, p. 94.

5

Rationality

Scientific Rationality and Ethnomethodology

The prestige of the physical sciences has not only ensured that the social sciences have tried to adopt their methods. It has also resulted in scientific standards of rationality being assumed to be the only ones. It appears rational to believe whatever science can establish and to dismiss as unscientific and hence irrational belief in anything beyond its scope. This raised problems in the study of 'primitive' societies which are motivated by beliefs that seem thoroughly unscientific. The African Azande are often quoted in this connection. They believe in witches and try to protect themselves against witchcraft. They consult oracles and use magic medicines. Apparently primitive beliefs can live on in more sophisticated Africans. One British Foreign Secretary thought Kwame Nkrumah, first President of Ghana, was fond of birds since he saw cages full of doves at his home. Nkrumah, however, only wished to consult their entrails, particularly before travelling in an aircraft.

This example indicates that any view of such practices which merely embeds them in a particular culture is too simple. Cultures intermingle. 'Superstition' and advanced technology can live side by side. No doubt some may consult birds' entrails before flying by Concorde. Such practices stem from a different background from that of technologically based society and perhaps can best be understood in their original context. In the end, however, we cannot ignore the question whether it is rational for anyone to hold such beliefs. Is a commitment to magic, or a belief in the power of witchcraft, mere superstition? Can we simply dismiss such views as primitive?

Winch is quick to point out that our criteria of rationality derive from the culture to which we belong. When we make the beliefs and practices of another society intelligible to ourselves, we try to make them satisfy our criteria of rationality. He remarks that our culture's conception of rationality 'is deeply affected by the achievements and methods of the sciences'. He goes on to say that it treats 'such things as a belief in magic or the practice of consulting oracles as almost a paradigm of the irrational.'[1] The question seems to be whether we are right to apply the standards of one culture to another. Yet this just raises the spectre of relativism again, since it assumes that cultures are monolithic, and indeed makes a large assumption about the standards of rationality in our 'culture'. It is false, as a matter of sociological observation, that our culture rigorously upholds the austere standards of scientific rationality, at least as understood by the empiricist. The popularity of astrology is hard to explain otherwise. It is even doubtful if science provides the unchallenged standard among those who aspire to rationality. In the heady days of positivism many championed scientific method as capturing the essence of human rationality. Once, however, empiricism is challenged, rationality can no longer remain the monopoly of scientists. The great danger, then, must be that the very possibility of rationality is denied. Many have tried to jettison the idea of rationality, as we have seen, instead of admitting that the methods of the physical sciences might provide too restrictive a model. The fact remains that humans may reason differently from each other, but some merely reason better than others.

The question of rationality challenges the social scientist at two levels. There is the problem of how rational are the people being studied, but there is also the question of the social scientists' own rationality. If scientific rationality is taken as the model, social scientists can both criticize those who fall short of the idea, even if they are quite oblivious of it, and attempt themselves to apply the rationality of science in their explanation of why some societies are so ridden with superstition. Once it is accepted that science merely forms one set of practices alongside others, social scientists are left without any standards for judging a society. This might appear a gain, but the corollary is that their own discipline can no longer claim to embody the application of any kind of rational principle. The aftermath of positivism can produce a paralysing nihilism. Understanding, instead of causal explanation, may seem to be the new goal of science, but mere understanding is of questionable value.

This is brought out particularly in some manifestations of what is called 'ethnomethodology', which studies everyday activities. When scientific pretensions are removed, all that seems to be left for a social scientist is to describe how participants in a society view their activities. The repudiation of causal accounts of how societies gain their character and the consequent distrust of any notion of rational standards allow little but the description of the varying viewpoints to be found and the recognition that the viewpoint of the social scientist provides one such example. Ethnomethodologists uphold a policy of what they term 'ethnomethodological indifference', and when they study what they term the 'formal structures' of everyday activities they restrict themselves to the task of describing members' accounts.[2] The point of their 'indifference' is that they wish to abstain in their study of such phenomena 'from all judgements of their adequacy, value, importance, necessity, practicality, success or consequentiality'. In other words, ethnomethodologists do not want to import any of their own assumptions about rationality into their descriptions.

Other writers on ethnomethodology say firmly that it 'treats social science as one more reality among the many'.[3] They criticize social science on the grounds that it 'distorts other realities because it views them only through the lenses of its own system'. Once again we must note the incoherence involved in talking of 'many realities'. Presumably if there *are* many realities we are forced to envisage one reality including them all. Just as crucial is the question what is the function of social science if it is prohibited from viewing other 'realities' through the lenses of its own system. The point is certainly being made that the assumptions of science should not be arbitrarily imposed on alien systems of belief. The authors complain that 'the scientific reality is used as *the* standard against which all other realities are compared'. For example, they say, native sorcery can be made to appear merely a bizarre example of aberrant drug use.

We may agree with the familiar objection that practices should not be torn out of context, but repudiating science can involve us in great difficulties. Many go much further than simply holding that science cannot give us all the answers and that human knowledge is obtainable from other sources. The reaction against science can produce the feeling that there are no answers. Mehan and Wood say that 'every reality is equally real', and further claim that 'no single reality contains more of the truth than any other'.[4] This introduces an odd notion of truth in addition to their curious idea of reality. They obviously wish to purge any belief-system of aspirations to superiority. They even attack Schutz for treating the reality of everyday life as the *one* paramount reality. Yet the way they put the matter suggests that truth is obtainable, whereas they clearly mean that there is no such thing. It is not that each system of belief has its own window on the same truth. What counts as true is different in different systems, so that no one can claim the others are mistaken. They go on, in fact, to quote Wittgenstein with approval, and equate 'forms of life' with 'realities'.

Ethnomethodology certainly takes the problem of reflexivity seriously, and encounters similar problems to the sociology of knowledge. Social science merely becomes one system of belief among many, at the same level as the Azande's predilection for oracles. Yet, however much we need to be wary of distorting other people's beliefs by imposing our assumptions on them, it is dangerous to argue that that is all that can happen. Mehan and Wood say: 'There is no way to look from the window of one reality at others without seeing yourself.'[5] Once this is taken to heart, an infinite regress seems inevitable. Ethnomethodologists must realize that any empirical findings they make are as much the outcome of their 'reality' as of the one they are investigating. Yet they cannot investigate their own reality without already bringing their assumptions to bear on it. It is hardly surprising that Mehan and Wood maintain that ethnomethodology 'is not a method of pursuing the truth about the world'.[6] Instead, they say, its task is to examine the many versions, including its own, of the way the world is assembled.

Why, then, should anyone practise ethnomethodology if it is understood in this way? Mehan and Wood admit that the problem of reflexivity has worried many, so that some have suggested that all 'empirical rhetoric' should be abandoned. The problem is how far any discipline which emphasizes that it is merely one form of life among many can get a grip on the world. Once experience of the world is explicitly relativized to a particular conceptual framework, empirical research is seen as merely the outworking of a particular system of belief. It cannot justify it, and it is difficult to find any answer when someone wonders why they should adopt or hold to such a system or what the point of any empirical research might be. Instead of being the paradigm of rationality, the methods of empirical science are reduced to the status of seemingly pointless ritual. Mehan and Wood admit that ethnomethodologists who become worried about the status of empirical ethnomethodology 'typically quit ethnomethodology and the academy in search of some other way of life'.[7] Nothing could demonstrate more strikingly the paralysing effect of relativism in the social sciences. It is one thing to assert that the physical sciences have no monopoly on truth but it is another to jettison the concepts of truth, reality and knowledge. It is one thing to resist a narrowly scientific paradigm for rationality, but it is another to widen the latter so that the most rigorous social scientist can be no more rational than the most superstitious tribesman. The only consequence of such a position is to cast complete doubt on the value or purpose of social science, or indeed of any intellectual activity.

Rationality as a Social Practice

The social sciences aim at more than a simple understanding of other cultures. Anyone can adopt the outlook of another society if they go to live in it and attempt to forget their own. It is possible to 'go native', and there are examples of Westerners even joining cannibal tribes and living like them. It would be ludicrous to suggest that the more cannibalistic someone became, the more successful he or she was as an anthropologist. Total absorption in a tribe cannot be the aim of social science, although demands for participation through fieldwork may have been an effective antidote to armchair anthropologists. One will find out more about New Guinea tribesmen in New Guinea than in Oxford. Yet the fundamental problem remains of how one treats the knowledge gained about the life of a tribe. Anthropology is a useless discipline if the assumptions of social science are dismissed at the outset as the product of a particular society. Some people may just happen to enjoy visiting exotic parts of the world and seeing strange customs, while others prefer to stay at home.

Something more is needed, and social scientists need to examine a culture with a certain detachment. The immediate response will be that they will not be detached about their own culture. The very notion of scientific detachment is itself a particular cultural assumption. Yet that contention is analogous to the response in a fierce argument that 'that is only *your* opinion'. Every opinion is the opinion of someone and the important question is whether good reasons can be produced for the belief. The point of any argument or discussion is lost if you are told that an apparent reason can only be what *you* think is a good reason. Without the ability to discuss what *are* good reasons, what *is* true or what *is* real, all talk becomes the expression of non-rational attitudes, or even tastes. Some may be culturally conditioned, others may be an individual matter, but all hold in common the fact that argument will not and cannot touch them. The treatment of the ideal of rationality as a cultural construction by Westerners, and only that, means that apparently rational discussion is the mere exhibition of culturally conditioned prejudices. They have been brought up to prefer that kind of intellectual game. While conditions in some societies may have favoured the development of rational thought, the question is whether such thought can claim any validity. Is the intellectual pursuit of 'truth' just an expression of the workings of one culture among many, or can it set standards to which all should aspire?

This question is of particular relevance to the study of other societies, but it does raise a very deep issue. The American philosopher, Richard Rorty, asks it in the context of a discussion about the purpose of philosophy itself. The repudiation of an empiricist epistemology with its sure foundations in experience leaves open the possibility that there may not be one overall framework in which rational discourse can take place. There could be many different kinds of discourse. Rorty uses the terms 'epistemology' and 'hermeneutics' to describe two different strategies. He writes about whether there can be common ground between various discourses or whether there cannot in fact be presupposed any 'disciplinary matrix which unites the speakers'. Is there a common rationality? He says:

> For hermeneutics, to be rational is to be willing to refrain from epistemology – from thinking that there is a special set of terms in which all contributions to the conversation should be put – and to be willing to pick up the jargon of the interlocutor rather than translating it into one's own. For epistemology, to be rational is to find the proper set of terms into which all the contributions should be translated if agreement is to become possible. For epistemology, conversation is implicit inquiry. For hermeneutics, inquiry is routine conversation.[8]

Thus he wishes to hold that conversation is 'the ultimate context within which knowledge is to be understood'.[9] Truth is not an objective matter arrived at through the correspondence of our ideas with reality. It is a matter of negotiation and of mutual understanding and compromise, if indeed it is possible to continue talking of truth at all. Rorty sees alternative social practices of justification, each presumably having to 'converse' with the other. Without any notion of objective truth, he still feels it important 'to keep the conversation going'.[10] Why, though, should philosophy have to keep on with what appears a pointless and trivial task? Even allowing for the metaphorical nature of the phrase 'the conversation of mankind', philosophy seems reduced to the level of the idle chatter of a cocktail party. What, indeed, is the status of Rorty's own philosophical arguments? If he is not attempting to provide rational arguments, it is difficult to see what he is writing for. If he is, he must himself be presupposing some framework of rationality.

The influence of Kuhn and the later Wittgenstein on Rorty is explicit. Yet whether we deal with the possibility of rationality at the most general level of all, that of philosophy and epistemology, at the level of scientific practice or at the anthropological level, the issue remains the same. Is rationality a social practice, historically conditioned, or is it possible to appeal to standards of rationality which transcend what may be accepted at a particular place and time? It is perhaps significant that questions about rationality are so often linked with questions about objective truth. The assumption of a reality independent of what we think itself provides a constraint on what it is reasonable to believe. Our standards of what it is reasonable to believe are adequate if reality is created or constructed by our beliefs, as an idealist might hold. If, on the other hand, what we believe in no way affects the nature of reality, as 'common sense' might assume and the realist maintains, it is completely possible that our assumptions about what it is reasonable to believe lead us far astray. Our beliefs may be totally false.

Rorty arrived at his position through repudiating empiricist views of knowledge. Yet philosophy seems cut adrift without the security of a foundationalist epistemology. Part of the trouble is that empiricism relied heavily on the notion of experience of the world to the detriment of any emphasis on the world as such. Consequently, once the theoretical or even cultural influences on what seemed 'raw' experience are exposed, it is difficult to recover any conception of the world or reality which does not itself seem to be merely a theoretical or cultural construct. Yet without such a conception the hopelessness which leads some ethno-methodologists to give up ethnomethodology can soon set in. What is needed is a concept of objective reality which is divorced from the presuppositions of empiricism and which, as a consequence, is not tied too closely to the methods and findings of empirical science. The latter may be a source of knowledge, but its claim to be the *only* source has undoubtedly led many to intemperate opposition to the idea of knowledge or of objective truth.

How far does this illuminate questions concerning alleged superstition and possible irrationality in 'primitive' societies? Someone with Rorty's views will not invoke rational standards and criticize a society for not abiding by them. Their standards are different from ours and we must, it seems, endeavour to enter a conversation with them without any comforting rational framework with which to assess their views. Yet is this position adequate when we are faced with, say, magic and witchcraft? Wittgenstein would have accepted that it was and was particularly critical of the anthropological work of Sir James Frazer: 'Frazer's account of the magical and religious notions of men is unsatisfactory: it makes those notions appear as *mistakes*.'[11]

Wittgenstein's own interpretation of such notions, however, rests on a refusal to accept that anything true is being claimed in religion. He refuses to accept that Augustine was mistaken in calling upon God, but this is not because he thinks Augustine was correct. He would not allow that a Buddhist or an adherent to some other religion was mistaken either. The concept of a mistake would be inappropriate in this area. He claims: 'A religious symbol does not rest on any opinion. And error belongs only with opinion.'[12]

This type of move is, in fact, extremely popular with modern social anthropologists. It is encouraged by a desire not to treat magical and religious practices as if they are just bad science. Frazer certainly seemed to be doing just that. Wittgenstein takes exception to his view that ceremonies to make the wind blow or the rain fall will persist because such occurrences will normally take place at some time. Frazer maintains that 'primitive man may be excused for regarding the occurrence as a direct result of the ceremony, and the best possible proof of its efficiency.'[13] Wittgenstein's rejoinder is that 'it is queer that people do not notice that it does rain sooner or later anyway'.[14] From a scientific point of view the conclusion has to be that the people concerned are irrational. Yet refusing to make this step must involve a refusal to impose our scientific standards on a 'pre-scientific' society.

The relativist reference to different realities will only lock different cultures in self-contained compartments, and it is perhaps not surprising if many social anthropologists prefer to stress the non-scientific character of much 'primitive' belief. We are told, for example, that 'magic is a symbolic activity not a scientific one'.[15] Thus, to save tribesmen from the accusation of being irrational, their activities are interpreted not as ways of making things happen but as ways of showing how they feel about events. The expressive and symbolic character of what is being done is emphasized. A rain-dance is, then, to be viewed not as an ineffective way of producing rain but as a ritual expressing a belief in the importance of rain and a desire that it should fall. In a drought-ridden society, any apparent rain-making rituals will embody these attitudes, and be potent symbols of something held very important. The problem is whether they are just that and whether the members of that society may not just be wrong in their beliefs about how rain can be produced. Even in Western societies, there may be prayers for rain when there is a severe drought. Sophisticated believers may feel that prayers of that sort are not means of altering the world but just express our deepest concerns. More likely, they will be reluctant to use them at all. Unsophisticated believers will certainly feel that such prayers may be answered. It is easy to assume that the latter are wrong, but it is inconsistent to think that of members of one's own society, while shrinking from judging apparently similar beliefs in other societies in the same way.

Why is it so easy to consider that prayers can make no difference to the world? The answer must surely be found in the prestige of science and in the prejudice that what cannot be explained by science cannot occur.[16] This is mere prejudice, since even scientists must admit that contemporary science has its limitations. If the belief is that science can *in principle* explain everything, even though some things will be for ever out of reach of flesh-and-blood scientists, this becomes vacuous. Whatever is real is scientifically explicable, it seems, but the snag is that *we* may never be able to explain it. We will not be so ready to equate science and rationality if we take the limitations of human science seriously. When science cannot at the moment, or in the foreseeable future, explain everything, it is not necessarily irrational to hold beliefs which are not provable scientifically. This does not thereby mean that it is automatically rational, but good and bad reasons for belief need not be restricted to what contemporary scientists would accept as such. It may be irrational to go against the findings of science, but it does not seem rational to be restricted by its limitations. We may not reasonably say that the earth is flat, but nor can we refuse to face all issues which have not been conclusively settled by science. Doing so would be merely to continue allegiance to a narrow positivism.

How does this affect our judgement of non-scientific beliefs? They cannot be judged irrational merely because they are non-scientific. The practical rejection of all religion, and indeed all metaphysics, embodied a commitment to the standards of science which could not itself be rationally justified. A persistent criticism of those who stressed that the meaning of a statement was to be understood by the way it could be scientifically verified was that this belief could not itself be scientifically verified. It was merely laid down from the beginning as an axiom, which others were accordingly free to reject. The determination to view metaphysics as nonsense, in the manner of the Vienna Circle, was simply a determination to count science as the source of rationality. It made scientific rationality synonymous with rationality. This defined certain positions as rational and others not, but its dogmatism left untouched the basic issue of whether all non-scientific beliefs about the world could be dismissed as irrational.

'Expressive' and 'Symbolic' Practices

The eagerness of many social anthropologists to emphasize the expressive character of many rituals and to stress the role of symbols in thought reflects both the influence of positivism and an unhappiness about its consequences. The same tendency is present in the way that some philosophers of religion try to interpret religion in Western societies. The first assumption made is that truth is the province of science, and that religious beliefs cannot claim 'literal' truth, whether they are about spirits in the trees or the Trinity. Then some hesitate to dismiss so completely the basic beliefs of so many. Saying that they are false, if not nonsensical, implies that those believing them are irrational. The next stage is to attempt to rescue the beliefs by showing that they have a definite function in the societies concerned and that the believers are in fact doing something perfectly sensible. Since questions of truth and falsity have already been handed over to science, explanations have to be given which show that the beliefs in question have nothing to do with beliefs about what is true. Rituals which are apparently designed to produce rain should not be understood in that way. Tribesmen do not have false beliefs about the weather but are, despite appearances, doing something perfectly sensible.

The same type of analysis can be, and is, given to religious beliefs in Western societies. The tacit assumption is often made that science cannot explain miracles or have any dealing with the transcendent or the supernatural. Therefore it seems that talk about God and divine intervention in the world cannot be literally true or false, and that if religious believers are not irrational they must be understood as doing something other than believing facts about the world. One of the most famous examples of this type of response to empiricism is that of R. B. Braithwaite, who said: 'The primary use of religious assertion is to announce allegiance to a set of moral principles.'[17] Religion is thus reduced to a determination to live a particular kind of life. Its apparent claims to truth are merely pictures, used as psychological aids. More recently, a radical theologian, Don Cupitt, has responded to what he sees as the challenge of science: 'Our highly refined and elegant scientific world-picture carries the clear implication that our moralities, art and religions are purely human constructions that are in no way endorsed by the universe at large.'[18] He recognizes that it is possible to refuse science the status of arbiter of truth, and to treat it as 'one human cultural activity among others'. Yet on either interpretation of science – the positivist one or the reaction against it – religion cannot claim objective truth. If positivism is correct, religion is strictly meaningless, since only science provides knowledge. If the reaction against positivism prevails, religion may be understood as part of forms of life, or as a distinctive one itself. The concept of objective truth has itself been banished.

Cupitt tries to save a place for religion by claiming that 'we have to come to see religious language as being not descriptive but expressive, action-guiding and symbolic'.[19] He says that 'the development of critical thinking and of the scientific outlook has now demythologized or demystified all the things that people have traditionally lived by.' Thus we can no longer think of God as a transcendent reality, let alone the ultimate explanation for everything. He offers the view that we have 'to make do with the use of the word "God" as an incorporating or unifying symbol connoting the whole of what we are up against in the spiritual life.'[20] It seems that believers in God cannot possess a putative fact about the world if facts are the province of science. Unless they are professing gibberish or holding irrationally to a belief which they should recognize as false, the belief must have some other function. It regulates their lives, and perhaps the life of their society, in some significant way, and without it they, or their society, would be different.

The significant feature of this type of analysis is that it is the same as that given by social anthropologists about 'primitive' religion. The same pressures to dismiss its beliefs as unscientific and hence false are exerted. The desire to compartmentalize areas of human experience, so that science is kept in its place, results in talk of different ways of life, and of symbolic and expressive speech. Social anthropology can insulate other societies from science by stressing the difference between those societies and its own. Some apologists of religion in Western society insulate religion by holding that science and religion, even within the one society, entail different practices or ways of life. In the end, however, the problem is the same. Armed with the insights of modern science, how are we to treat the persistence of practices which cannot be justified scientifically? The issues encountered by social anthropologists are no different in kind from those we encounter in Western societies. How is it that some people are able to hold beliefs which cannot be judged rational according to a strictly scientific understanding?

Two philosophers, MacDonald and Pettit, writing about the problem of cross-cultural understanding, suggest that, 'in fastening on the religious/scientific contrast, anthropologists have been led to over-emphasize the differences between our culture and more traditional ones.'[21] They consider that in the latter there would be no tradition of reflecting on the rationality of particular beliefs. The occurrence of contradictory beliefs might perhaps be less surprising in these circumstances. They conclude that 'it may be that the anthropologist, or at least the atheist anthropologist, will find the sharpest challenge to the assumption of human rationality not in researches among the alien, but in investigations among her own.' This is fair comment in so far as it points out that the same type of problem recurs when religion and science confront each other in Western society as when science meets primitive religion and magic. If what is at issue is the repudiation of all beliefs which are not scientifically supported, it is a clear error to assume that all Western society functions according to the presuppositions of positivist scientific method. Indeed, as we have seen, few now believe that even science does.

Many of the problems of interpreting 'primitive' cultures have arisen because they have been judged according to narrowly scientific standards, as understood by positivists. Challenges to assumptions about human rationality appear more acute because scientific procedure is taken as the paradigm of rationality. The cultural relativist would limit the criteria of science to Western societies, but that does not remove the problem, since non-scientific beliefs occur there too. The view that all religious beliefs, wherever they occur, are merely symbolic accepts the positivist claim that only science can provide a path to truth. It is similar to relativist views in that it provides religion with its own set of standards so that 'symbolic truth' or 'religious truth' can still be talked about in a way that science cannot touch. There is, though, the strong implication that 'real' or 'literal' truth has been passed over to science.

What is needed is a conception of reality, and hence of truth, which is not restricted to the present findings of science. Modern science has proved a powerful technique for making important discoveries about the world, but the view that it is the only path to knowledge can result in grave distortions in the interpretation of non-scientific belief. 'Scientific realists' may still be inclined to restrict the concept of reality to what science can discover, but this is prejudice. We dare not assume that all non-scientific beliefs must be false or that their holders are thereby shown to be irrational.

Charles Taylor points out that modern science has been able to develop only because we have disciplined ourselves to 'register the way things are without regard to the meanings they might have for us'. A chasm has appeared between the detached view of reality exemplified by science and a richly meaningful world as delineated by symbols: 'This kind of contrast is one that has developed out of our form of life. But exactly for this reason, it is probably going to be unhelpful in understanding people who are very different from us.'[22]

Thus the very idea of a symbol, as opposed to what is literally, or scientifically, true itself arises from a scientifically based society. It is obvious that it must do, since otherwise the contrast could not be made. Rightly or wrongly, we have learnt to make such a dichotomy, while other cultures will not have done so. Yet it may be suggested that this is beside the point, unless we are conceptual relativists, restricting the application of concepts to the societies in which they originated. A valid distinction should be applied even to those who would not apply it to themselves. Other cultures may not recognize the symbolic nature of their beliefs. This is one of the major problems in interpreting other cultures. Are we entitled to describe or explain practices in terms that would not be accepted by the people we are investigating? Can we say that prayers for rain are purely symbolic or expressive, even if those using them do not accept that interpretation? They may not accept it because they do not possess our concept of symbol, but many who do share the concept would still reject it as inapplicable to their prayers. Alternatively they might stop praying for rain precisely because they come to see that it does correctly describe them. In either case, categorizing the prayers in this way involves more than a neutral description. It does not allow that anyone could intelligibly try to use prayer to alter the world by supernatural means.

By definition science cannot cope with the supernatural, so that kind of prayer is not in accord with a scientific view of the world. What is at issue is whether humans may in fact use prayer for this purpose. They may also use magic or witchcraft to attempt to alter the world. The automatic assumption that all of these practices must be irrational and are therefore unlikely to occur is a mere application of a prejudice in favour of science. In fact some of the practices may be surprisingly rational, given a fairly profound ignorance about the physical forces at work in the world. Even the objection that magic often does not work derives from a scientific training in which predictive success is recognized to be of primary importance.

Belief and Rationality

Rationality is a relative concept. What it is rational to believe depends on what you know already. Scientists can easily dismiss primitive belief in the power of magic as irrational because they possess greater knowledge about the world. From their point of view such beliefs are mere superstition, and perhaps the scientists are right. Sometimes, however, scientists have been tempted to claim knowledge they do not possess. A scientist may find it impossible to explain the apparent efficacy of prayer on some occasion, and be unhappy that the alleged effects of prayer cannot be reproduced under laboratory conditions. Yet this might just as well point to the limits of science as to the shortcomings of prayer. This is an exceedingly controversial matter, but this very fact suggests that it cannot be solved by treating certain beliefs as unscientific and therefore not really about the world. The controversy arises precisely because science cannot take account of forms of explanation which are at variance with a scientific outlook. Interpreting them in such a way that they do not conflict is a subtle way of re-asserting the supremacy of science in an alarmingly positivist manner. Accepting the conflict as real need not make us lose our bearings about what it is rational to believe. The scientists could be right, and those disagreeing with them wrong. The symbolist approach makes it impossible to expose false belief and ignorance, since all beliefs are made to express sensible attitudes.

John Beattie argues that 'Magic is the acting out of a situation, the expression of a desire in symbolic terms; it is not the application of empirically acquired knowledge about the properties of natural substances.'[23] He is right to suppose that native magic is not just a silly scientific theory, since this imports our ideas of Western science to an inappropriate situation. What he fails to realize is that, when he concludes that it must therefore be totally different, he is still applying the distinction between science and non-science. Yet the point is not that native magic occurs in a society which does not have scientific beliefs, but that the very distinction between science and non-science does not apply there. It certainly would follow that if only scientists can have access to the nature of reality, native practices cannot be understood as involving conceptions of reality. This is, though, a travesty of the situation.

Once it is accepted that science is just a particularly efficient method of obtaining knowledge, we may reasonably expect to find knowledge in other cultures. The corollary of this is that we shall also find ignorance. Nevertheless, when our beliefs conflict with theirs, the view that reality is as independent of our views as it is of theirs has salutary consequences. We cannot be certain that our methods of obtaining knowledge are always superior to theirs. We may be able to learn from them. Traditional remedies in tribal medicine, for instance, may actually sometimes *be* remedies. Too great a reliance on the impressive technology of modern surgery might blind us to important facts that simpler societies may long have known.

The assertion that 'pre-scientific' societies somehow could not have any knowledge about the world, but are involved in practices that make sense only in their society, itself involves the application of positivist distinctions. Yet although a culture's grasp on reality may be slight, and although it proves unable to control powerful natural forces, there may often be the glimmerings of deep insight. It is a gross error to say that either a belief is scientific or it cannot be concerned with reality. When we see a tribal society relying on magic, it is inappropriate to impose our theoretical categories on it, even if we merely intend to exonerate it of the charge of irrationality. An analogous situation arises when we study the early days of philosophy and of science in Ionia in the fifth century BC. It is difficult to determine whether some beliefs were scientific or metaphysical. Science, with its empirical methods, had not been explicitly distinguished from the simple exercise of human reason. Saying that the early atomic theory of Democritus, not to mention Thales' theory of water as the underlying reality, was scientific merely imposes categories not recognized at the time. From our point of view there may be scientific elements involved, but the imposition of anachronistic categories does little to assist our understanding.

The basic question should be the truth of beliefs rather than their rationality. Given a deep enough ignorance about the world, many practices which seem obviously irrational to us are, in fact, perfectly rational. If I do not know how to cope with the contingencies of my life, and am totally at their mercy, I might indulge in what seem weird practices in an attempt to gain some control. Winch suggests that the magical rites of the Azande 'express an attitude to contingencies'.[24] He describes the attitude as one involving recognition that one's life is subject to contingencies rather than an attempt to control these. Yet the tribesmen used sarawa leaves in the apparent belief that they made things flourish. Evans-Pritchard quotes how the Azande address a leaf of sarawa: 'Medicine, you protect my ground-nuts from witches, you make my ground-nuts flourish.'[25] Only someone in the grip of a philosophical theory could think that this does not result from a genuine fear of witches and a belief that sarawa leaves would make the ground-nuts grow well. Similarly, only someone who was already in the grip of the assumptions of modern science could think of a prayer for rain as anything other than a request to a supernatural power to produce rain. The view that the people concerned would surely see that these methods did not 'work' merely imports a rigorously scientific view into the situation. If they had possessed that sophisticated a view of cause and effect, they would probably not have had the beliefs they did have in the first place. Anyway, often the ground-nuts would flourish.

The very fact that missionaries in the nineteenth century and scientists in the twentieth have been able to convince many people that some of their beliefs are primitive and should be discarded bears witness to the rationality of their holders. It is surprising how rapidly the beliefs can be discarded when irrefutable evidence is provided that the witch-doctor does not have the power everyone believed he had, or that rituals can be discarded without ill effects. South Sea Islanders discovered after the arrival of missionaries that the taboos and rituals connected with sailing and fishing could be given up without anything terrible happening.

Once one seaman had the courage to omit the practice and still did well, everyone else would follow. Their reasons for participating in the traditional rituals were shown to be grounded in false beliefs.

Symbolist interpretations of traditional beliefs may be intended to protect the holders of such beliefs from the charge of irrationality, but what they do is to ignore the fact that people hold beliefs for reasons, good or bad. The explanation given by many social anthropologists for the persistence of practices in a society often ignores the individual understanding of the participants. Just as the later Wittgenstein thought that beliefs gain their significance from their social role rather than from what they purport to be about, a symbolist understanding of belief ignores its actual content and looks for the truths expressed about that particular society. Individual belief when seen from a holist standpoint may well have a certain role in society, but the ordinary believer may not be aware of it, and certainly does not hold a belief for that reason.

The Explanation of Ritual

D. Z. Phillips gives a Wittgensteinian account of ritual when he says:

> Where rituals express a wish, to know in what sense the ritual acts out the wish, we would have to take account of the role played by the ritual in the details of the lives of the people who celebrate it.[26]

From the standpoint of an anthropologist, the social context may be illuminating, but unless the ritual is a *mere* ritual the viewpoint of the individual participants must be different. Phillips, however, refers to an example, also used by Winch, of mountain-dwellers 'who, before specifically religious expressions develop in their language, contemplate the mountains, prostrate themselves before them, celebrate rites in relation to them, in such ways that we call them primitive religious responses'. Phillips continues:

> Later, they come to speak of gods in the mountains. Rituals and stories develop which can be said to be *about* these gods. Must we then say that talk of the gods expresses the existential presuppositions of the primitive reactions?

Phillips's conclusion is that it is wrong to *explain* their looking to the mountains in terms of their reverence to the gods. There is in fact a 'conceptual connection' between their ritual and what they understand by their gods, so that the two cannot be separated. The conclusion is that 'a decline in the religious practices would be an aspect of loss of belief in the gods, not a consequence of it'.[27] The practice embodies the belief, and is not justified by it as if the latter was something separate. Yet this account is at variance with what Phillips posits as the account given by the mountain-dwellers themselves. When they speak of gods in the mountains, they presumably believe that there are gods in the mountains. The fact that this belief was expressed in religious practices before it was properly articulated does not mean that, when it is articulated, it should be rejected. Phillips would doubtless claim that what is meant by 'there are gods in the mountains' can only be understood by locating the ritual in the life of the people. Yet what the belief *says* is very different, and the ritual would not be the same without that belief. In fact, identifying religious practices in some respect with belief in gods makes it difficult to see how a ritual could live on without the belief. What, though, is to prevent a sophisticated tribesman participating in the ritual and even encouraging it, even though he knows full well there are no gods in the mountains? His reason may well be that he has read the works of modern anthropologists and he realizes the wider social significance of the rituals. Perhaps the ritual becomes something different for him and he may find it difficult to be gripped by it in the same way. It becomes a *mere* ritual. The difference, though, is that an existential belief has been removed.

Once a practice is consciously recognized as a ritual, or a symbolic activity, it is very difficult for it to play the same part in the life of a society. Religious rituals that presuppose a belief in gods or a god are different from rituals that do not. It becomes very difficult to participate in them in the same way once it is recognized that they do not. No doubt Sunday worship in a Christian church plays a particular role in society and the lives of those participating in it. Once, however, a 'sophisticated' philosopher of religion accounts for it as a purely expressive or symbolic activity, with no presupposition that God is being worshipped, it becomes much more difficult to participate on the same terms as before. It is an intriguing point that again and again the same issues confront social anthropology and modern philosophy of religion. Phillips himself remarks that where philosophers stand on issues concerning anthropological understanding 'determines the treatment of some of the deepest issues in contemporary philosophy of religion'.[28] In other words, what provides difficulty in the understanding of the religious practices of other cultures is not that they are embedded in other cultures, but that they are *religious*. The positivist assumption persists that no religious belief, when taken at face value, can be rational, whether it is about gods in the mountains or the Christian God.

Some rituals *are* mere rituals. When the British Parliament is opened in state by the monarch, she summons the House of Commons by sending Black Rod to fetch them. When he arrives at the door of the Chamber, it is ceremoniously and defiantly slammed in his face. This expresses the independence of the Commons from interference by the Crown. The Queen's messenger can only enter when invited. Memories of Charles I linger on. Yet, while this ritual expresses a constitutional fact and has a social role, it is performed self-consciously as part of the picturesque traditions of Parliament. No one is really trying to keep Black Rod out or wishes to refuse to go to the Queen's presence in the House of Lords. No one believes that Elizabeth II is a menace to the power of Parliament. Members of Parliament are in fact eagerly waiting in their best suits to process in front of the waiting television cameras. The ritual is viewed as such. When religious practices come to be seen in the same light, as picturesque traditions expressing truths about our society, religion will be in an advanced state of decay. Its whole basis, namely a belief, whether true or false, in an independently existing God, will have been eroded. After that, nothing can be the same. The role played by a ritual in people's lives is the result of their beliefs about what is true.

The social role of belief should not be confused with the reasons why a belief is embraced. Its content is distinct from its consequences. Here, as so often, there can be a subtle slide from what is believed to the fact that a certain belief is held. The social sciences may legitimately have ambitions to explain the latter. Social anthropologists will probably throw light on why primitive beliefs and practices could persist even though they were poor ways of manipulating the real world. A symbolist interpretation of, say, the casting of a spell on crops helps to explain why members of a society go on doing it. The spell is an expression of the dependence of their society on the crops, and collective rituals always help to enhance loyalty to the group. Other plausible explanations may locate the practice firmly in its social context. The society would be a

very different one without such rituals, and might eventually fall
apart. Yet, however persuasive such explanations may be, they only
explain why beliefs *of that sort* may be held and rituals *like that* performed.
Many other similar types of belief would do just as well. Any religious
ritual would probably be equally successful in reinforcing group
loyalty. Indeed, the conversion of tribes to Christianity and the replace-
ment of one set of rituals with another need be of little importance to
the symbolist anthropologist. One set of symbols is replaced by
another, but it might appear that much the same thing is being symbolized.

Sometimes not enough weight is put on the intrinsic nature of the
symbol. The fact that participants in a ritual may not be conscious of
what is being symbolized (the unity of the tribe, for instance) suggests
that, whatever the social context of their actions, further explanation is
needed. Why do they choose this ritual rather than another? Why is a
particular incantation used? Unless we treat the participants as automata,
the perspective of the individual cannot be ignored, and the content of
his or her belief becomes relevant. What do the participants think they
are doing? Treating individuals as merely agents caught up in a social
process of which they understand little, takes too little account of their
own rationality. If a religious believer becomes convinced that prayer
cannot be understood as a definite request for supernatural help which
may be successful, he or she will probably stop using such a prayer. One
has to be a very sophisticated theologian to be able to go on using
language to make requests in prayer, while knowing that is not really
what one is doing at all. No doubt many prayers could be interpreted by
such a theologian as simply expressing our dependence on God, or,
more radically, showing our attitude to the contingencies of life. That,
however, is not what the prayers say. It is hard not to conclude that the
reluctance of many to use such petitionary prayer stems from the fact
that they no longer believe what they would be saying. Whatever the
social context and however much an individual's rational processes are
influenced by it, the beliefs of individual participants in a society cannot
be ignored. What they believe and their own reasons for believing it are
not unimportant. The identification of a particular belief cannot be made
by simply appealing to its social role. The slot it fills in a society does not
explain why *it* rather than another belief fills it.

The social sciences in general and social anthropology in particular
face limits to what they can explain. Explaining the social context of a

belief is not the same as assessing the rationality of the belief itself. The latter is outside the professional competence of social scientists. In the end, we cannot sidestep questions about individual rationality. The temptation in the past has been to deal with questions of such rationality by either bluntly applying contemporary scientific standards or by refusing to accept that our standards apply at all. Either way, the problem has been seen as a clash of systems of belief. It has then seemed inevitable that social scientists produce explanations for the existence of such systems. If, instead, we assume that humans are everywhere much the same and face the same reality that we do, we can conclude that varying practices exhibit varying beliefs about the nature of that reality. Without the benefit of sophisticated ways of gathering knowledge and of controlling the world, many humans quite rationally react to the world in what seem to us to be futile ways. They hold their beliefs not because they live in a different world from ours, but because they inhabit the same one but do not possess our knowledge of it. Sometimes they may know things which we wrongly reject.

The assumption that, although anyone can be stupid or foolish, by and large all humans share the same ability to reason and adopt the same basic standards of rationality is a crucial one in understanding alien societies. We shall never find them intelligible unless we can build a bridge between them and us. One such point of contact might be that they and we agree in most of our beliefs, particularly everyday ones about the world as we perceive it. This assumption is embodied in Donald Davidson's 'principle of charity' according to which, if we want to understand others, we must count them right in most matters. This seems implausible, since we may in fact be able to find others intelligible precisely in the cases where we do disagree with them. In place of the principle of charity, Richard Grandy has proposed a 'principle of humanity'.[29] This is 'the condition that imputed patterns of relations among beliefs, desires and the world be as similar to our own as possible'. Rationality has to be presupposed before translation can begin. We must think what we would do if we had the relevant beliefs and desires. Obviously it is of great assistance if the people we are trying to understand share our beliefs and desires. Too great a divergence will prove troublesome. Yet, if the world we each confront is the same and we share the same kind of desires, it should prove possible to find alien beliefs intelligible without pretending that they are something other than they are. Moreover, we find them intelligible precisely because we assume the rationality of the person holding them. Irrational beliefs are much more difficult to find intelligible and translate.

As has been pointed out by MacDonald and Pettit, the principle of humanity rests on a 'belief in the unity of human nature' – 'a belief that people in different cultures are essentially similar'.[30] They elucidate this by saying that 'any differences there are across cultures, or at least any differences central to the attitudes and actions of people, should be explicable by reference to different circumstances'. In other words, if we were in the same situation as, say, tribesmen, without our technology, we might very well have adopted a similar way of life. They are not different kinds of creatures from us. This assumption of a common human nature is an important one, needing further justification. One retort could be that, as there is no such thing, we must expect to find major difficulties in understanding other cultures. Questions about human nature cannot be ignored by the social sciences. If the assumption of a universal human nature is necessary, it could be argued that, even when the social sciences are demonstrating the supposed radical differences between cultures, they are, through their understanding of those cultures, bearing witness to the fact of human nature.

Notes

1   P. Winch, 'Understanding a Primitive Society', 1972, p. 9.
2   H. Garfinkel and H. Sachs, 'On Formal Structures of Practical Actions', in J. C. McKinney and E. A. Tiryakin (eds), *Theoretical Sociology*, 1970.
3   H. Mehan and H. Wood, *The Reality of Ethnomethodology*, 1975, p. 37.
4   Ibid., p. 37.
5   Ibid., p. 31.
6   Ibid., p. 114.
7   Ibid., p. 167.
8   R. Rorty, *Philosophy and the Mirror of Nature*, 1980, p. 318.
9   Ibid., p. 389.
10 Ibid., p. 379.
11 L. Wittgenstein, *Remarks on Frazer's Golden Bough*, 1979, p. 1.
12 Ibid., p. 3.
13 James Frazer, *The Golden Bough*, 1922, p. 59.
14 Wittgenstein, *Remarks on Frazer's Golden Bough*, p. 2.
15 J. Beattie, *Other Cultures*, 1964, p. 209.

16 See my 'The Limits of Science' in H. P. Duerr (ed.), *Science and the Irrational*, 1984.

17 R. B. Braithwaite, 'An Empiricist's View of the Nature of Religious Belief', in I. T. Ramsey (ed.), *Christian Ethics and Contemporary Philosophy*, 1966, p. 63.

18 Don Cupitt, *The World to Come*, 1982, p. viii.

19 Ibid., p. xiv.

20 Cupitt, *Taking Leave of God*, 1980, p. 97.

21 G. MacDonald and P. Pettit, *Semantics and Social Science*, 1981, p. 54.

22 Charles Taylor, 'Rationality', in M. Hollis and S. Lukes (eds), *Rationality and Relativism*, 1982, p. 97.

23 Beattie, *Other Cultures*, p. 207.

24 Winch, 'Understanding a Primitive Society', p. 40.

25 E. Evans-Pritchard, *Witchcraft, Oracles and Magic among the Azande*, 1937, p. 452.

26 D. Z. Phillips, 'Primitive Reactions and the Reactions of Primitives', Marett Lecture, Oxford, 1983, p. 18.

27 Ibid., p. 22.

28 Ibid., p. 4.

29 Richard Grandy, 'Reference, Meaning and Belief', *Journal of Philosophy*, 70, 1973, p. 443.

30 MacDonald and Pettit, *Semantics and Social Science*, p. 31.

6

Facts and Values

'Value-free' Science

When the beliefs of apparently primitive societies are judged by the standards of scientific rationality, they can seem singularly foolish. If they are treated as scientific hypotheses, we might well wonder why they continued to be held in the face of what seem to us to be so many counter-instances. We have seen how the influence of positivism has resulted in the restricting of rationality to the procedures and techniques of modern science. Forcing primitive belief into the mould of hypotheses to be tested by experience only assumes that scientific method is the unique path to truth and the only proper expression of human rationality.

The categories of empiricism and positivism are also applied in another way which has a fundamental effect on the social sciences. It is a dogma, often repeated unthinkingly, that facts and values are logically distinct. Science seems to deal with facts, but the values placed on them cannot be logically deduced. The argument continues that we must have, as a result, much greater freedom to choose our values than to decide what the facts are. The latter is an objective matter, susceptible to scientific verification and falsification. Scientific method can provide an agreed procedure in case of factual disagreement, but there is no such procedure to settle differences about the values to be ascribed to the facts. Hume's injunction that what *ought* to be the case must not be confounded with what *is* the case epitomizes the empiricist approach. Whether we talk of 'ought' and 'is', or emphasize that values can never be deduced from facts, or stress the distinction between description and evaluation, the message is the same. Science can tell us what the facts are, but people's reactions to them are subjective matters, perhaps emotional reactions or feelings.

It is real enough that people make evaluations, but it appears that they can equally well view the same thing as good or bad. Some will see it one way and some another, and there is no way a scientist could suggest any procedure for setting the issue. Therefore there is no real issue, and it is not a factual matter, or so the positivist would say. Just as, if I hate bananas and you like them, there is no way it can be shown that I am right and you are wrong, the most basic human judgements about what is worth pursuing or to be avoided are reduced to mere matters of taste. How they arose may be explicable scientifically, but they cannot be justified. The sociologist may be able to explain why they have been produced. Hume himself tended to assume that basic desires were shared by all humans, so that we all naturally approve and disapprove of the same things.

This picture of the different status of what is factual and of what happens to be valued by humans comes from a particular view of science, which assumes that 'values' have no part in the operation of science. It has always seemed harder to exclude values from the social sciences because they deal with human concerns. The quest, though, of a 'value-free' social science has seemed indispensable if the social sciences were to acquire parity of esteem with the physical sciences. Yet just as a social anthropologist's approach to a culture is bound to be coloured by how far he or she considers it to be relying on false beliefs, so an estimate of how worthwhile some of its practices are must enter into attempts to explain them. For a start, it will influence what the anthropologist selects as in need of explanation. Time spent on growing crops for food hardly needs to be explained, since the activity is necessary. The very fact, though, that an anthropologist might be bewildered at a neglect of crops in favour of an involved religious ritual means that he or she will search for an explanation of the ritual. Yet the search is a reflection of what that anthropologist considers important. In other words, it is a reflection of values.

The desire to purify the social sciences of all values stems entirely from the assumption that the physical sciences have achieved the total separation of fact from value. Science appears to embody the dispassionate search for truth, abstracted from the partiality of particular points of view. If that is not so, the social sciences may themselves be aiming for something impossible by wishing to be 'value-free'.

The major shifts in the philosophy of science away from empiricism
are relevant to this issue. The question of the place of values in science
particularly arises when we ask what constraints there are on the adoption of new theories. A consequence of the new philosophy of science is
that theories, and not passively received experience, are given priority.
Yet, because of the underdetermination of theories by data, there must
be a gap between a theory and the empirical evidence for it, even if the
latter is not already 'theory-laden'. Theories cannot be deduced from the
evidence, and so a gap is opened up between evidence and theory which
is in some respects similar to the one allegedly existing between facts and
values. It therefore does not seem very extraordinary to hold that values
are needed to close the gap between the evidence and an underdetermined theory. Indeed, the very way we perceive the world is itself
impregnated with values if our language is already theory-laden and
our observations theory-dependent. The risk is that the notion of
empirical evidence can get completely lost, so that it is impossible to
talk of a theory being underdetermined by anything outside itself. There
are just different conceptual schemes positing different worlds. The
distinction between facts and values breaks down because no sense can
any longer be given to the notion of 'fact'.

The challenge to empiricism remains, even if the depths of conceptual
relativism are not plumbed. It seems that choice between theories is
influenced by values, rather than determined by rules. This distinction is
one that Kuhn invokes in an article which goes some way to making
room for the rational assessment of theories. He wants nothing to do
with positivist conceptions, but is happy to allow that characteristics such
as accuracy, consistency, scope, simplicity and fruitfulness can all be
relevant for evaluating the adequacy of a theory. This still will not
serve to reduce disputes between scientists, but the different weight
given by different people to the various criteria may well explain why
the disagreement has arisen. Kuhn writes:

> I am suggesting that the criteria of choice . . . function not as rules which
> determine choice but as values which influence it. Two men deeply
> committed to the same values may nevertheless in particular situations
> make different claims, as, in fact, they do.[1]

Mary Hesse concludes that, 'if we take the thesis of underdetermination
of theories seriously, relativism is a consequence that is inescapable in

some form.'[2] This may partly stem from a view that what cannot be deduced from empirical evidence must be consigned to the realm of value. She refers to comprehensive theories in the human sciences as 'ideological' on the grounds that they incorporate evaluations of their subject-matter. She then says: 'Evaluations may be constrained by facts, but cannot be determined by them.'[3] Values are apparently guides to our choice to theories when the facts do not settle the matter. Perhaps they could be defined as such. Mary Hesse also maintains that, 'as in the natural sciences, social theories are constrained but not determined by facts'.[4] She assumes that the theories involve evaluations, but this means that what she terms our 'criteria of acceptability' for theories in social science are pluralist. She says that they are as pluralist as our choices of value goals and continues: 'If we wish to talk of *choice* of values, it also follows that we presuppose a certain area of freedom in the activity of theorizing.'[5]

The view that emerges is that both the natural and social sciences are impregnated with values, and might even be termed 'ideological'. Empirical facts do not suffice to explain the adoption of theories. We are apparently free to choose our values, and this entails that different people may make different choices. Yet it appears that these are left with no rational basis and cry out themselves for the kind of sociological explanations beloved of the sociologist of knowledge. Although Mary Hesse believes that a strongly determinist view is self-defeating, incurring all the problems of reflexivity, she concedes that theories may be shown to be 'partially determined' by the social environment.

Scientific Values

Many contemporary philosophers no longer make any clear distinction between what is factual and what is not. This is not just because they find it hard to draw the line between the categories of fact and value. They cannot give any clear sense to the notion of anything being factual, and 'values' cannot any more be compared unfavourably with 'facts'. The one is not subjective and the other objective. What people choose to regard as real and what they view as important, valuable or worth pursuing cannot be regarded as belonging to two different types of discourse, the descriptive and the evaluative. Even the suggestion that scientific theories are value-impregnated from the beginning itself relies on a distinction that cannot be made, since values cannot in principle be separated from other ways of selecting what we are to believe. It seems likely that reference to values only makes real sense as a contrast to the scientifically established world of facts. It is difficult to destroy conceptions of the latter merely by talking of 'value impregnation', since values seem by definition to be non-factual. Without facts there is a sense in which there can be no values either. The concept of value is itself imbued with positivist assumptions.

People judge some things worth pursuing and others not, and they adopt some beliefs while rejecting others. We are all faced with choices at different levels which are not wholly determined. Our choices are very often governed by what we judge important or 'value'. Once the contrast with facts is discarded, though, there is no reason why what we value may not be as rationally based as any existential belief. Our valuings are no longer understood as taking place in some epistemological vacuum beyond the reach of respectable science. They need no longer seem merely subjective, and the possibility of rational justification for our valuings has to be looked at again. This is crucial for the question of the rationality of science itself, since, if the adoption of different scientific theories depends on what we judge important, any arbitrariness about the latter will infect science itself. If, on the other hand, choices between theories are made on the basis of rationally adopted criteria, science will remain the outworking of human rationality. It may, though, be only one expression of that rationality, instead of providing its standard.

The most obvious 'value' at the root of science is truth itself. The whole purpose of any science must be the pursuit of truth, and any understanding of science which ignores it runs the risk of undermining the whole edifice which scientists have constructed. This is the reason why the sociology of science can have a corrosive influence. Truth, of course, can itself be understood in various ways, and the great temptation is to identify it with one of the proven routes to it. In the end, however, the nature of reality becomes irrelevant to science if truth is not understood as some form of correspondence with reality. What, then, are the proven routes to truth in science? Western science has through the centuries tried to filter out prejudices and assumptions which have proved bad guides. Scientists have realized, for instance, that religious and political beliefs may incline them to one theory rather than another in ways which can be unhelpful to the basic aim of acquiring knowledge.

A desire for predictive accuracy has proved a good guide, although it is *only* a guide. A new theory may yield predictions which are not borne out. A strict falsificationist, like Karl Popper, would hold that the theory must be discarded. It may nevertheless be the case that there is more right than wrong with the theory, and a scientist who perseveres in the face of adverse results may still be more likely to acquire knowledge than one who gives up at the first setback. The theory might be better modified rather than totally rejected. The ability to give correct predictions is one test of truth but it should not become a substitute for truth. Similarly the internal coherence of a theory is important and is rightly valued by scientists. Unless reality is fundamentally chaotic, coherence within a theory and between theories will be a precondition for understanding the world. If a theory actually contradicts itself, it may not actually be stating anything. Yet the popularity of the coherence theory of truth bears witness to the readiness of many to substitute a test of truth for truth itself. Such tests always seem inadequate to those who want rigorous definitions and strict rules for the adoption of theories.

Scientists also value other features of scientific theories. The ability of a theory to bring together aspects of knowledge which were previously separate is important, as is its ability to generate new theories and research programmes. Many have valued simplicity, though this sometimes seems more like an aesthetic criterion than a method of searching for truth. It is a criterion which can result in the ruthless dismissal of superfluous entities in a crude reductionist manner. In our quest for the nature of reality, it can be disastrous to assume that it is less complicated than it is. Nevertheless, this example itself shows how scientists may legitimately disagree about which criteria of choices between theories are more likely to lead to knowledge or have led to knowledge in the past. There is no clear way of resolving such disagreement or differences in emphasis. From the viewpoint of anyone influenced by positivism, these criteria can only be seen as values influencing our choice of theories. It is no simpler to resolve a dispute between scientists about the importance of predictive accuracy in a particular case than is to resolve an overtly moral dispute. Whereas the positivist must hold that all such disputes are beyond the scope of rational resolution, we are under no such constraint. Once we realize that scientific method is the product of human rationality, rather than what defines it, disputes about scientific method and its application can themselves be regarded as part of our attempt to understand the world better.

The idea that scientific method demands the filtering out of 'extraneous' values, irrelevant to the pursuit of truth, is itself controversial. Once positivism is discarded, it is difficult to maintain a clear distinction between 'internal' and 'external' reasons for adopting theories. Some philosophers lump all 'values' together as playing a part in conditioning choices, without recognizing that some are more relevant to the pursuit of truth than others. When truth disappears as a goal, as in some sociology of knowledge, it becomes impossible to distinguish between values on that basis. Yet, if we maintain a realist perspective, it should be obvious that some reasons for preferring one theory over another may not be very good ones. The world is not always as we want it to be.

To a convinced feminist, the fact that a modern scientific theory, such as sociobiology, contains certain assertions about the nature of women is a conclusive reason for rejecting it. She is so convinced of the truth of her belief about the female predicament that she is unwilling to accept anything conflicting with it. Similarly a fundamentalist Christian will wish to reject the theories of modern evolutionary biology because he is so sure that God made the world in a different way. This is not an arbitrary, or even necessarily irrational, thing to do. He is convinced of what is the truth of the matter, and will not listen to modern scientists who disagree. The problem is not that he is basing his views on 'values' rather than 'facts' but that he disagrees with scientists about the facts, just as scientists disagree with each other. They each put weight on different criteria of truth, and the argument should be about which criteria have proved to be the best guides to truth.

Scientific theories about the origin of the universe are themselves sometimes influenced by theological or anti-theological criteria. Some scientists may oppose, say, the theory of the universe beginning with a 'big bang' because they feel that such a theory might give comfort to theists. Others might put it forward partly because it coincides with their belief in a God who created the universe. Both positions may appear unscientific and therefore wrong, but this must be too hasty a conclusion. It is not irrational for those who consider they have grounds for certain metaphysical beliefs to allow them to influence their scientific work. It is not a matter of shame that they are governed by factors external to science. What would be irrational is if they carried on their scientific work in a manner which detached it completely from all their other beliefs. If people know what is true in some area, they must let that knowledge impinge on their scientific work when relevant. Otherwise the latter cannot itself hope to produce truth. The catch is whether someone really possesses knowledge in the first place. Science has proved a successful way of challenging prejudice and bigotry, even though it can itself also generate bigotry. Those who allow their scientific outlook to be governed by other beliefs have to be very certain that they do have good grounds for them and must be prepared to justify them in open, rational argument.

Objectivity in Social Science

Anyone who subordinates the proper methods of science to the demands of certain preconceptions must have good grounds for thinking that the preconceptions help rather than hinder in the search for truth. Otherwise the rational person will abandon them. Some may wish to suggest that science is itself imbued with non-rational values and that any attempt to prove otherwise is merely to indulge yet again in a rational reconstruction of science that pays scant attention to the way science has actually developed. Yet this position not only removes science as the paradigm of rational activity but is liable to undermine the very idea of rationality. It suggests that scientists see what they want to see because of their values and cannot change them rationally.

Why must it be assumed that such values cannot be changed? They may be so much part of the fabric of one's conceptual scheme that it could be impossible to know one has them. Even the interests governing one's quest for knowledge may not be made explicit. However, the ambition of many sociologists of knowledge is to perform precisely this task and unmask the ideology at work in different cases. It seems arbitrary to rule out this possibility at the outset. Much more likely an explanation for assuming that values are beyond the scope of reason is the lingering shadow of positivism, according to which one cannot use reason to change values because only value-free science is genuinely rational. If positivism is repudiated, but reason is still excluded, some deterministic thesis is being put forward, according to which the values people have are totally the product of, say, their economic background. The drawback of such global claims is their reflexivity. The person making the claim is also the prisoner of his or her own economic background, and so the claim itself will be infected with values.

One writer, Loren Graham, on the connection between science and values contrasts two approaches to the problem which he dubs 'expansionist' and 'restrictionist'. Expansionists 'cite evidence within the body of scientific theories and findings which can supposedly be used, either directly or indirectly, to support conclusions about sociopolitical values'.[6] Graham cites sociobiology as an example of science encroaching on territory which previously belonged to values, because it attempts to provide scientific explanations of sociopolitical values. On the other side is 'restrictionism', 'an approach that confines science to a particular realm or a particular methodology and leaves values outside its boundaries'. One example he gives is the view that science and religion cannot conflict because they are concerned with entirely different things. Scientists found that they were better able to continue their work unmolested, by keeping away from religious and social controversy. Similarly defenders of existing social values benefited by a clear demarcation between science and values. Graham remarks: 'If you insist that science and values do not mix, then the antecedent values of society are protected.'[7] This perhaps suggests that the idea of science as 'value-free' is itself the result of a human decision about values.

While trying to move away from what he terms the 'polarities' of 'value-free science' and 'science-free values', Graham is apparently still in the grip of positivist prejudices about science. He assumes that science is the source of knowledge and that the problem must be basically how far it encroaches on other areas. When he talks of values he means 'social values',[8] so that, if science is seen as a spectrum, fields such as astronomy and physics will be at what he terms 'the far "value-free" end'. Yet, if we take values to encompass the strategies adopted in the pursuit of truth, physics is far from value-free. The whole idea of values being mixed with science to a greater or lesser extent itself trades on the assumption that facts and values are in principle separable. The concessions made by writers like Graham amount to little more than a demonstration that this is very difficult to achieve in practice. In fact he begins his book by accepting that 'the intellectual prohibition against confusion of "is" and "ought" still reigns.'[9] Modern philosophy of science has to question this distinction, since 'facts' are established by processes of human reasoning identical to those which establish 'values'. One possible response to this is to conclude that science rests on the same shaky subjectivist foundations as morality. That appears to be the position of Feyerabend.

A more obvious conclusion must surely be that questions of values need no longer be compared unfavourably with scientific questions, so that it appears that only the latter are capable of rational resolution. Disagreement between scientists is not only healthy but may itself be an indispensable part of scientific method. There are, however, no set procedures for resolving such differences, despite what traditional philosophy of science has maintained. When one scientist rates accuracy of prediction more highly than another, it may be impossible at that stage to say who is wrong. Similarly, when conflict arises in areas beyond science, the mere fact that immediate resolution of the difficulty seems unlikely does not mean that it is all a matter of subjective taste and that human reason must be impotent.

Some wish to preserve the distinction between scientific and non-scientific method, by accepting that science depends on values, but asserting that some are internal to its method – as when scientists value truth – and others, such as political values, are external. 'Value-freedom' for science would then involve the removal not so much of all values as of those that are considered inappropriate. That involves accepting that values as such are integral to science and govern what we accept as a fact. Once the argument is seen to be not about purifying science of the taint of 'values' but about which values are essential to its purposes and which bias us away from them, any distinction between fact and value becomes irrelevant.

Graham remarks that in the social sciences 'some concepts are irretrievably value-laden'.[10] This phrase itself reflects positivist prejudice. If no part of the quest for human knowledge can fail to be value-laden, it seems pointless to regret the fact. Each quest for knowledge involves the selection of some features as relevant and the dismissal of others. Sometimes, as in the physical sciences, the criteria for this can be made explicit, but in other cases this may be harder. The social issues are concerned with human activities, and it is inevitable that social scientists are influenced by their own views about our place in the world. Religious and political issues can never be far away. To many imbued with positivist principles this will seem dangerous and unscientific. What is more dangerous, however, is that methods developed by the physical sciences for predicting and controlling the physical environment are assumed to be the only ones available for gaining knowledge in other areas.

The quest for a 'value-free' social science has permeated all the social sciences. The scientific outlook appeared to dictate that personal viewpoints and all contents of consciousness were subjective and to be ignored in a properly scientific account. What people valued, and indeed the value to be put on people, seemed to be part of this. True scientists, it seemed, should not be concerned with mere feelings, whether their own or other people's. As Habermas remarks in connection with the whole issue of value-freedom, 'positivism has permeated the self understanding of the social sciences'.[11]

One consequence has been the unfortunate use of the concepts of objectivity and subjectivity. Science is concerned with what is objective, and therefore true. Questions of value are to be consigned to the category of the subjective, and therefore unconnected with any claim to knowledge. Yet there can be a marked slide from one meaning of 'objective' to another. Malinowski, writing about culture, flatly says: 'Nothing can be objective which is not accessible to observation.'[12] This links objectivity with detachment from any particular point of view, so that what is objective has to be public. Yet this is a different idea of objectivity from that invoked in a claim to objective truth. The latter is what is true, whatever people may happen to think. The dispassionate, detached objectivity of a scientist at work in the laboratory does not confer a monopoly on objective truth. If I have a pain, it is real enough, even though it may not be examined in a laboratory. What is objectively there may not always be divorced from all particular points of view.

The physical sciences may have good reason for seeking the kind of objectivity which ruthlessly ignores the perspective of the individual. When scientists investigate the properties of matter, their own experience of the relevant stuff is irrelevant, since that will tell us about the scientists and not about matter. When social scientists investigate the functioning of some aspect of human society, it is much more difficult to maintain that human experience and the perspective of individuals must be ruled out of account. Such a view may have seemed scientific, and it is obvious that, in so far as social scientists are investigating other societies, their own perspective should be excluded as far as possible. Yet there is a danger in treating human beings and human societies in the way physicists deal with physical objects. Behaviourist and reductionist methods have at times seemed the only ones which social science could use if it were to be recognized as genuine science. The measurement of publicly verifiable behaviour seemed the hallmark of an objective approach. The task of the social sciences appeared to be the discovery of laws governing human behaviour.

A genuinely objective and scientific approach to the study of human society will not copy the tactics of the physical sciences, but is constrained by the nature of what is being studied. If the social sciences are governed by the reality they are investigating, they must recognize the differences as well as the similarities between social and physical reality. The desire of natural scientists to predict and control their environment need not automatically be shared by social scientists. In some areas general regularities in human behaviour may be discovered and some predictions may be successful. Mary Hesse remarks about this: 'Where these things are the case, we may speak of "objectivity" in the social realm, in whatever sense we wish to speak of it in the natural realm, and we *may* (not *must*) make the same choice of value goals for the social as for the natural sciences.'[13] This perhaps suggests that the term 'objectivity' should only be used when the social sciences ape the natural sciences. In fact, if the natural sciences are being truly objective, they are paying attention to the nature of what they are studying. If the social sciences adopt the same policy, they will be emulating the method of the physical sciences by reflecting the nature of social reality, even though this may mean treating it as very different from physical reality. Genuine objectivity involves being true to the reality under investigation.

The Values of Social Science

Our choice of theory will be guided by values which themselves are linked with our understanding of the reality we are studying. The criteria adopted by physical scientists for what constitutes a good theory are shaped by the desire to gain knowledge; the criteria for the choice of a theory by social scientists must be similarly shaped. Views about the adequacy of a theory will inevitably be influenced by assumptions about the nature of human beings and their relationship with society. There may seem an element of circularity about this. Surely the social sciences are going to discover for us some of the answers to this kind of question? Yet the physical sciences have progressed through a continuous winnowing of good theories from bad, and our understanding of physical reality is increased as our initial assumptions are modified. The way we evaluate a theory is itself the product of scientific progress. Only slowly has it been realized that theological preconceptions about the way the world was created may hinder rather than help our understanding of physical processes.

In the same way, the assumptions of the social sciences and our ideas of what makes a good social theory may have to be modified in the light of increased knowledge. This does not alter the fact that philosophical assumptions about human nature are built into any understanding about the way society works. Behaviourist views, like any others, coupled with an eagerness to quantify results in social research, undoubtedly carry with them basic conceptions about human nature.[14] All private and individual perspectives are ignored unless they can be expressed in behavioural terms. The result seems to many to be profoundly dehumanizing, in that anything distinctively human is ignored in the name of science.

Richard Rorty refers to the controversy in the social sciences between what he terms 'objectivity' and 'hermeneutics', the quarrel between those who wish to model the social sciences on the physical ones and those who emphasize the importance of achieving 'understanding':

> Foucault is doubtless right that the social sciences have coarsened the moral fiber of our rulers. Something happens to politicians who are exposed to endless tabulations of income levels, rates of recidivism, cost-effectiveness of artillery fire, and the like – something like what happens to concentration camp guards.... The rulers of the liberal democracies come to think that nothing matters but what shows up in the expert's predictions. They cease to think of their fellow citizens as fellow citizens.[15]

These are harsh words, and Rorty himself recognizes that it is important to 'take hold of social forces and use them to alleviate human suffering'. Mere hermeneutics is not enough. Nevertheless a scientific emphasis on prediction and control can lead to a desire to manipulate people as if they were mere physical objects. The attitude is justified if that is all people are, but it is significant that policy-makers cannot in all consistency apply that analysis to themselves. They have to see themselves as rational and responsible agents, deciding, perhaps in good faith, what is best for others.

Treating people in a scientific and detached manner can result in not treating them as persons at all. How, though, are they to be viewed by social scientists and those they advise? Social scientists cannot avoid facing the most basic questions about human nature, any more than they can avoid making choices between different sets of values. The pretence that social science can be 'value-free' itself results in a definite set of values and a distinctive way of regarding human beings. The scientific detachment of the social engineer, bleakly manipulating the lives of others, is even more horrifying when it is honestly considered that this represents some ideal of scientific neutrality.

The urge in social science to aim for successful prediction and control as basic values may not be linked just to explicit beliefs about human nature but also to a desire for some kind of professional expertise. The physical scientist knows how to manipulate the physical environment, and it might seem to follow that if social science is to be a source of knowledge it has to aim for similar control of social reality. High hopes vested in subjects such as sociology, or even economics, and later leading to disillusionment have very often depended on this simplistic view. The search for laws of human behaviour has seemed an integral part of the pursuit of knowledge, and the future of, say, sociology has appeared to depend on deterministic assumptions about human beings. Moreover, sociology had to prove that the most important causes of human behaviour were social if it was to be respected as a discipline. Perhaps, however, human beings are able to direct themselves on occasions in a rational manner and are not wholly determined by causes outside their control. If scientific knowledge is not the only kind of knowledge, the scarcity of laws on human social behaviour need not involve the collapse of social science.

The values of social science have to be rooted in its subject-matter, to enable it to see more clearly the nature of society. Anything distorting its vision must be bad, while anything helping it to discover truth must be good. The possibility of scientific neutrality is an illusion, if only because no scientist can be neutral in respect of truth and falsity. What, then, is the truth about society? As in physical science, we shall expect considerable disagreement to arise as different theories are adopted or rejected. In one respect, the social sciences have a harder job than the natural sciences. It can be argued that the latter must assume the existence of an independent physical reality.[16] The social sciences, however, cannot just assume the existence of 'social reality' as an independent entity. One of the major arguments in the social sciences is how much content can be given to this notion. It is possible to be a realist without accepting it. Even though it might appear that, if the physical sciences are concerned with physical reality, the social ones are concerned with social reality, this immediately weights the question in favour of holist views as opposed to individualist ones. The respective attention to be given to the individual and the society itself involves a major decision about values. The ontological priority given to one of them will undoubtedly be reflected in political views. There is a major divide between those tracing the ills, and goods, of society back to the activity of individuals and those locating them in the structures of society. This is not a mere choice between 'values', but is also a factual matter about the working of society.

Ideology

Are we to say that all social theories are irredeemably ideological? Much depends on the meaning given to the term. In one sense, the term means no more than 'conceptual scheme'. People with an ideology think they know while others with different ideologies will not see things from their point of view. An ideology on this understanding could never be shown to be mistaken, and there could be no such thing as false consciousness. We could not talk of minds so distorted that they falsify everything they come across. Ideas of distortion and falsity could have no application.

Karl Mannheim tried to avoid the use of the word 'ideology' in his sociology of knowledge. He preferred to speak of the perspective of a thinker, meaning by that 'the subject's whole mode of conceiving things as determined by his historical and social setting'.[17] As a result, his approach was different from that of Marx. Mannheim comments:

> The sociology of knowledge actually emerged with Marx. . . . However
> in his work the sociology of knowledge is still indistinguishable from the
> unmasking of ideologies since for him social strata and classes were the
> bearers of ideologies.[18]

Marx thought ideology involved false belief, and this implied he had a standpoint from which to distinguish truth and falsity. Mannheim was more concerned with relating beliefs to their overall perspective. He thus invites the rejoinder that nothing can be claimed to be true if everything is perspectival. His 'relationism' can easily collapse into relativism. Whatever is claimed cannot 'be formulated absolutely but only in terms of the perspective of a given situation'.[19] He gives as an example of what he means the case of a peasant who moves to a city after growing up in the narrow confines of his village. Gradually he becomes more detached from rural ways of thinking and perhaps quite consciously distinguishes between 'rural' and 'urban' ideas. He can no longer take for granted what he previously believed. He has seen an alternative set of ideas, and the mere knowledge of their existence helps to undermine the absolute character of what he was brought up to accept without question. Mannheim comments that the distinction between 'rural' and 'urban' demonstrates the beginnings of the approach that the sociology of knowledge wishes to develop. He continues: 'That which within a given group is accepted as absolute appears to the outsider conditioned by the group situation and recognized as partial.'[20]

We have already seen how the sociology of knowledge has been used in an attempt to explain science as a social activity. This example shows how it can easily explain all human activity by relating it to its social background. Mannheim insists that all assertions have to be related to 'the perspective of a given situation'. Yet, if this is so, the familiar problem of reflexivity reappears, since we can say that his own claims about the sociology of knowledge are the expression of *his* perspective. Mannheim himself hankers after the possibility of a position 'from which a total perspective would be possible'.[21] He thinks of 'unattached intellectuals' as a group which might be able to transcend the narrow vision of particular classes and interest groups. He says hopefully: 'Thus they might play the part of watchmen in what otherwise would be a pitch-black night.' Yet intellectuals themselves form a class that can develop very definite interests which are economic as well as academic. The danger is that their viewpoint is as partial as that of anyone.

The more beliefs and ideas are related to their background instead of being examined on their own merits, the more truth becomes inaccessible. Our attention is directed at the social pressures on people rather than on the validity or otherwise of ideas. If we are convinced that we have no choice, since the possibility of independently assessing truth is an illusion, we are still being governed by an idea which claims some kind of validity. In fact, the view that everything is ideological is a very corrosive belief, striking at the very basis of our reasons for believing or doing anything. Once I realize that my beliefs are *only* the product of my background, I can have no grounds for continuing to believe them. Even Mannheim's peasant who goes to the city does not go this far, because he presumably thinks that city ideas are better. He is impressed by them and perhaps feels rather contemptuous of his simple origins, using words like 'unsophisticated' to criticize them. Only, perhaps, if he becomes a sociologist, will he relate the ideas of the city to urban styles of living just as rural ones are related to the simplistics of country life. Then a certain contempt of *all* ideas could set in, as he concludes that even the perspective of sociology is conditioned by its background.

Social scientists face a difficult task, since they are supposed to be detached and see how many viewpoints are partial and socially conditioned. They must be able to compare different cultures. Yet their insights must somehow be liberating rather than paralysing. Berger and Kellner insist that 'sociology is a science, not a set of doctrines',[22] but realize that this view stands in tension with what they term 'the "debunking" or negative threat of the sociological perspective'.[23] The trouble is that sociology seems to expose the way in which the world is 'made' by different cultures. It apparently demonstrates that absolute standards which we take as self-evidently valid, whether in religion, morality or science itself, are merely the result of the way a particular society has developed. What is good or true or rational seems to be merely what we have been trained to accept without question as such. There may too be forces at work in society sustaining these beliefs of which we may be totally unaware. Social reality may be only the visible part of a building with a complicated structure of interests and causal mechanisms. The apparent reality may not be the genuine one. Berger and Kellner sum up the way in which sociology can even play a subversive role, undermining our own confidence in our beliefs and even hankering after a total change. They say that sociology can show us that 'not only is the world not what it appears to be, but it could be different from what it is'.[24]

This approach, however, is not necessarily the same as that of Mannheim. The 'relationist' gambit relating everything to its social context certainly shows the arbitrariness of any social system. When everything is ideological, ideology ceases to matter. There is no way that it can be 'unmasked', and all that will happen is that one ideology may be replaced by another. The concept of ideology is only useful if it means more than a definition of reality. Ideology must be contrasted with a correct understanding of reality. The definition given by Berger and Kellner is that 'an ideology is a set of definitions of reality legitimizing specific vested interests in society'.[25] They hope to avoid vexed questions in sociology about who is right about reality, while still being able to say whether a particular standpoint is ideological. They regard a belief-system as an ideology if it explains and justifies the vested interests of a group. They continue by referring to a claim that a system is ideological.

> Such a proposition, assuming that it is empirically grounded in evidence, is an objective and 'value-free' statement, despite the fact that the proposition brackets the question as to whether the belief system is finally valid or not.[26]

The relationship of a particular belief to vested interests can be shown, independently of whether it happens to be true or not. Whether a belief is ideological thus appears to be an ordinary matter of fact. Even a true belief could be ideological. Such an interpretation steers a middle course between the view that everything is ideological and the position that ideology is false belief. It seems to preserve the cherished neutrality of science while not undermining all notions of reality. In particular, it treats social reality as a reality about which discoveries can be made.

However attractive such a position may be, the argument of this chapter must raise questions about it. The association of what is empirically grounded with what is objective and value-free is itself unwarranted. The values of positivist science are conveyed only too clearly by it. No statement can be value-free in the sense required. We need to discover the appropriate values for the pursuit of truth in sociology. The desire for 'value-freedom' may often be an expression of fear that the wrong values will be adopted. Which are the right ones is itself controversial. If physical scientists cannot agree on the criteria for a good theory, we are unlikely to find agreement in the more recently established social sciences. There is broad agreement in the physical sciences on the kind of criteria to be used, but the social sciences may not even have reached that stage. A Marxist social scientist might make faithfulness to Marxist doctrine a criterion of a good social theory, while the liberal will feel that this is to allow political values to enter social science in an illegitimate way. Yet the liberal's desire for political neutrality can equally be seen as a 'value'.

Disputes about the distinction between facts and values are themselves usually disputes about which values are important for social science. They in turn depend on questions about the nature of the reality being investigated by social science. Whatever else it is, it must be social, and this means that the social sciences need not be called upon to adjudicate the truth of every belief in society. The social characteristics of a religion, for example, will be a fit object of study for sociology or social anthropology, and they exist because the religion is believed by its practitioners to be true. Whether it is actually true is a separate issue which cannot be settled by social sciences. Yet this very admission can be the source of trouble. 'Bracketing off' questions of truth may be a legitimate method in social science, since it ensures that social science deals only with social reality. Otherwise every sociological investigation of religious practices will become a debate about the existence of God. Yet 'bracketing off' may be the result, whether intended or not, of making the real nature of religion to appear a social matter, explicable by the sociologist. Because questions of the truth of a particular belief have been put on one side as being beyond the professional competence of the sociologist, it may seem as if it does not matter whether the belief is true or not. Theology seems irrelevant, and religious studies all-important. Social influences become central, and it is somehow forgotten that the belief is held because it is thought to be true.

Unless sociology embraces relativism, it must remember that the rational pursuit of truth may be a prime characteristic of those it studies. The scope for sociological explanation of particular phenomena may thereby be lessened, but sociology itself can claim truth for itself without blushing. In social science the 'values' or criteria for the choice of theories that are adopted must be subordinated to the quest for truth. They can then genuinely claim to be sciences in as full a sense as the physical sciences. This is not because they have the same methods. That would be inappropriate, because their objects of investigation are different. It is because both in a systematic manner tailor their methods and their 'values' to the nature of their subject-matter.

Notes

1 T. S. Kuhn, 'Objectivity, Value Judgments and Theory Choice', in his *The Essential Tension*, 1977, p. 331.
2 Mary Hesse, *Revolutions and Reconstructions in the Philosophy of Science*, 1980, p. xiv.
3 Ibid., p. xxiii.
4 Ibid., p. 201.

5   Ibid., p. 202.
6   Loren Graham, *Between Science and Values*, 1981, p. 6.
7   Ibid., p. 29.
8   Ibid., p. 356.
9   Ibid., p. 1.
10 Ibid., p. 9.
11 J. Habermas, *Knowledge and Human Interests*, 1972, p. 303.
12 B. Malinowski, *A Scientific Theory of Culture*, 1944, p. 69.
13 Hesse, *Revolutions and Reconstructions*, p. 200.
14 See my *The Shaping of Man*, 1982, ch. 2, for a discussion of the views of B. F. Skinner.
15 R. Rorty, 'Method and Morality', in N. Haan et al. (eds), *Social Science as a Moral Inquiry*, 1983, p. 164.
16 See my *Reality at Risk*, 1980.
17 Karl Mannheim, *Ideology and Utopia*, 1936, p. 239.
18 Ibid., p. 278.
19 Ibid., p. 254.
20 Ibid., p. 253.
21 Ibid., p. 143.
22 P. Berger and H. Kellner, *Sociology Reinterpreted*, 1982, p. 17.
23 Ibid., p. 13.
24 Ibid.
25 Ibid., p. 70.
26 Ibid., p. 71.

7

Economics and Society

Rationality and Desires

The question of value-freedom is intimately connected with views about the nature of human society. Empirical disciplines which proudly eschew all values inevitably run a risk of applying inappropriate values to the task in hand. This is particularly so in the social sciences, where the methods, and hence the values, appropriate to the study of inanimate objects are sometimes adopted without question. Max Weber has been influential in the advocacy of value-freedom for the social sciences, considering that the choice of values must be left to the individual. He concluded that 'value-freedom' was a requirement in empirical matters, and that any debate about values could only have the purpose of understanding what each of the parties to a dispute really means. This presupposes, he says, an 'appreciation, quite simply, of the possibility that ultimate values might diverge, in principle, and irreconcilably'.[1]

According to this view, questions about the ends to be pursued in any empirical discipline can never be squarely faced. The empiricist, following Hume, can only be concerned with the means to given ends; the true scientist, *qua* scientist, must never consider what ought to be done but only show how people may obtain the objects of whatever desires they happen to have. The scientist's role is seen as similar to that of a senior British civil servant, who is supposed to devise means to whatever ends are chosen by the government of the day, and not play any part in the formulation of policy. The same civil servants can survive changes of government and advise on the undoing of the very policy they previously helped to implement. Whether this admirable neutrality is in principle possible is a further issue.

Weber had no doubts of the possibility of separating value judgements from empirical disciplines. He says:

> It seems to be possible to establish without a shadow of doubt that in the area of practical political value-judgements (especially in the fields of economics and social policy), as soon as guidance for a valued course of action is to be sought, all that an empirical discipline with the means at its disposal can show is (i) the unavoidable means; (ii) the unavoidable side-effects; (iii) the resulting conflict of several possible value-judgements with each other in their practical consequences.[2]

Economists who allow themselves to be influenced by political judgements may be pursuing a dangerous course. This is not because economics can somehow be separated from values and put on a strictly 'factual' basis, but because political considerations, particularly those connected with short-term party interest, are irrelevant to the practice of economics. What a particular political party would like to be true, in order to facilitate the implementation of its policy, may not be the same as what is true. The economist should not get trapped into telling politicians only what they want to hear. If economics is truly a science, it must be geared to what actually happens in society, rather than to particular political interests. Of course there is bound to be disagreement about what does actually happen, and there will probably be connections between disagreements among economists and wider political arguments. This will at least partly be because of the underdetermination of economic theory by the facts. To put it another way, economists do not possess the requisite knowledge of the phenomena they are studying. Sometimes this will be because of the complex nature of the interactions involved, and it could also be that human beings are in the last resort unpredictable. Like all social sciences, economics often tries to discount the fact of human freedom of choice, because its desire to be a precise science seems threatened by a recognition of this. Yet, by the way it chooses to view humans, 'values' can be built into the nature of the discipline from the start. That may be unavoidable, but it is essential that the values aid the acquisition of knowledge and do not hinder it.

Weber advocated 'value-freedom' because of the empiricist assumption that agreement is possible about facts but may in principle never be reached about 'values'. The breakdown of the distinction between facts and values has had the result in some modern philosophy of science that agreement about what was considered a 'factual' matter seems impossible at times. It is, however, equally possible to see that obstacles to reaching agreement about values have been removed. They are expected to live up to an impossible standard. The existence of apparently irresolvable disagreement does not mean that there is no truth to be discovered in the area. Without any values to begin with, we have no guidance about where to start looking.

The assumption that ends cannot be rationally chosen and that we are restricted to discovering means to set goals is contentious. Philosophers have for long argued about whether human reason can establish what is worth pursuing or whether human desire provides the necessary and unalterable framework for the exercise of reason. Some desires themselves seem irrational, or even evil, and these are open to criticism. Must reason only show us how to obtain what we desire most efficiently, and how to eradicate conflicts between different desires? It is hard to avoid the conclusion that the subordination of reason to desire in empiricist philosophy often stems from the difficulty of resolving disagreements. Again and again we come back to the alleged fact that there are settled procedures in science for coming to agreement. Where agreement cannot be reached, the matter seems outside the scope of science, and hence neither factual nor a matter of reason. We are just left with the fact that different people want different things. We cannot go on to talk of what they should want, since that will merely reopen the disagreement. Science can deal with the fact that people do have varying desires, and may explain why they do, but it seemingly cannot cope with the question of what they ought to desire.

The dichotomy between fact and value, and reason and desire, goes very deep. It not only explicitly governs the way social scientists view their own activities but also influences the way they study human behaviour. If desire is logically prior to reason, it appears to follow that we act as we do because we want to, rather than because, at least on occasion, we rationally believe we ought to. What we want determines what we try to get, and our reason merely provides us with the means of getting it. If, though, we each act because of what we want, does not that inevitably show we are all ultimately selfish? It seems that we are each trying to get as much as possible of what we want. This is almost a travesty of an argument. Just as we can only think about what we think, and jibes about being imprisoned within our own conceptual scheme are misplaced, we can only do what we do. The rejoinder that we must have done what we wanted because that is what we chose to do reduces the idea of doing what one wants to utter triviality. The man who throws himself on a grenade to save his comrades is in a sense doing what he wants. He was not pushed. Saying that he is motivated by desire, and therefore by implication is selfish, is ludicrous. Wanting to save others at the expense of oneself is altruistic, not selfish.

Most people may indeed be selfish, but they do not have to be. If it becomes true by definition that everyone is selfish, the point is not worth making. It is important to distinguish the claim about how people happen to behave from a methodological assumption about how they behave. Governments may well be called on to cope with the ingrained selfishness of their citizens, and perhaps exploit it by means of incentives to work harder. This is a distinct question from the way the social sciences should approach the matter. In trying to understand or to explain human behaviour, they have to make assumptions about the nature of human rationality and its effect on human action. They have to face the issue whether the rational policy for anyone is to maximize one's own personal advantage. In other words, is getting as much as possible of what one wants, even at the expense of others, not just a widespread human trait but a normal feature of human action? Such an assumption is a very large one to make about human nature, but it appears to be made by much modern economics. Amartya Sen writes:

> While consistency is taken in economic theory to be a necessary condition of rationality, it is usual to supplement that requirement by some substantive view as to what the individual would maximize. The regularity of consistent pursuit of self-interest is a frequently used assumption of rational behaviour.... It is implicitly present in much of traditional economic theory.[3]

The possibility of prediction seems much greater if humans do indeed act in this way, since, if you know what they want, you know what they will try to obtain. On the other hand, what they try to get is by definition what they want. Desire is revealed in behaviour, and economists can keep well away from the difficulty of trying to grasp the contents of other people's minds. Their beliefs about priorities and their reasoning processes can seem irrelevant except in so far as they are exhibited in behaviour. The methodological demand for scientific objectivity excludes them, since they are inaccessible to the scientist.

Economics and Egoism

Economists are not just cynical about the prevalence of human self-ishness but often make it a condition of rationality. The rational person becomes the one who seeks to satisfy his or her desires regardless of the impact this will have on others. Two economists feel able to refer to the 'archetypal economic man'. He seeks 'to maximize his own welfare without concern for how this compares with the welfare of others.'[4] They are themselves critical of this notion and point out the difficulty of providing 'public goods' if each person is assumed to be concerned only with personal advantage. No one will be willing to pay taxes merely to provide services for others. They also remark: 'Elemental personal values of honesty, truthfulness, trust, restraint and obligation are all necessary inputs to an efficient (as well as pleasant) contractual society, but all are without significant direct pay-off to the individuals providing them'.[5]

There may be an indirect pay-off. Theories about self-interest usually have to acknowledge that enlightened self-interest demands a different policy from the ruthless pursuit of what is immediately in my interest. Co-operation with others is sometimes necessary for the achievement of long-term desires. It may be a disadvantage for me now to help you, but you may help me later if I do. Similarly, I may make more money now by being dishonest, but lose it all when others find that they cannot trust me. The maxim 'honesty is the best policy' could be fervently held by a very selfish person.

However this may be, economists make predictions on the assumption that all individuals are 'maximizing utility' for themselves. In other words, we each pursue a policy which we hope will obtain the most possible of what we want and the least of what we do not want. This can be put in mathematical terms, with weight given to different probabilities. Sometimes it is thought that the aim is to maximize overall utility, so that one's own interests are not counted as more important than those of anyone else. I can thus weigh costs to a society against total benefits, or I can restrict my vision to what will or will not benefit *me*. In both cases it may seem as if I merely reveal my own preferences. In the one instance I exhibit a preference for my own welfare, while in the other I show a preference for the welfare of others as well. Indulging the latter might seem selfish because it is my preference, whereas it is precisely the opposite. It may be for this reason that talk of behaviour revealing preferences seems so easily and so explicitly to lead to the assumption of egoism.

Sen suggests that the concept of preference is made to carry too much. It can be defined merely in terms of choice in such a way that I show that I prefer whatever I happen to choose. Saying that preference can be understood in a mathematical operation as the binary representation of individual choice, he comments: 'The difficulty arises in interpreting preference thus defined as preference in the usual sense with the property that if a person prefers x to y then he must regard himself to be better off with x than with y.' Sen himself points out that the separation of the concepts of choice, preference and welfare may make things less simple but produce an important conclusion. Economic incentives may not be the only means of affecting human behaviour. I may be open to influences other than appeals to my own material self-interest. References to the general good may not be as irrelevant as is assumed by 'traditional economic theory'.

Apart from the assumption that everyone acts in accordance with what they most want (and that is equated with the most powerful desire), much economics is firmly committed to explanation in terms of atomic individuals with fixed desires. Features of society are explained in terms of the desires, and are not allowed to explain them. Rationality involves working out the means to given ends as set by desire. In this respect, economics treads firmly in the empiricist tradition set by Hume. Like him, it can assume that desires remain constant, and there is thus a suitable basis for economic explanation and prediction. If tastes and desires were subject to change, the scope available for economics would be correspondingly reduced. Its prediction could only be valid given a particular set of human desires. What held in one society might not hold in another.

Given an assumption about the stability of human nature, the economist can be much more confident. Stigler and Becker explicitly propose the hypothesis that 'widespread and/or persistent human behaviour can be explained by a generalized calculus of utility-maximizing behaviour, without introducing the qualification "tastes remaining the same".'[7] By positing stable preferences, and assuming people act in accordance with them, the economist can remain on firm ground.

Stigler and Becker were afraid that admitting a difference in tastes meant
economists would have to hand explanations of behaviour over, as they
put it, to 'whoever studies and explains tastes (psychologists? anthropologists? phrenologists? sociobiologists?)'.[8] They claim that on their preferred interpretation the economist never reaches this impasse, but goes
on looking for differences in prices or incomes to explain differences in
behaviour. They are against abandoning 'opaque and complicated problems with the easy suggestion that the further explanation will perhaps
someday be produced by one of our sister behavioural sciences'.[9]

Any social science can quite reasonably take as part of its methodology
the policy that it should not give up too easily. Saying that a particular
matter is inexplicable by economists stops them looking for further
explanations. As a result, they could be handing over to other social
sciences issues which may after all be within the scope of economics.
Nevertheless, refusing to admit the relevance of other social sciences can
be equally dangerous. Stigler and Becker appear to be saying that
economics has no need to take any notice of, say, sociology. Because
they believe that human preferences remain stable even in different ages
and times, they leave no room for a sociological understanding of the
way desires can be created by society. It is often held, for instance, that in
a consumer society advertising can create wants that were not there
before. Stigler and Baker explicitly reject this.

One writer on the philosophic assumptions of economics notes that
the methodological roots of the subject are highly individualistic. He
says flatly that 'the tendency in economics is to explain society as the
product of individual choice'. He continues: 'But in accounting for
wants, the fact that they are in major part a reflection of cultural and
social phenomena that precede the individual cannot be overlooked.'[10]

This is the edge of the large controversy about the forces at work
shaping human nature.[11] The crucial point is that the assumptions made
about the issue determine the character of any social science. Indeed, it
sometimes seems as if the assumptions determine which social science
one turns to. It is only a slight exaggeration to suggest that someone who
believes that humans are rational agents, and that society is the result of
their interactions, will be drawn to economics, while anyone convinced
that humans are primarily moulded by their social background will be
likely to be more sympathetic to sociology. Yet the social sciences should
not provide alternative, conflicting viewpoints of human societies.
There is something basically at fault with any methodology which

invites confrontation with the other social sciences. Even ignoring the findings of other disciplines is an error. Economics cannot be right to view society in an individualist manner, if sociology is right to look at it from a holist point of view. Sociology cannot be right to talk to the social creation of wants, if economics is right to see everyone as having the same wants.

These disputes can break out within disciplines as well as between them, but it is important that the social sciences aim for a unified theory of society and our place in it. Economics can be tempted to claim a monopoly of knowledge. Like, say, the sociology of knowledge, it produces all-embracing explanations which ignore the role of other branches of social science. For example, it cannot allow for alternative views of rationality, because of its equation of human rationality with a certain form of egoism. Either other subjects conform to the economist's idea of 'rational man', or they are dismissed as merely dealing with irrational aspects of human behaviour. McPherson comments:

> Extending the scope of rational explanations of conduct beyond the sphere of markets, as in the 'rational choice' theories of politics, has really meant pushing aside other modes of explanation in these areas and substituting economic methods. . . . When (as in the received view of economics) sociology or psychology are seen as sciences of the irrational and economics as the science of the rational, prospects for meaningful communication between them seem pretty bleak.[12]

The economist's notion of 'rational man' is deficient, even according to its own criteria. The well-known example of the 'prisoners' dilemma' provides an illustration of this.[13] There are different versions but, put briefly, the situation is that two prisoners are known to be guilty of a serious crime, but there is not enough evidence to convict them of it, unless one gives evidence against the other. They are kept separately and told that they may confess and implicate the other. If neither does, they will each only be convicted for a minor crime and be given two years' imprisonment. If one does confess, he will go free and the evidence will send the other to prison for twenty years. If both confess, they will each be convicted but, because of their co-operation, the sentence will be reduced from twenty to ten years. As a result, each prisoner has a considerable incentive to confess so that he himself can go free. The situation is as follows.

If neither confesses:	2 years each
If A confesses, B does not:	A goes free, B gets 20 years
If B confesses, A does not:	B goes free, A gets 20 years
If both confess:	10 years each

If A is going to confess, it is in B's interest to do so as well. Otherwise he will go to prison for twenty years rather than ten. If A does not confess, it is still in B's interest to do so: he will go free, even though A will then go to prison for twenty years. A will reason in the same way about B and so they will both confess. It seems as if the rational strategy is to confess, whatever the other prisoner can be expected to do. Yet this produces a situation in which each will go to prison for ten years instead of two. The ruthless pursuit of egoism produces undesirable consequences even for the egoist.

It may not be sufficient for them to trust each other not to confess. Although mutual trust is of great importance in such situations, it will still be possible for one of the parties to trade on it. After all, if A can trust B not to confess, the rational course is then for A to confess and go free. His penalty for remaining silent would be two years' imprisonment. Yet B may well reason in a similar way. Mere confidence about the other's course of action will not necessarily help. Some feeling of an obligation which is binding, even if one is thereby worse off, appears to be essential. Moral standards of one kind or another are often invoked at this point.

The paradox seems to be that, if someone single-mindedly pursues his or her own interests, regardless of the cost to others, those interests will not in fact be served very well when everyone else is doing the same. Some form of co-operation becomes inevitable. The example of the prisoners' dilemma has suggested to many that society must provide the essential framework for the pursuit of one's own interests. The reasoning is similar to that of the seventeenth-century political philosopher, Thomas Hobbes, who tried to base the concept of political obligation on prudential considerations. He firmly believed in human egoism, but saw that in a 'state of nature' disaster would follow. Life would be, in a famous phrase, 'nasty, brutish and short'. It is therefore in one's own longer-term interest to co-operate with sanctions, such as the punishments meted out by a state for those who do not. This would certainly alter the situation, and the egoist would have to take into account the likelihood of being found out and hence punished. As long, though, as one's only motive is one's own interest, there are going to be many situations, even in a social context, where egoism will only serve to undermine society, even if it is in no one's interest that this occurs. There will always be circumstances where I can uphold society only by deliberately forgoing my own immediate interest. The question must then be faced how far egoists can do this, particularly if they expect to gain from it. Indeed, they might even be called on to sacrifice their own long-term interests for the sake of society, perhaps even by laying down their own lives. Yet no egoist could consistently do this. It can never be guaranteed that the 'general good' and 'my good' will coincide.

Economists try to meet difficulties such as those illustrated by the prisoners' dilemma in various ways, but there seems to be a fundamental weakness in the whole notion of self-seeking rationality. It is certainly true that indirect consequences have to be taken into account as well as the direct ones, but even so the 'rational' course of action cannot be relied on to produce the best result. The insight that we do better through co-operating than by going it alone lies at the root of the formation of society. Nevertheless, if we are all only concerned for other people's interests as a means to furthering our own, we can easily produce a situation where everybody loses. Our commitment to the demands of society cannot be viewed according to the standards of rational egoism, of self-seeking 'economic man'. No doubt, if economists were right in their estimate of the motives of human behaviour, there would still have to be a certain measure of co-operation, but social arrangements would be in constant jeopardy, as each tried to gain an advantage over the rest.

Illustrations can be produced from many different contexts. In an arms race, two superpowers may aim for nuclear superiority at minimum cost. It is therefore in the interest of each to break any arms agreement fixing parity of weapons in order to get ahead of the other. It may be presumed that they will do so if they can without being detected. Unfortunately, however, this will not give them superiority if both reason in the same way. If each assumes that the other will break the agreement, they still have to continue the race, for fear of being left behind. Yet this will involve parity at great expense, whereas if they had both kept to the agreement they could have achieved the same result at a fraction of the cost. 'Rationality' apparently can produce a state of affairs which is not desired. Given a choice of superiority, parity at low cost, parity at great cost, and inferiority, it has only produced the third best possibility out of four options.

One practice at the heart of democratic society, that of voting in elections, itself often seems hard to explain if all the voters are self-seeking egoists. Not only does it become irrational for people to vote against their own interests and in what they conceive as the national interest, but it even seems hard to understand why many people vote at all. If the result of an election seems in doubt, most people will be anxious to cast a vote. Yet why should anyone suffer, say, the inconvenience of going out to vote on a wet night, when it is quite clear what the outcome is going to be? Predictions can sometimes be wildly inaccurate, but even so one vote is probably insignificant in a large election. Yet many still persist in voting. Suggesting that they are irrational seems to strike at the roots of theories about the working of democracy. The exercise of a political right like that would appear to many to need no further justification.

Amartya Sen is ready to consider the possibility of people making choices against their own interests, and suggests that we should not ignore what he terms 'commitment' in human behaviour. This notion appears to involve acting on principle, regardless of the consequences to the individual agent. The agent may thus act in a way expected to leave him or her worse off than available alternatives. Sen comments: 'The characteristic of commitment with which I am most concerned here is the fact that it drives a wedge between personal choice and personal welfare, and much of traditional economic theory relies on the identity of the two.'[14] He points out that, in the example of voting, people may be guided not so much by a choice to maximize expected utility but by a mere wish to record their preference. It must be a matter of some concern that such a normal and intelligible piece of human behaviour would be judged irrational in traditional economic theory.

Private Interest and Public Goods

Internal consistency is not enough to assure rationality. Some people may be completely consistent in the ordering of their preferences and the steps they take to achieve their goals. The preferences themselves, however, should not be regarded as necessarily fixed in human nature. Some may be, but others may themselves be the result of reason. Suggesting, as Hume did, that reason is the slave of the passions renders us powerless to modify our preferences or adopt new ones. His view was ameliorated by his belief that humans naturally felt sympathy for each other. If, though, it is assumed that our preferences are inevitably self-seeking, we seem to be left with a situation where rationality is construed as the most efficient and consistent way of destroying society through the ruthless pursuit of one's own short-term interests.

It has been suggested that one reason economists are reluctant to examine the origin of wants is that 'to do so would be to undermine a commitment to view the economic agent as an autonomous, free, chooser'.[15] Yet refusing to accept that human reason has any control over our desires strikes at the roots of all freedom. It merely locates the causes of our behaviour in whatever produces our desires. Transferring the causes from society to the individual organism does not make the position any less determinist. Denying the social determination of wants does not thereby increase the autonomy of the individual. Indeed, there are many who would feel that locating the origin of behaviour in society held out the possibility of change. They imagine that because societies can be modified there is the hope that, by changing society, they might eventually change the individual. By contrast, the ability to do what we want does not constitute freedom, if our wants are fixed and unalterable. We seem then to be mere puppets acting according to the dictates of something beyond our control – perhaps evolution through natural selection. In fact our autonomy seems undermined, whether our wants are created by biology or society. Impersonal forces seem to be moulding us, whether we are aware of it or not.

The economist's notion of rationality is a very widespread one, and it is often taken as self-evidently correct. John Rawls's theory of justice, for instance, explicitly makes use of a similar view. With the proviso that he believes a rational individual does not suffer from envy, he defines rationality as follows, saying it is 'the standard one familiar in social theory':

> Thus in the usual way, a rational person is thought to have a coherent set of preferences between the options open to him. He ranks these options according to how well they further his purposes: he follows the plan which will satisfy more of his desires rather than less, and which has the greater chance of being successfully executed.[16]

There is nothing in this to suggest that preferences need be selfish. As I have suggested, I could have a preference for the welfare of others.

Egoism is a further ingredient, although a tempting one to add once reference is made to 'preferences' and 'desires'. Rawls's version of liberalism leaves plenty of room for altruism. His focus of concern is not whether people should be altruists or egoists, but rather on the prior need that everyone should have equal liberty in which to make their choices. He wishes to achieve the kind of social co-operation in which each person is as free as possible to seek the satisfaction of his or her desires, whatever they may be. The only constraint is that others enjoy a similar liberty. The position is in many ways classically liberal, ensuring maximum freedom for individuals to implement their own choices. Since no conception of what is good is presupposed, everything depends on the preferences held by individuals. Some may very well seek to promote the welfare of others. Such a happy chance is not, however, enough to create a society. If any kind of community needs a willingness on the part of its members to sacrifice their own interests, there has to be a link between the existence of human society and the occurrence of altruism. The former is dependent on the latter, and so altruism must be more than a chance occurrence. It cannot be the result of randomly adopted choices. We need some theory which explains the connection between the claims of society and the wants of individuals.

This problem does not arise if individuals are considered abstractions from society, because society can then be assumed to create human desires. If we start with the individual, we need to close the gap between individual desires and the need for co-operation. This may be more than a theoretical matter, since individuals may have to be shown why they should care for the welfare of others at some expense to themselves. It is sometimes thought that laws and government exist for the precise purpose of plugging the gap. Hobbes believed, indeed, that rational egoists could remain true to their views and create such a government. Yet it remains problematic how viable a nation of rational egoists would be. Co-operation against one's immediate interest would always have to be enforced. Since it may be in the interest of each to obtain the fruits of co-operation without the cost, there will still be considerable incentive to break the law if it appears possible to escape detection. Much would depend on the efficiency of enforcement. It seems likely that a society would be very unstable if there was respect for the law only as a means to the furtherance of private interests, rather than as an end in itself. Law cannot be a substitute for morality, and no law can make people altruistic. It can serve as an important restraint, but there is no way it can make anyone act for the interests of others. Even if someone is compelled by law to make a contribution, he or she does not become an altruist. The effect of the action may be good, but because the person acted out of fear of legal sanctions, he or she is still pursuing a course of unremitting self-interest, and is likely to evade the law if possible.

The difficulties that arise when we envisage self-seeking 'economic man' in society can be shown by what has been called 'the free-rider problem'. Let us imagine a public good, such as the need for clean air. It is very often a characteristic of such goods that, while they are available to all, they can be produced by some without the participation of everyone. Yet there is often no way of preventing everyone from benefiting. The result is that individuals who refused to contribute to the production of the good may still share in the fruits of others' efforts. The problem arises why people should pay the undoubted cost of contributing if they can obtain the same benefits without doing so. Why should they not let others do the work? One smoking chimney may not make the air appreciably dirtier, and one outflow of sewage may not pollute the river unduly. One tax dodger will not bring the functioning of government to a halt. Why should one not use a hosepipe for one's garden in a drought, or use electricity in a power shortage? Why should one not seek a pay rise when general pay restraint is demanded? The problem is all too familiar. Each of us may find occasions when we are tempted to trade on the fact that others are contributing.

One stock retort to these questions is 'What if everyone did that?' A children's story once told of how a king wished the fountains of his capital city to flow with milk on a particular day of celebration. Everyone was to pour a contribution into the cisterns supplying the fountains. When they had done so, the fountains were turned on again, and flowed with water as clear as the previous day. Each person had reasoned that one pitcher of water, instead of milk, would make no difference. The 'free-rider problem', however, takes this type of possibility into account. Each member of a group is assumed to reason as follows. Either enough of the others will contribute to produce the desired results or they will not. If enough will, it is not necessary to contribute, as the good will be provided without cost to oneself. If enough will not, there is no point in contributing anyway. It seems, therefore, as if rational self-interest demands that one does not contribute.

The problem appears in a similar guise if we are concerned with maximum overall utility rather than just our own welfare. There still seems no point in contributing, because either enough others will contribute or they will not. It is often suggested that this is a question of rationality. One writer comments: 'The point is not that inaction is *compatible* with rationality. Rationality requires inaction.'[17] Something must have gone wrong with our conception of rationality for such a result to be produced. Any procedure which starts weighing costs to oneself against possible benefits may *seem* rational, but it is implicitly equating rationality with self-interest. The assumption is that those who prefer the interests of others to their own are irrational. Unless contribution to the public good can be immediately justified in terms of the pay-off to the individual, it is rational not to contribute. Individuals' it is assumed, can each exist in isolation from their community and decide how far they will contribute to it. Individualism can join forces with egoism in a manner which is supposed to be the epitome of rationality.

A rejoinder to this could be that, even if one is altruistic and genuinely seeks to further the interests of others, there seems little point if one's action is going to be ineffective. Unless my contribution is the one that tips the scales, I am incurring a cost without any corresponding benefit. Is it not right to conclude that such pointless behaviour is irrational? Wasted effort hardly seems rational even if rationality is not defined in terms of self-interest. Part of the trouble lies in the fact that we cannot often be certain our effort is wasted. The matter may seem to have been dealt with, in the initial calculation of costs and benefits, in terms of the probability of an outcome being achieved. Despite the apparent mathematical precision of this, it still remains true that we can often be wildly inaccurate in foreseeing the consequences of our actions, particularly when this involves predicting what others are going to do. The question of example, too, is often important. If we incur costs in cutting down pollution, others may be encouraged to do the same. Just because, on an individualist view, the community is nothing more than the combination of its members, what happens in it depends entirely on what each of its members does. Some may, quite unfairly, get a 'free-ride', and the resentment this causes is itself an important factor in society. The conclusion seems inevitable that an individualist understanding of society assumes a strict code of morality among its members, if public goods are to be provided. A sense of duty will ensure that everyone contributes. The alternative would be a chaotic situation in which everyone is trying to benefit at the expense of others' efforts.

Individualism

The demands of society are very often at odds with the consistent pursuit of self-interest. Moral principles may certainly be important in the commitment of an individual to his or her society, and there is a close relationship between the notion of a morality and that of a society. It even seems doubtful if there could be a society without some form of morality encouraging its members to be willing to sacrifice their own interests. Yet there are two problems which have been lurking in the background. The first is that questions about egoism and altruism will inevitably be linked with issues about human nature. Exhortations to consider the good of society are unlikely to be effective, if as a matter of fact human beings are basically selfish. Once more, a major problem about the functioning of human society appears to depend on considerations about human nature.

The second issue raises questions about the very basis of assumptions concerning the rationality of an individual contributing to society. Nowhere does the distinction between holist and individualist views of society become clearer than here. The problem has appeared to be one of inducing autonomous individuals to contribute to society, but, if society defines the nature of an individual, the latter's autonomy is a mere abstraction. The individual, it may be argued, has no existence outside his or her context in society. The very concept of an individual is perhaps the creation of particular circumstances in a particular type of society. The emphasis of both Marx and Wittgenstein on the priority of the social appears to undermine any view of atomic individuals coalescing to form a society. For Marx, the social context is specifically the socio-economic structures which have changed through history. They determine the way we think and will have to be changed if human life is to be improved. This means that Marxists should always be more concerned with changing the structures than changing the ideas that are produced by those structures. They will regard ideas as being more significant as symptoms of underlying social and economic relationships than as worthy of study in themselves.

One writer comments: 'Historical materialism is a substantive critique of ideologies which is premised on the denial of that ideological separation of ideas *as ideas* from the relation of ideas to their materiality as social praxis.'[18] Thus the more such ideas are examined in isolation, the more we allow our view of social reality to be distorted. Such a view trades on a strong distinction between appearance and reality. What appears to be the case to participants in a society may be far from what is actually going on. Marxism, as a science, is hence required to show the real nature of social relations. That view is controversial, even among the followers of Marx, since it is a strongly realist position, asserting that there is one reality underlying the various ideologies. Marxist theory, it is alleged, can claim to be scientific since it helps us to see this. Other views seek to modify this position by, for instance, attempting to overcome the distinction between the subject and object of knowledge. Marxists, however, face a dilemma, since they risk the threat of relativism if they give up their claim that their theory gives a unique insight into the nature of social reality, and stress the social origin of *all* ideas. On the other hand, claims to special knowledge can give rise to elites, who can become exceedingly ruthless in the pursuit of their aims because they are secure in the knowledge that they are right.

The shift of emphasis to structures in society empties the concept of an individual of any real content. All attention becomes focused on the social and historical preconditions for consciousness of different kinds. Marx was, particularly in his later work, opposed to any conception of fixed human needs or desires persisting through changed circumstances. He says, for instance, in *Capital* that, by acting on the external world and changing it, man 'at the same time changes his own nature'.[19] In an often quoted passage which serves as an inspiration for the sociology of knowledge, Marx says:

> The mode of production in material life determines the general character of the social, political and spiritual processes of life. It is not the consciousness of men that determines their existence, but, on the contrary, their social existence determines their consciousness.[20]

The stress on the priority of the social entails the repudiation of any conception of individuals exercising rationality in a vacuum beyond the reach of the influences of their time. Their reasoning will be the product of the society of which they are members, and Marx's materialism traces the form of society to the underlying economic factors moulding it. His thought is given many different interpretations, but a common one is that he does not base the economic substructure on anything else, least of all human biology. If he had, the social character of some human needs and wants might thereby have been put in question: they might turn out to be grounded in something transcending the vagaries of history.

The abstract individual, as favoured by classical economists, was an explicit target for Marx. In fact in the *Grundrisse* he tries to trace the development of the idea of the abstract individual, showing how in the past the individual appeared inseparable from the social whole.[21] First society was just the family, then the family expanded into a clan, and then it was formed through communities arising from various combinations of clans. Individuation only arises, holds Marx, with the rise of bourgeois society, characterized by free competition. In such a society, he says, 'the individual appears detached from the natural bonds etc. which in earlier historical periods made him the accessory of a definite and limited human conglomerate'.[22] The point is, though, that this is an illusion created by the particular conditions of a particular economic structure. Belief in the abstract individual is itself the product of a definite kind of society.

This is a radical challenge to the individualist assumption of many economists. Far from the 'rational' individual being the origin of the economic facts of life, it is alleged that the conditions of Western capitalist society have given rise to the idea in the first place. This is not just a controversy in economics, since it matters enormously in society at large, whether we regard the individual or the structures of society as prior. Is society the creation of the interrelated effects of individuals, or are individuals only to be understood in their social setting, since they are themselves the creation of that setting? We have encountered this problem before, but in this instance it should be clear that the argument has political implications. If we wish to change society in some way, how is it to be done? Do we attempt to change individuals first, or do we change the economic structures of society? The latter is the Marxist way. The former is less catastrophic, but just because it is more gradual it may appear less effective.

If Marxists are right, the individual will only be changed by altering economic structures. If, however, they are wrong, and individuals are at least partly formed by other factors, whether their biology, or even their own rational choices, changing society will be somewhat irrelevant. If individuals are egoists, changing the system will leave their egoism untouched. It is a common criticism of Marxist theory that it is utopian because it assumes human perfectibility, in that it takes for granted that the achievement of a perfect society will of itself produce perfection in human beings. Yet it might be that people turn out as greedy and selfish under a new system as they were in the old. The cynic will observe that communist systems can apparently be exploited by party bosses for their advantage just as easily as a capitalist system may be manipulated by industrialists or bankers for theirs. Marxists will retort that existing communist systems are not necessarily good examples of Marxist theory put into practice. Nevertheless the difficulty of ever putting revolutionary ideals into practice may very well have something to do with basic facts about human nature. Too great an emphasis on socio-economic structures may ignore the brute fact of human selfishness.

Christian theologians express much this view of human nature when they refer to 'original sin'. They would certainly expect to find it reflected in the structures of human society, but would not expect to cure it by means of social change. What is needed is rather the kind of change expressed by the word 'redemption'. As a result, a theological understanding of humanity takes human selfishness seriously, but also assumes that it can be dealt with. Because of the latter, they are far from any notion of 'rational economic man' of the kind I have been discussing.

Christian theology, to the Marxist, is a prime example of ideology, an effect of social and economic conditions blinding us to their true nature because of the operation of vested interests. Because of this viewpoint, genuine dialogue between Marxists and non-Marxists would seem difficult. It would not involve a simple disagreement about what is true, which could be discussed reasonably. Marxists would trace their opponents' alleged distortions to their social background, while non-Marxists are, on their assumptions, still able to examine Marxist theory on its merits.

Rationality and Revolution

The difference between a Marxist and non-Marxist view of the relationship between individual and society can be illustrated, for example, by the Christian idea of love. In particular, the love of neighbour exemplified by the parable of the Good Samaritan seems to be a matter of how individuals should treat each other, regardless of such factors as race or religion. It might even be plausible to suggest that the point of the parable is that individuals matter regardless of their socio-economic background, and regardless of what the power structures of society happen to be. Yet it is easy for those influenced by Marxism to insist that such love is pointless, and even illusory, if it allows socio-economic structures to continue which legitimize forms of oppression and exploitation. One writer, describing 'structures of domination', maintains:

> These structures are such that it can be only ideological to speak of loving within them. . . . Consequently, one side of Christianity – a sorely understressed side of it – shares a parallel conviction with the Marxist, that it is in the business not of *loving*, but rather of securing the conditions of the possibility of loving.[23]

There is a major philosophical difference between a view stressing the significance of the individual, and the alternative position stressing the importance of having the right social structures. An emphasis on the individual need not involve ignoring the importance of wider social and economic considerations, but it may induce some scepticism about how much can be achieved by social and economic change alone. On the other hand, emphasizing the priority of society may involve absolving the individual of any responsibility for social evils. Whether the traditional Christian belief in the importance of the individual can easily be combined with a Marxist emphasis on the effects of the structure of society seems unlikely. Needless to say, this is a highly contentious issue.

There is another illustration of how individualist and collectivist perceptions can differ. It may seem puzzling sometimes why members of an exploited class should continue to support the very conditions which are responsible for their exploitation. Why, for instance, should members of the menial castes in India fervently uphold the caste system? Marvin Harris puts it this way:

> Members of impoverished menial castes avidly uphold the rule of caste endogamy and insist that marriages be legitimized by expensive dowries. Abstractly, it would appear that the members of such impoverished castes would be materially better off if they practised exogamy and stopped insisting on big marriage payments. But the victims of the caste system cannot base their behaviour on long-term abstract calculations. Access to such menial jobs as construction worker, toddy-wine maker, coir maker and so forth depends on caste identity validated by obedience to caste rules.[24]

Anyone breaking ranks will be penalized by the system. Therefore, although it is oppressive, each individual has an interest in perpetuating it rather than lose all prospect of employment. Those at the bottom of the society have not the power to throw off all the privileges of the upper castes. Harris comments that, 'perverse as it may seem, those who benefit least from the system ardently support it in daily life'. This position is clearly intelligible from the standpoint of 'rational economic man'. No doubt the caste system could be broken if enough people refused to abide by it, but individuals would have to be willing to suffer to produce an eventual change, and they have not so far been prepared to do so.

At this point, a Marxist would speak of the necessity of revolution, but this is the nub of the matter. Are the members of the proletariat perhaps in an analogous position to the members of Indian lower castes? Those initiating a revolution may well have to suffer, and they might not be prepared to do so. The doubt arises if one assumes the kind of egoism already referred to. Altruists may be ready to die for the benefit of others, but those intent only on maximizing their own utility will not. The problem has been summed up as follows:

> Even if revolution is in the best interests of the proletariat and even if every member of the proletariat realizes that this is so, so far as its members act rationally, this class will *not* achieve concerted revolutionary action. This shocking conclusion rests on the premise that concerted revolutionary action is for the proletariat a public good in the technical sense.[25]

Thus, in addition to the question of altruism, all the paradoxes connected with 'the free-rider problem' come into play. Is it reasonable to expect anyone to attempt to establish new social structures regardless of what others do, particularly when death is a more than likely outcome? The 'rational man' might prefer survival under an unjust system to such a gamble. Yet this would suggest that it could be irrational to participate in a revolution, and such a conclusion would obviously be uncongenial to Marxism. However, assumptions have been made which Marxists would not accept. Apart from the picture of a society as a group of individuals, they would also reject the notion of rationality as maximizing utility. Rationality, in Marxism, is not a matter of finding the most suitable means for the satisfaction of personal desires. Since Marxists believe the latter are socially conditioned, their attention is directed at producing the best kind of society. That would, they think, be unlike a capitalist society in that apparent and real relations between people would coincide in it. There would be no room left for ideology, but we would be in conscious control of society, since our understanding of it would reveal the true state of affairs. This is the rational end sought by Marxists, and it thus defines rationality for them. As one writer puts it, 'From Marx's perspective the idea that rational action could lead to socially non-optimal – indeed disastrous – results is a *reductio ad absurdum* of the individual utility maximizing conception of rationality.'[26]

Marxists could also suggest that the very notion of rationality as maximization of utility, especially when combined with egoism, is itself produced by a particular set of socio-economic circumstances. It is, they would argue, a typical product of capitalist society, portraying people in terms which merely reflect the prevailing spirit of competition between individuals in a market economy. As such it is a good example, from the Marxist point of view, of ideology. It disguises what to a Marxist is the real situation in a manner which allegedly serves the interests of the existing power structure of that society. It sets as standards of human rationality what are apparently only the local conditions in a particular society, and seems to restrict the possibility of change. The argument that revolution is irrational further helps prevent any radical alteration of existing social relations.

Thus we are faced with two utterly different conceptions of human society and the nature of human rationality, the one based on the individual and the other on society. Yet although the views are in many respects polar opposites, rejecting one does not necessarily entail accepting the other. Not all positions emphasizing the priority of the individual are egoist. It is perfectly possible to hold that individuals need to use their reason concerning the ends to be pursued and to consider the interests of others as well as themselves. Similarly not all holist views need adopt a Marxist stance about socio-economic causation. It is possible, as Wittgenstein did, to root the notion of rationality in social practice, without accepting Marxist theory about the relation of ideas to the material substructure of society.

Both the economist's conception of 'rational man' and Marxist theories about society make assumptions about human nature. For the economist, human desires are fixed and unalterable, setting the stage for the living of human life, while for the Marxist they are the creation of a particular society. The assumptions about the nature of rationality made by each stem from their respective views about individuals. Can they be intelligibly viewed in isolation from society or not? The social theory we adopt, and even the economic system we prefer, depends on our answer to this question.

Notes

1 Max Weber, *Selections*, 1978, p. 61.
2 Ibid., p. 85.
3 Amartya Sen, *Choice, Welfare and Measurement*, 1982, p. 5.
4 F. Hirsch and J. H. Goldthorpe, *Political Economy of Inflation*, 1978, p. 273.
5 Ibid., p. 274.
6 Sen, *Choice, Welfare and Measurement*, p. 67.
7 G. Stigler and G. Becker, 'De Gustibus non est Disputandum', *American Economics Review*, 67, 1977, p. 76.
8 Ibid.
9 Ibid., p. 89.
10 M. S. McPherson, 'Want Formation, Morality, and Some Interpretive Aspects of Economic Inquiry', in N. Haan et al. (eds), *Social Science as Moral Inquiry*, 1983, p. 107.
11 See my *The Shaping of Man*, 1982.
12 McPherson, 'Want Formation', p. 102.
13 e.g. as given by Sen, *Choice, Welfare and Measurement*, p. 62.
14 A. Sen, 'Rational Fools', *Philosophy and Public Affairs*, 6, 1977, p. 329.
15 McPherson, 'Want Formation', p. 98.
16 John Rawls, *A Theory of Justice*, 1972, p. 143.
17 A. Buchanan, 'Revolutionary Motivation and Rationality', *Philosophy and Public Affairs*, 9, 1979–80, p. 66.
18 D. Turner, *Marxism and Christianity*, 1983, p. 181.
19 K. Marx, *Capital*, 1967, vol. I, p. 177.
20 K. Marx, *A Contribution to the Critique of Political Economy* (1859), 1970, p. 21.
21 K. Marx, *Grundrisse*, Harmondsworth, 1973, p. 84.
22 Ibid., p. 83.
23 Turner, *Marxism and Christianity*, p. 214.
24 Marvin Harris, *Cultural Materialism*, 1979, p. 62.
25 Buchanan, 'Revolutionary Motivation and Rationality', p. 63.
26 N. Holmstrom, 'Rationality and Revolution', *Canadian Journal of Philosophy*, 13, 1983, p. 324.

8

Culture: Function and Adaptation

Social Function

Whenever human nature is discussed, one fundamental feature is invariably mentioned. We are remarkable for the manifold ways in which we express ourselves in culture. Social scientists have to give some form of unifying account of this if they are to do more than catalogue the myriad ways in which human life is lived. One major issue is just how much of human behaviour is based on biology and how much on culture. Allowing that human genes, for instance, explain a fair proportion of human activity would suggest that the differences between cultures are more apparent than real: the same biological needs would underlie what are apparently different customs. On the other hand, insisting that human nature is socially produced would imply that biology is largely irrelevant to the understanding of social practices.

The argument is often presented as a choice between alternatives, so that one is governed either by biology or by one's cultural environment.[1] One is moulded either by one's genes or by one's society. For example, Marvin Harris puts forward a view called 'cultural materialism', and quarrels with sociobiologists who, he alleges, 'actively seek to expand the list of genetically determined traits whenever a plausible opportunity to do so presents itself.' He writes:

> Cultural materialists pursue a strategy that seeks to reduce the list of hypothetical drives, instincts and genetically determined response alternatives to the smallest number of items compatible with the construction of an effective corpus of sociocultural theory.[2]

As a result he looks primarily to non-biological factors in his aim 'to account for the origin, maintenance and change of the global inventory of sociocultural differences and similarities'. In particular, he examines the causal factors of culture in what he terms 'the infrastructure', which comprises 'patterns of production and reproduction'. Since this infrastructure is, as he admits, 'the principal interface between culture and nature', it remains problematic just how much influence human biology will have.[3] It transpires that Harris's disagreement with sociobiology is one of emphasis rather than of principle. He believes that most human culture is not under genetic control, and holds that '*Homo sapiens* has been selected for the capacity to acquire and modify cultural repertoires independently of genetic feedback.'[4] He points out the massive variety of cultures exhibited in the world, all of which can be acquired or wiped out within the space of a single generation. The language one speaks and the food one eats are matters of how one is brought up rather than of who one's parents are.

It is in fact exceedingly difficult to maintain either that human culture is totally unaffected by human biology or that it is totally determined by it. The fact of cultural variation seems sufficient to refute the latter. As to the former, it is only necessary to wonder what human life would be like if we were all ten feet tall, or if there were three sexes, to realize that biological factors do at the very least set the stage for human life. Partly, perhaps, because social scientists are not biologists, they have preferred to look at human culture in its own terms, taking the biological background for granted. Many suspect that treating cultural categories in biological terms will only squeeze out of them all that is most significant for humanity. There is the constant fear of reductionism, whereby reference to human concepts becomes transmuted into talk of genes and biochemistry. Since, too, the biologist will always speak of the individual organism, any switch from the social sciences to the biological ones apparently involves conceding that the individualist is right in his argument with the holist. Moreover, if society cannot be reduced to its individual members, a scientific study of the biology of individuals is not going to help in understanding the functioning of society.

Any study of human society is almost bound to have to deal with two pervasive features. Most humans live in family groups and most human societies profess some sort of religion. Whether these two traits are universal, rather than merely widespread, is controversial. It is possible to define the terms so that they become universal. Is state atheism a type of religion? Is a commune a family? Whatever the answer, social scientists will wish to give explanations for these widespread social phenomena, and will tend to restrict themselves to social, rather than biological or physical, explanations.

One very popular form of explanation has been in terms of social functions. The point of culture has been taken to be the way it contributes to improving what Malinowski termed 'the individual and collective standard of living'.[5] He linked culture with human needs and concluded: 'Function cannot be defined in any other way than the satisfaction of a need by an activity in which human beings co-operate, use artefacts, and consume goods.'[6] Some needs, he thought, were biological and others were 'derived', that is, created by culture, as the theory could afford to be fairly neutral about the relevance of biology. He was convinced of the crucial importance of the family in society. Its function, he believed, was to supply citizens to the community:

> From the very outset of culture the family has been the institution in which most of the fundamental needs of human beings have been satisfied. It is the institution primarily based on the reproductive need, but also directly associated with the production, distribution and consumption of food.... Custom, order and authority are embodied in the family.[7]

With this kind of account, Malinowski explicitly attempts to fit all human cultures, with their manifold differences, into one universal scheme. A family may take many forms in different cultures, but Malinowski would assume, for instance, that its function of training children will always be performed. His search for the nature or 'cultural reality' of human marriage and the family will involve discounting the differences between societies, and attempting to find 'valid scientific generalizations' about the functioning of institutions. Like many other social scientists, he tried to copy the methods of the physical sciences without relating his work to them in any direct way. Yet the search for a common factor in what appeared to be great cultural variation explicitly leads to the search for the lowest common denominator in, say, different forms of family, or of religion. Malinowski wrote:

> When E. B. Tylor inquired at the beginning of his great work on 'Primitive Culture' into what religion was, in the widest sense of the

term, or in his own words, when he attempted a 'minimum definition' of this subject, he was a genuine functionalist.[8]

This approach is illustrated further by Durkheim's treatment of religion. In attempting to show the function of religion, he inevitably considered the differences between religions as of little account. What was relevant was their similarity, and, since he approached the matter as a social scientist, he looked only at their social effects, which he felt were of the greatest importance: 'If religion has given birth to all that is essential in society, it is because the idea of society is the soul of religion.'[9] He believed that all societies have to reaffirm at regular intervals their collective sentiments and ideas. The unity of a society depends, he thought, on individuals assembling to participate in ceremonies which serve to draw it together:

> Hence come ceremonies which do not differ from regular religious ceremonies, either in their object, the results which they produce, or the processes employed to attain these results. What essential difference is there between an assembly of Christians celebrating the principal dates of the life of Christ or of Jews remembering the exodus from Egypt or the promulgation of the decalogue, and a reunion of citizens commemorating the promulgation of a new moral or legal system or some great event in the national life?

The answer may be: very little, in terms of social function. Religions, like other institutions, do have social functions, and not all of them are obvious to participants. A distinction has been made by Merton between 'manifest' and 'latent' function, between, as he puts it, 'conscious motivations for social behaviour and its objective consequences'.[11] There is a perpetual problem, particularly at a time of rapid social change, that social institutions will be deliberately altered without any awareness of their latent functions. The family provides one obvious example. Radical change can be made in patterns of family relationships without any conscious thought being given to the wider effects on society.

A social scientist can, and should, observe the social effects of social institutions, even when they are religious. Yet ignoring the major differences between religions with a view to stressing the basic similarity of their influence on society is a perilous undertaking. Identifying religion with its social role ignores the very different claims being made about the world in different religions. We have seen before that social scientists are very tempted to ignore the content of belief and concentrate on the fact of belief. Durkheim in fact deals with public ceremonies indiscriminately, whether they have a religious purpose or not. The function of an institution so overshadows it that it appears to cease to matter what kind of institution it is. The only significant question is whether the function is fulfilled.

Functionalism is sometimes alleged to have a conservative bias because it seems to approve of whatever institutions a society possesses on the grounds that they are meeting important needs. Yet the emphasis on social function can actually serve to weaken commitment to the institutions in question. The importance of religion in society might seem to be emphasized when its function is shown. Since, however, it does not matter which religion is invoked, it seems that any kind will do, and perhaps non-religious creeds may be able to fulfil the same function. Claims to truth by religion are put aside as irrelevant. The *real* explanation for religious commitment is, it appears, social, and no room is left for beliefs to be held on the grounds that they are true. Functionalism can have similar effects to those of the sociology of knowledge. In both cases, sociological explanation seems to replace explanation in terms of reasons. I cannot reasonably believe that God exists if I become convinced that the reason for belief is God has nothing to do with what is transcendent and everything to do with the needs of society. The great danger is that social scientists both dismiss questions of truth and falsity as being outside their professional competence and assume that they can still deal with the central issues of religion. There is bound to be an element of distortion in sociological accounts of religion if it is taken for granted that the social function of religion is its most important feature. Social science must also recognize that it is an important task to show why one religion, rather than another, has been adopted.

Even if it is accepted that any society needs religious institutions to remain in equilibrium, there remains the question why a particular society has one institution rather than another. As George C. Homans remarks in the course of criticizing functionalism: 'I take it that what sociology has to explain are the actual features of actual societies and not just the generalized features of a generalized society.'[12] He feels that in the end functional explanations have to rely on psychological explanations about what people are or are not likely to do. Discussion in terms of abstract social systems and the functions of institutions explains nothing beyond why a society is enabled to continue working. Causal explanations about the origin of institutions or indeed about social change seem to get short shrift from functional analysis. Religion may serve to integrate society, and the decline of religion may, as a result, have a disintegrating effect, but that does not wholly explain why people are religious. Given the existence of religion, the functionalist account can help to explain its persistence. Institutionalized forms of atheism can no doubt be devised to serve the same social function. Whether atheism satisfies other human needs is a further question. Because it may be outside the province of sociology does not mean it is not a real one.

The Role of Consciousness

The distinction between manifest and latent functions entails that participants in a social system may not always fully understand the significance of what they are doing. This involves a similar question to that of false consciousness. An institution could be different from the way it is perceived by its members. They may support it for one reason while in reality it may possess functions that are quite different. Social science may be able to reveal that this is so. One apposite comment on the situation was: 'Nowadays with sociologists busily ferreting out latent functions in every nook and cranny of society and their writings gaining general currency, latent functions are not likely to stay latent for long.'[13] The fact that such knowledge becomes widespread itself becomes an important factor in society, and some may consciously try to preserve institutions merely for the sake of such previously latent functions.

We have already seen how controversial this distinction can be between what is happening in a society and what its participants understand. Some sociologists would not accept that there is a difference. For instance, Peter and Brigitte Berger say flatly that 'our epistemological assumption is that society is not a functioning system, but a meaningful construction'.[14] They apply this particularly to consideration of the family: 'To the extent that people perceive the family as a major source of meaning, value and identity, *that* is what the family is – no matter what a systemic analysis might have to say about its functioning.'[15] This can be seen as a correction of the functionalist approach rather than a total repudiation of it. The institution of the family might have latent functions, but the central point remains. Just as a religion typically makes claim to truth, it can be argued that the central features of a family lie in the conscious relationship of its members with each other. In each case, social science can distort rather than clarify.

Peter and Brigitte Berger are particularly concerned that talk of the family as a system interacting with other systems itself encourages mechanistic imagery. As a result, social workers can approach the family with 'services' to fulfil its needs, without looking at 'the importance of meanings and values in human life'. The dehumanizing methods of bureaucrats can finally destroy what they were supposed to help. This is a good example of how philosophic positions about the foundations of the social sciences can affect social policy. Peter and Brigitte Berger take it as axiomatic that the understanding possessed by individuals determines the nature of the practices in which they engage: 'The situation cannot be understood except "from within", that is, by understanding what the situation means to those who are in it.'[16] This is a familiar point, often made by those influenced by phenomenology, but it becomes vital when an institution such as the family is being studied. It is apparent that ignoring the perspective of the individual can misrepresent the nature of the human family. Peter and Brigitte Berger deny that notions of 'systemic' functionality can be helpful if they ignore what individuals mean and intend. They comment that people are unlikely to see themselves as operating units in a social system, unless they have taken too many sociology courses.

Giving individual consciousness this kind of priority raises again the problem of the relation between social structures and consciousness. What is the role, for instance, of consciousness in initiating social change? Peter and Brigitte Berger see social change 'as the result of the interaction (or, if one prefers, of a dialectic) of institutions and consciousness'.[17] This contrasts with views which would regard consciousness as perhaps nothing more than a by-product (or epiphenomenon) of underlying structural changes in society. Even if the link between such changes and consciousness were weakened, there is still the question whether consciousness can itself be an agent of change. The rise of feminism provides a pertinent example. There has been a marked change in recent years in the way many women, particularly those with a higher education, perceive their role. Peter and Brigitte Berger acknowledge 'the difficulty of determining to what extent feminism *caused* changes in behaviour or merely legitimated changes that were happening anyway'.

Their philosophical assumptions would leave open the possibility that consciousness can create social change.

Against such a position would be ranged many who, like Marvin Harris, stress the importance of infrastructure in determining consciousness. He himself also uses the example of the raised consciousness of women, and significantly traces it back to changes in the conditions in which contemporary life is lived, rather than to the inherent force of ideas. He points out that women's role has changed with increased urbanization. A society based on agriculture, particularly a frontier society, would emphasize the woman's role as mother and housekeeper. The conditions of living in cities, with greater opportunities in employment for women, combine with the increasing cost of having families when compared with the benefits received. Large families are not as important in the city as in a homestead. Harris looks to the vast changes in technology as part of the explanation for women's changed role, and is convinced of the asymmetrical nature of causal relationships between 'infrastructure' and 'superstructure'. In other words, the material conditions of life will influence the content of consciousness, rather than consciousness changing the conditions of life. To illustrate his case, he asks whether groups of males could succeed in reviving the sex roles of the nineteenth century. Would a decisive factor be how far they were committed to their goal? Or, we might add, could ideas themselves be judged to have power, whatever the prevailing social conditions? Harris believes that the men would stand no chance 'as long as the present urban industrial infrastructure holds sway'.

This controversy is, in essence, the traditional argument between 'materialists' and 'idealists'. Can ideas, or the power of human reason, influence human life, or are they themselves under the control of material forces, which shape society in their image? The power of ideas can certainly be enhanced or checked by the general condition of the society in which they are presented. What is at issue, however, is not the truism that some societies will be more receptive than others to the force of particular views. The question is whether the way people think can itself initiate change in society. Thought may itself be only a symptom of currents already strongly flowing. Yet those who preach various brands of materialism hardly seem to believe this themselves: they certainly see fit to write and to argue in order to convince others. While such doctrines may be more acceptable in some types of societies than in others, most materialists bear witness to the effective power of thought by the very fact of their efforts to convince others. The fact that they themselves present rational arguments suggests that they are not content with what society may predispose us to believe.

Attempts to explain the contents of human consciousness will always be self-defeating since they are themselves the products of consciousness. As a result, social scientists may change the subject and talk of systems, structures and functions without doing justice to the nature of what they are investigating. Alternatively, they may feel that their task is not one of explanation at all, but of understanding the meanings of participants in society. The former course succeeds in examining society while apparently leaving the men and women who make it up out of consideration. Yet the second seems to offer little scope for the construction of any theory about human social behaviour. It is hardly surprising that there have been in recent years attempts to link the social sciences with the physical sciences, particularly biology. The disadvantages of merely aping the physical sciences and copying their methods in an appropriate context may disappear if social science is treated, at least to some extent, as a continuation of the rest of science. It would then be not so much a parallel enterprise trying to do for human society what physics does for the material world, but would actually use the insights of physical science in dealing with human behaviour.

Biology and Social Science

Applying biology to social science may appear unpromising at first. How can the scientific study of biological organisms throw light on the complicated organization of human society? The approach needed for the study of insects or animals appears irrelevant once human consciousness and its products become objects of study. Admitting the relevance of biology seems to involve both reductionism and individualism. Reductionism is involved as all social categories have to be translated into something else if they are to be brought within the ambit of biological and hence physical explanation. Since, too, modern biology is concerned with the reproductive success of individuals, all its explanations will have to proceed through the behaviour of individuals.

The whole new discipline of sociobiology has grown up on the assumption that social behaviour does have a biological basis and that even complicated social arrangements may be illuminated by biological theory. The latter is, of course, essentially Darwinian, upholding evolution through natural selection. Unlike Darwin, modern biologists can refer to genes and even link differences in behaviour to genetic difference. Things are rarely so simple that one gene could be identified as the cause of a particular type of behaviour. Anyway, all genes interact in a complex way with their environment, so that even simple creatures under tight genetic control react to environmental stimuli and do not blindly act whatever the circumstances.

Sociobiology is devoted to the study of the biological basis of behaviour. Such a task is uncontroversial when insects, birds or animals are under scrutiny. It is easy in such cases to accept that natural selection influences the spread of some behaviour and impedes others. Birds with a taste for harmful food or without any desire to look after their young will normally leave few descendants. Even the cuckoo has to rely on other birds raising its young. If other birds had not been so gullible, cuckoos would have quickly died out. Similarly, if there were too many cuckoos, and the other birds only raised cuckoos at the expense of their own offspring, other species would quickly be at risk, so that there would soon not be enough to raise young cuckoos. In fact, a delicate compromise has been reached, which has been termed 'an evolutionary stable strategy'. There are sufficient cuckoos to perpetuate themselves, but not enough to put other species in danger.

Behaviour does have consequences. Some kinds of behaviour can further reproductive success and genes encouraging it will spread, but other kinds can have such deleterious effects that the agents or their offspring fail to pass on their genes to further generations. The inevitable result is that genes encouraging harmful behaviour will die out. Natural selection will encourage some forms of behaviour and discourage others. With regard to non-human organisms, this appears to be the sensible application of Darwinian principles. It shows why animals naturally prefer their kin according to degree of relatedness, and look after their offspring. There has been a tremendous outcry, however, at the suggestion that sociobiology can also explain human behaviour.[18] Many believe that human beings cannot be simply classed as one kind of animal among many. Cultural variation seems difficult to explain solely in terms of genetic variation. Sociobiology, at least in its early stages, has certainly seemed to treat humanity as just another biological species. Yet the agility of the human mind, coupled with the fact of human culture, has ensured that human behaviour is much more flexible and variable than that of animals. It is easy to assume, with many social theorists, that humans are infinitely malleable, so that we are merely the product of a particular culture.

If, however, sociobiology is even only partially correct, our genetic inheritance gained over many thousands of years will predispose us to some patterns of behaviour and make us find others distasteful. This will both limit possible variation in culture and cause strains in a society when the prevailing culture begins to go 'against nature'. We would expect an underlying similarity between all human cultures, however great superficial differences may be. Different customs may be mere fronts for the same impulses governed by the same genes.

This is not to advocate a simple-minded genetic determinism in opposition to an equally simplistic environmental determinism. Humans are educated within a culture. Nevertheless, the suggestion is that culture does not exist on its own, and cannot be understood except as an environment in which human genetic impulses can be thwarted or find fulfilment. In other words, it has the function of serving the biological needs of individuals. Sometimes, however, it is allowed to stray a little. Lumsden and Wilson have referred to the 'leash principle', according to which 'genetic natural selection operates in such a way as to keep culture on a leash'.[19] This allows a certain independence to cultural development, and means that not everything in a human society can be explained from the standpoint of neo-Darwinian biological theory. It has been alleged, for instance, that the contemporary willingness to use contraceptives is not something that could be explained on sociobiological principles, despite its cultural importance. Is not the voluntary limitation of a family, or even the refusal to have one, inexplicable by a theory which preaches the importance of maximizing reproductive advantage? Sociobiology, however, has always recognized that maximum parental investment in a small number of children may be wiser than less care spread around a larger family. Even among animals, there is a difference between species, like rabbits, that find safety in producing large numbers of offspring, few of which are likely to survive, and a species such as an elephant which invests its care on few offspring, on the assumption that they will survive. It will not be surprising if humans consciously choose to adopt the latter strategy, if they are able.

A total refusal to have children raises a more difficult question, and it is here that the leash principle may be relevant. It is clear, according to neo-Darwinian theory, that an unwillingness to have children could not be encouraged genetically. Indeed, the reverse must be the case, since we should expect genes encouraging care for children to spread. Since children will be likely to possess half of a parent's genes, those who are cared for by parents, because the latter have genes prompting such behaviour, are likely to inherit the same genes. They are likely to survive to pass on their genes, while neglected children will be unlikely to do so. How then can people choose not to have children? A desire to have children is much more likely to be genetically based than indifference to children. Any genetic mutation encouraging parenthood would soon become established in the gene pool.

The leash principle acknowledges that culture is not totally dependent on genes. A simple model of genes causing behaviour is inappropriate for most aspects of human behaviour, particularly because of the influence of culture. Human consciousness has an active role to play, but that does not mean that culture is totally free of genetic constraint. It is not just a question of humans evolving to the point when they create culture and break free of genetic influences. Human genetic make-up does not just grant the ability to create culture and be influenced by it, but it must also be responsible for at least some of the content of human culture. The point of the leash principle is to assert both that culture can go against the promptings of the genes and that, if it does, it is eventually going to be pulled back. Whatever humans naturally desire, they can resist. Going 'against nature' will usually produce a cost. Individuals who rationally decide not to have a family may still find themselves sometimes yearning for one. Even if they do not, a culture encouraging childlessness is going to find itself in trouble. It will be possible for a small minority to choose not to have children, but, when a significant number do, the culture is signing its death warrant. It will be progressively debilitated, as it is passed on to fewer and fewer children. No culture can go against basic facts of human nature for long and hope to flourish.

Human Sociobiology

E. O. Wilson, the 'founding father' of sociobiology, began by studying insect societies and then extrapolated his findings in a controversial manner to mankind. He has, however, modified his previous position to take into account the distinctive features of human consciousness. Writing with Charles Lumsden, he refers to the 'remarkable fact that sociobiology has not taken into proper account either the human mind or the diversity of cultures'.[20] This admission marks the introduction of human sociobiology as a distinct branch of sociobiology. Humans cannot be studied as if they are insects or birds, and attempts to explain human behaviour as if it is merely an example of animal behaviour are bound to fail. The existence of human consciousness and its products creates a new environment in which natural selection can operate for the most part only indirectly.

Indirect operation is still significant and will influence the content of culture. Any social science ignoring biological theory is bound to be grossly hampered. Treating culture and human society as phenomena to be studied in their own right will be bound to tell only half the story. Our understanding is going to be severely restricted if all explanation for the characteristics of society are to be sought only in social terms. The current orthodoxy in the social sciences, suggesting that biology is irrelevant, must be challenged. One does not need to be a reductionist, dissolving culture or consciousness into something quite different, to feel uneasy about dismissing biology. Lumsden and Wilson lay themselves open to criticism on this issue. While insisting on what they term 'gene-culture co-evolution' and giving culture an active role in human development, they appear, as we shall see in the next chapter, to want to reduce talk of culture to talk of individual human brains. They thus both reduce culture from the social to the individual level and reduce reference to the contents of the individual mind to talk of brains. Many will rightly repudiate this conversion of the study of culture into the study of the brain. Yet that does not mean Lumsden and Wilson are wrong in their general thesis. Culture and genes may not develop in total independence of each other. Cultures provide the environment in which genes can be passed on or in which they can die out.

Do genes predispose us to some forms of culture rather than others? The argument of Lumsden and Wilson is that, even if humanity had started in a *tabula rasa* state, completely malleable by the environment, genetic mutations would inevitably have begun to bias individuals towards some features of culture rather than others. They would have flourished if the features were beneficial and done significantly less well if they were deleterious. Some mutations would establish themselves in the gene pool and others would be quickly eliminated. Gradually cultural predispositions would be passed on genetically. A good example of a case where this kind of reasoning seems to work is incest.[21] Social scientists have often investigated incest taboos with the assumption that, because they are cultural, they can be explained only at the level of culture. Yet, once it is recognized that close inbreeding reduces biological fitness, it becomes obvious that a sociobiological account may itself help to explain this aspect of human culture. It seems fairly straightforward to explain avoidance of incest by means of genetic predisposition. Those indulging in incest have less fit offspring than those who do not, and their preference will not be passed on genetically for very long. There even seems to be evidence of positive aversion to incest.[22]

This type of sociobiological account seems very compelling, but it has its critics even in the case of incest. Marvin Harris asks: 'If incest avoidance is part of the human biogram, why are there, conservatively estimated, several hundred thousand cases of father-daughter incest in the United States each year?'[23] This point need not alarm sociobiologists. Unless they are putting forward a very simple version of genetic determinism, they must acknowledge that humans are perfectly capable of going against inherited tendencies. It is only necessary to insist that they will inevitably pay the price of doing so. Incest can have catastrophic biological effects. Harris's own explanation for incest taboos ignores the genetic costs and concentrates on the economic infrastructure. He suggests the following:

> Restrictions on brother-sister, father-daughter, and mother-son sexual intercourse within the nuclear family probably reflect selection against groups who failed to develop inter-band marital alliance and who therefore suffered from a lack of lability and mobility and who consequently had a constricted resource base and lacked trading partners and allies in the event of armed conflict.[24]

However valid these points may be, a sociobiologist will feel that they refer to secondary factors and do not mention the principal cause. Nevertheless the very fact that incest does occur suggests an answer to one important question. Why are cultural taboos necessary, if we are genetically 'programmed' to avoid incest? Human desires may be strong but they can always be overridden. A culture which reinforces natural aversion will do better than one which either ignores the question or positively encourages incest. The members of the former will be biologically fitter, while the cost paid in the latter is likely to be enormous. Van den Berghe says in his survey of inbreeding avoidance: 'Human nature and culture are inextricably interlinked to produce fitness-optimizing solutions.'[25] He believes that incest taboos are a product of puritanical societies and are a substitute for natural aversion. His view is 'that such taboos arise in societies that frown on nudity and sex play and segregate children by sex'. In other words, because familiarity breeds contempt, the lack of such familiarity particularly in this context prevents the conditions in which natural aversions develop in a subtle interplay of genes and environment. His conclusion is:

> Culture clearly has the potential of interfering with nature, and when it does, it often creates new problems down the road. Incest taboos are an example of a rather clumsy solution to the problems created by a puritanical way of raising children.[26]

Human flexibility ensures that we can resist natural tendencies, even if it is at a cost. In this case, however, there is no reason to link incest taboos with a puritan attitude in this manner, even if there were a general empiricist correlation. Puritanical societies may be more conscious of sexual 'dangers' and may be more ready to reinforce certain natural tendencies with explicit rules. Van den Berghe suggests, however, that somehow a natural tendency has been thwarted by puritanism. His argument is that such societies have to introduce taboos because of the arrested development of any ordinary natural aversion. Apart from the implausibility of a view which suggests that puritanism is accompanied by a greater natural readiness to indulge in incest, Van den Berghe makes the mistake of assuming that a natural tendency *removes* rather than *reinforces* the need for a cultural norm. Yet the very conditions which ensured that revulsion to incest would be under genetic control also serve to emphasize the importance of the problem for a culture. It need be hardly surprising if societies hedge their bets by forbidding what evolution has already decreed to be 'unnatural'. This is a mere consequence of the fact that simple genetic determinism is totally ruled out in the human context.

It may be suggested that, if a sociobiological account does not work in the case of incest, it will not work anywhere, because of the connection between incest and loss of biological fitness. Similar accounts, however, in terms of natural selection can explain many widespread human traits, particularly those important for self-protection. Fear of dangerous situations is an advantage from an evolutionary point of view. Fear of snakes, of running water, of heights or of thunder can all be explained in this way. Such fears seem to be inherited from our remote ancestors, and significantly we do not possess the same instinctive fear of contemporary situations which might be equally dangerous. Children will not, for instance, react initially to an electric socket as they would to a snake.

Biology and Altruism

Many might accept the power of sociobiological explanation for taboos and phobias, while feeling it must be irrelevant to the understanding of the complicated structures of modern society. Perhaps most important for the very existence of society is a willingness to co-operate with each other and perhaps subordinate one's interests to those of others. Can sociobiology explain that? The family is the most basic unit where co-operation occurs, and we have already noted that it is a source of perpetual interest to social scientists. Sociobiology may throw considerable light on family relationships, since the regulation of sexual liaisons and provision for the care of children must be central issues for any theory concerned with the transmission of human genes.

A general preference for kin may have a biological base. Our relatives are more likely to share our genes than our non-relatives, and an abstract love of humanity is difficult to pass on genetically. That would involve sacrificing our genes for those who are unlikely to share them. Concern for relatives, on the other hand, involves caring for those who may themselves possess a gene prompting such concern. Sociobiologists have introduced the notion of 'kin selection' to explain a natural preference for relatives, and they further differentiate between close and distant relatives. The basic question always asked is, What is necessary for genes to spread? Sociobiology has to take into account the likelihood of a relative sharing our genes. If I sacrifice myself for someone unlikely to share the genes prompting such behaviour, the argument is that these genes are going to die out. Lumsden and Wilson refer to altruism towards relatives, meaning by it any action that increases their biological fitness at the expense of that of the altruist. Since a man's brother or sister will share half their genes with him through the fact of common descent, they say:

> If a man makes a sacrifice on behalf of his brother or sister, and as a result of his act the sibling has more children, the man's altruistic act will cause

an increase in the number of genes that are identical to his own. . . . The sacrifice of an altruist must result in at least a doubling of the number of the brother's offspring for the altruism carrying genes to spread. A first cousin has one eighth of genes identical: if the altruism is directed at first cousins alone, their offspring must be increased at least eightfold for the altruism genes to spread. And so on.[27]

Thus we would expect greater affection and concern for the welfare of brothers and sisters than for first cousins, and a much weaker concern still for more distant relatives. Nevertheless, the conclusion of socio-biology seems to be that love of one's family is natural, and an altruistic concern for those who are unrelated is not. This, however, fails to explain how societies can successfully work if they are composed of more than one family, however extended. Room is therefore made by sociobiologists for the strangely termed 'reciprocal altruism'. That enables them to explain co-operation in complex societies which are not tribally based. Indeed they accept that animals co-operate when it is to their mutual advantage, perhaps by grooming each other. Among humans there is a similar readiness to do favours as long as some are expected in return. Yet suggesting that I shall be altruistic to you only if you will be altruistic in return means that I am not being altruistic at all, but selfish. What is prompting me may be enlightened self-interest but it is still self-interest, and not the disinterested and even self-sacrificial concern for others which is the hallmark of genuine altruism. How far society can function if it is composed of rational egoists remains an acute question, and we have already seen how economic theory has found it difficult to account for 'public goods' using the assumptions made by sociobiologists in formulating their principle of reciprocal altruism.

Sociobiology thus raises in an acute form the question of what kind of society is possible. Is it going to be a purely competitive one, in which individuals try to get as much of what they want for themselves and their families, without caring for the interests of others as ends in themselves? Is co-operation itself merely a means to personal gain? The problem arises because contemporary biology tends to view selection as operating at the level of the individual organism, or even the gene, rather than at the level of the group or species. The notion of the individual being sacrificed for the good of the species is inexplicable from the standpoint of natural selection. The individual has probably benefited unrelated members of that species so that genes encouraging that behaviour will soon die out when they have to compete with mutants causing selfish behaviour. Similarly, 'group selection' is difficult to uphold, since sacrifice for unrelated members of a group seems self-defeating. Some groups may be sufficiently close-knit for every member to be related to every other, and group selection is then merely an example of kin selection. A group could flourish because it was in fact a large family.

Why, though, should not the unselfish behaviour of the members of one group enable it to succeed where competing groups fail? The group might enable its members to achieve greater biological fitness because of the self-sacrifice of some, even though the genes encouraging such altruism were not passed on. The group might have been able to seize more fertile land, even though some of its members were killed. Another group whose members were unwilling to take such risks might find its hold on natural resources weakened. In the end, even those who preserved their lives may find their future, and that of their children, at grave risk. A sociobiologist might still insist that this is all intelligible because of the way the biological interests of the *individual* are affected. The fact of a group flourishing or failing is still only important in so far as its members flourish or face difficulties. The group is nothing more than the individuals making it up. Even when we talk of one group succeeding and another failing, we only mean, it may be maintained, that the members of each are enabled or not to obtain biological advantage. The reason for this is quite simply that groups do not have children, but only individuals do.

Group selection may be normally unacceptable as a biological theory, but there may be good social grounds for the encouragement of altruism. It may be dangerous to reify societies, but nevertheless there is a sense in which societies teaching altruism may do better than those which do not. What is meant by that is that the members of an unselfish society will gain advantages which those in a selfish one will not. The sociobiologist may still be worried that an altruistic action which is not done for a relative or with the expectation of any favour to be returned cannot be explained genetically. Indeed it may not when there is competition between different kinds of genes, but there may be good reasons for the encouragement of such actions in a culture.

Sociobiologists are often tempted to conclude that what cannot be explained genetically must be of little account. As a result, they fail to take seriously the possibility of genuine altruism towards non-relatives. E. O. Wilson is even forced to say of Mother Teresa in Calcutta that she was motivated by basically selfish concerns.[28] She was committed to the supremacy of Christianity over its rivals, he thinks, and was no doubt striving for personal immortality. Altruism of this notable kind to people of a different race who can have no way of repaying the kindness done to them may seem puzzling from the standpoint of strict evolutionary theory. Yet the very fact that complicated beliefs, such as those of a religion, are invoked makes clear the relevance of cultural considerations. Human beings are not merely under the influence of genes. The very fact that Lumsden and Wilson now talk of 'gene-culture co-evolution' emphasizes that in the long run cultural considerations can have as great an effect on genetic development as the other way round.

A culture in which unselfishness is extolled as a virtue, and selfishness and nepotism frowned upon, will be radically different in its effects from one where selfishness is held to be the norm. Some sociobiologists have proved so enamoured of a simple form of their theory that they have dared to suggest that everyone is really selfish, even if we have been programmed by our genes not to realize this.[29] Much more likely is the possibility of cultures inclining humans away from what may have been an inherited tendency to selfishness. Our biology may encourage us to care only for ourselves and our relatives. What we are taught in the form of culture may grant a different vision, as for instance in the injunction to love our neighbour, even if he or she is not a relative and is in no position to repay our kindness. Sociobiology may explain why this is often difficult for us, and why we may just not want to because of our genetic inheritance. Saying it is an impossible demand requires further argument, since this involves denying that culture is a formative influence on human behaviour, although paradoxically the very denial might have the effect of making people more selfish. Unselfish behaviour has been advocated in many cultures, and if it is impossible a significant element of culture has been exposed as a sham. The real influences on human beings, it seems, must lie elsewhere.

If we accept this conclusion, we have to face the question why this kind of ineffective exhortation should have ever been incorporated in culture. Why do we possess forms of culture at all? The mere ability to create culture certainly gave humanity an evolutionary advantage. It is only a short step from this to seeing that different cultures may themselves vary in their biological effects on their members. Even if some individuals may do worse by being unselfish, the benefits to the majority will outweigh the disadvantages. The culture is not sowing the seeds of its own destruction by encouraging all its members on a course which is destructive of reproductive advantage. Sociobiological misgivings about this can only arise if it is assumed that even the content of effective moral exhortation has to be under genetic control, so that genes encouraging altruism have to be passed on if altruism is to be advocated. Yet this is to reduce the cultural level to the genetic and to refuse to accept that a form of culture can be passed on irrespective of whether genes encourage it or not. In fact, it seems quite likely that the purpose of many cultural norms is to restrain natural human impulses rather than merely to reflect them. The genetic constitution of humans was formed in conditions very different from those of contemporary civilized society, and many societies may find that human nature is not the best guide as to how to co-operate in modern circumstances.

Notes

1   See my *The Shaping of Man*, 1983.
2   M. Harris, *Cultural Materialism*, 1979, p. 127.
3   Ibid., p. 57.
4   Ibid., p. 123.
5   B. Malinowski, *A Scientific Theory of Culture*, 1944, p. 116.
6   Ibid., p. 38.
7   Ibid., p. 206.
8   Ibid., p. 148.
9   E. Durkheim, *The Elementary Forms of the Religious Life*, 1971, p. 419.
10 Ibid., p. 427.
11 R. Merton, *Social Theory and Social Structure*, 1968, p. 114.
12 G. C. Homans, 'Bringing Men Back In', in Ryan, *The Philosophy of Social Explanation*, 1973, p. 55.
13 R. P. Dore, 'Function and Cause', in Ryan 1973, p. 67.
14 P. and B. Berger, *The War over the Family*, 1983, p. 202.
15 Ibid., p. 203.
16 Ibid., p. 144.
17 Ibid., p. 90.
18 e.g. by E. O. Wilson, *On Human Nature*, 1978.
19 C. Lumsden and E. Wilson, *Genes, Mind and Culture*, 1981, p. 13.
20 Ibid., p. 13.
21 See P. Van den Berghe, 'Human Inbreeding Avoidance: Culture in Nature', *Behavioral and Brain Sciences*, 6, 1983.

22 Ibid., p. 97.
23 Harris, *Cultural Materialism*, p. 132.
24 Ibid., p. 80.
25 Van den Berghe, 'Human Inbreeding Avoidance', p. 99.
26 Ibid., p. 98.
27 C. Lumsden and E. Wilson, *Promethean Fire*, 1983, p. 30.
28 Wilson, *On Human Nature*, p. 165.
29 e.g. R. D. Alexander, 'The Search for a General Theory of Behavior', *Behavioral Science*, 20, 1975.

9

Sociobiology and Determinism

The 'Leash' Principle

I accepted in the last chapter that much of human culture is not under direct genetic control, and have remarked that social scientists feel that they can safely ignore biological theory. It even looks as if cultural norms may be so far from being under genetic control that their purpose might sometimes be to control the desires that still are. How does this match with Lumsden and Wilson's view that the genes hold culture on a leash? Van den Berghe has enlarged on this by picturing genetic evolution as a man taking a dog for a walk, with the dog representing culture. The dog has a certain limited range of choice about its direction, but can soon be pulled back by its master. Van den Berghe comments:

> What many social scientists have long tried to do is to explain the movements of the dog by rubbing out the man and the leash. What the sociobiological paradigm is suggesting is that we regard man, leash and dog as an integrated system in which the motions of the dog are always to be explained by interrelated motions of the man and the dog, mediated by the leash. What we can legitimately argue about is whether we are dealing with a Great Dane held by a toddler, a Chihuahua held by a Sumo wrestler, or some more likely pairing in between.[1]

On occasions, the dog can pull the man, instead of the man controlling the dog, and this accords with the contention of Lumsden and Wilson that culture can itself create an environment in which genetic evolution can take place. Nevertheless, as the leash principle indicates, sociobiology maintains that genetic evolution is the predominant factor in our understanding of culture. The dog does not usually take the master for a walk.

Natural selection does not merely provide the stage on which the drama can take place, but it influences the course of the play. A sociobiologist must cast doubt on the wisdom of social scientists who ignore the findings of biology. The fact that human cultures can only vary within limits provides an underpinning for our assumption that we can understand the members of alien cultures.[2] Cultural relativism is challenged by human sociobiology, since all cultures can ultimately be measured by the success or failure with which they respond to the basic human genetic constitution. The leash is slack enough to allow for different kinds of cultural development, but if some serve the demands of human biology badly it can be sharply pulled in.

We have already seen how a culture which does not allow its members to survive and have healthy offspring will not itself survive long. No culture could advocate youthful suicide and last, while a tribe too given to making war may find itself exterminated. More complicated elements in culture may have more subtle effects. Even living in high-rise flats might have an eventual biological cost. Certainly the type of diet favoured by a culture is relevant to its survival. Nevertheless, whatever the validity of particular examples, different forms of culture do make a biological impact, which will eventually become manifest. Cultures can become so debilitated that they change or die, while other cultures may allow their members to flourish, and in consequence become more firmly rooted.

Is nothing, then, beyond the scope of sociobiology? E. O. Wilson thinks not. While accepting that religion appears to offer the greatest challenge to sociobiology, he tries to show that even that can be explained in terms of its biological effects.[3] He finds it difficult to see how religion could be such a widespread human phenomenon if it had not proved advantageous to people. His conclusion is that 'the highest forms of religious practice . . . can be seen to confer biological advantage.'[4] He suggests in a quaint phrase that 'above all they congeal identity'. In this he is following functionalist explanations of religion, such as that of Durkheim, although he differs from functionalism in so far as he is not talking of societies or systems, but traces the benefits of religion back to the individual biological organism. There are clear reductionist and materialist overtones. He argues that 'sociobiology can account for the very origin of mythology by the principle of natural selection acting on the genetically evolving material structure of the human brain'.[5]

The biological effects of religion can be examined by sociobiology, just as the social sciences can investigate its social effects. Some religions could go beyond the limits of what is biologically acceptable, by advocating complete celibacy or mass suicide. Such positions cannot be maintained for very long. Conversely, just because of the central biological importance of such questions as abortion, contraception and the regulation of sexual relations, religion could be expected to offer guidance on such matters. Religious rules which adversely affected the biological fitness of individuals must eventually be changed. Any religion would itself begin to lose ground if its members failed to flourish. From a theological standpoint, indeed, this is not surprising. It would be strange indeed if any religion which preached the love of God for humans championed a code of conduct which in the long run actually harmed its adherents.

Wilson, however, is *only* concerned with questions of biological advantage. He brushes aside questions of the truth and falsity of beliefs to the extent that, like some functionalists, he classifies together systems of belief which directly contradict each other. Yet, once a role is given to culture and the contents of consciousness, one cannot deny that truth matters and concentrate attention on the biological consequences of belief. Wilson even argues that, as in the case of communist commitment, 'the blinding force of religious allegiance can operate in the absence of theology'.[6] Even if we suppose that communism and different religions can ultimately have similar biological effects, this only illustrates the fact that biology, even in the guise of sociobiology, can only have a limited usefulness. The role of culture has to be emphasized because the substance of beliefs is important. The basic question must be not whether a religion is biologically advantageous – any more than whether it has been produced by a particular kind of society or fulfils an important social role – but whether it is true or not.

Sociobiology and reductionist views of culture themselves involve beliefs that are entertained for reasons, good or bad. They are themselves part of the variegated pattern of human culture, and are not held merely as a result of some biological process. Dismissal of questions of truth and falsity can only be accomplished from the standpoint of a position that implicitly claims truth regardless of the ultimate biological consequences.

What sociobiology can assert is that, however widely human reasoning may range, its results as laid down in culture must interact with human genes.

Opposition to Sociobiology

Many would hold that the existence of sociobiology as a discipline itself demonstrates that society is the major influence on human reasoning. They would say that it merely applies the presuppositions of the society which produced it. There is a remarkable similarity between some of the basic assumptions made in economics about the nature of human rationality and those made about the behaviour of biological organisms in sociobiology. Both are attracted by the view that forms of egoism constitute the most intelligible type of behaviour. The economist considers that people merely seek to satisfy their desires or fulfil their preferences, and can easily slip into thinking that these must be selfish. Indeed, there appears to be no reason why they should not be. The sociobiologist thinks that all action must ultimately further biological fitness. Both find the spectacle of people deliberately going against their own interests to help others difficult to explain. Sociobiologists tend to dismiss pure altruism towards non-relatives as an impossible state of affairs. They sometimes cloak this by redefining the term, but their notion of reciprocal altruism would be familiar to any economist espousing egoism.

The sociobiologist would partially deal with the 'free-rider problem' by assuming that evolution inhibits animals (or humans) from helping a second time those who have deliberately refused to return favours. This presupposes the ability to remember, and so it is not an account that could be applied to lower forms of animals. It is easy to see how resentment towards those who receive advantages without contributing may be natural. There would have been an evolutionary advantage in encouraging co-operation and in refusing to allow some to benefit from the contribution of others. Parasitical behaviour has to be restrained, since parasites would flourish at the expense of those contributing, because they would receive benefits without the cost of taking their share of the burdens. All the individuals in the group would begin to be weakened, because the parasites would become too numerous to receive proper benefits, and there would not be enough contributors left. It could recover its equilibrium only if those contributing tried to ensure that only those who gave their labour received advantages. A minority might always try to exploit the situation, and research into animal behaviour shows how this can happen. Nevertheless this type of reasoning shows how evolution, through natural selection, can restrain the development of uncooperative behaviour.

Thus the problem which economists raise at the level of what it is rational to do is dealt with by sociobiologists at the level of the evolution of social behaviour. Their perspectives, however, are remarkably similar, since each sees society in exclusively individualistic terms. The problem then is inevitably raised as to why individuals should contribute to society. Since society can be built up only by the efforts of individuals, explanations have to be found as to why it is in their interests to strive to this end. The egoist flavour is also significant. Not only is a community conceived as being constituted by atoms, but the atoms tend to be colliding with each other. There is bound to be conflict because each person is concerned only with his or her own interests, whether consciously or not.

One of the interesting aspects of animal behaviour is ritual conflict, where animals fight to find a winner but rarely mortally wound each other. They thus achieve the benefit of conflict without incurring the losses. A willingness to retreat can clearly be passed on genetically as the animal is likely to produce offspring on another occasion even if it fails to mate on this one. An 'all or nothing' strategy, however, is likely to result in an animal dying before it can pass on its genes to its offspring. If human behaviour is looked at in this way, in terms simply of costs and benefits to the agent, the result will be a picture of a strongly competitive society. It may even appear that some people will naturally 'know their place'. Social relations will be described in terms suitable for the behaviour of stags in the rutting season. Each individual has to adopt the strategy which will gain the most advantage. The strong will grab what they can, and the weak will try to pick up whatever crumbs are left. Such an account may be appropriate for animal behaviour, which is not complicated by the intervention of culture. For example, one zoologist writes about the current stress on individual strategies in animal behaviour:

The emphasis is now on selfish individuals competing to maximize their gene contribution to future generations. If some males are attracting females by calling, then we now expect to find other males parasiting their efforts and behaving as satellites.[7]

He goes on to give an example of how old male elephant seals, as well as red deer, can fight successfully to defend groups of females. Younger, smaller males that cannot hope to obtain a harem for themselves 'hang around the edge of the harem and attempt to sneak copulations'. Among animals, strategies can evolve which trade on the behaviour of the majority, but checks and balances have had to develop to ensure that the underlying 'selfishness' of each animal is not disastrously destructive in its consequences.

There are obvious dangers in extrapolating from the animal world to human social reality, but critics of sociobiology are making a more profound point. The nub of the matter is where the categories of sociobiology come from. Their similarity with those of economics might arouse a suspicion that they are derived from the economic conditions of the society in which sociobiologists happen to live. Might they not even be projecting those categories on to animal societies? Moreover, the allegation continues, are they not then using the apparent types of animal behaviour as an actual justification for what happens in Western capitalist society? If certain forms of behaviour are made to appear 'natural', nothing will be done to change them, because it seems that nothing can be done.

This criticism typically comes from those Marxists who are able to demonstrate to their satisfaction that, far from being science, sociobiology is mere ideology. It is seen as disguising the true conditions of capitalist society and serving as a legitimation of the existing structures of society. Indeed, Marxists have no alternative but to view sociobiology as a product of capitalism, since their emphasis on holism cannot coexist with the rampant individualism of sociobiology. Paradoxically, however, both espouse different versions of materialism.

It could be significant that sociobiology originated in America. Perhaps the conditions of their society, with its emphasis on the individual, will predispose many Americans to look favourably on the discipline. That is a sociological question, and unless we are ready to embrace relativism we should hold it to be strictly irrelevant to questions of truth. The roots of sociobiology are very firmly in biological theory, since it is above all an application of Darwinism to social behaviour. Mixed with the insights of modern genetics, this produces the very emphasis on individual selection which many find objectionable. No doubt some are tempted to grant that animal behaviour can be understood in sociobiological terms, but refuse to accept that this has any bearing on human behaviour. The distinctiveness of human society could then be guaranteed. Many in the social sciences will make just such a stand, and claim the irrelevance of biology. Unless, however, social science is willing to make use of biology it is going to be completely cut off from the physical sciences. Instead of merely adopting the *methods* of the physical sciences, the social sciences may well find themselves considerably helped by using some of the *knowledge* gained by biology. Understanding those human needs and interests which have developed through natural selection will help us to understand the societies which have grown up to deal with them.

Sociobiology has sometimes tended to make extravagant claims to have superseded the social sciences. This view is particularly attractive to those who believe that the physical sciences set the only standard for knowledge.[8] As a result, social and cultural categories have to be reduced to terms which exclude reference to anything mental. The meaning of actions to the agents has to be ignored. It is hardly surprising that sociobiology has aroused fierce opposition for its uncompromising reductionism. The acceptance by Lumsden and Wilson that mind and culture have to be taken into account appears at first to remove this spectre: 'Culture is not just a passive entity. It is a force so powerful in its own right that it drags the genes along. Working as a rapid mutator, it throws new variations into the teeth of natural selection.'[9]

This appears to allow plenty of scope for the study of culture in its own right, rather than as a by-product thrown up by our genes. Advocates of 'gene-culture co-evolution' must be wary, though, of laying too great an emphasis on the effects of culture on genes. Culture may have had an effect on human genetic evolution over many thousands of years, particularly if the environment was stable enough. It seems very dangerous, however, to correlate cultural variation with genetic variation in the contemporary world. Mobility and intermarriage over the centuries serve to keep the human gene pool from being partitioned into separate compartments. Significantly Lumsden and Wilson themselves admit this and give as an example the Indian caste system, which I referred to earlier. They say that, despite its rigidity and the fact that it has persisted for two thousand years, it is maintained by cultural conventions. They continue:

So far as is known (although the matter has never been thoroughly studied), members of different castes differ from one another only slightly in blood type and other measurable anatomical and physiological traits.[10]

It seems safe to assume that much the same mixture of genes is likely to be present in any human society. Sociobiology seems to emphasize the essential oneness of humanity, rather than giving comfort to any brand of racialism. Cultural differences will never become very great before they are sharply pulled back by the leash. They are, however, real enough, and cannot be explained by biologists. No doubt the interaction of the same genes with different environments will suffice to explain some differences. The thesis of 'gene-culture co-evolution' entails, however, that some cultural differences are inexplicable in biological terms.

Determinism

The assumption that causal explanation is the only proper kind of explanation can lead to a desire for a simpler scheme of causal explanation. Sociobiology seemed to offer just such a scheme with its original tendency to favour a biological determinism which claimed that everything can be explained in terms of genes. Others look for causal explanations in other directions and adopt some form of environmental determinism, looking to society or economic systems as their source of explanation. Marvin Harris, for instance writes:

> In its commitment to the rules of scientific method, cultural materialism opposes strategies that deny the legitimacy or the feasibility of scientific accounts of human behavior – for example, humanist claims that there is no determinism in human affairs.[11]

Assuming that determinism is the thesis that every event has a cause, a belief in determinism embraces the claim that all human behaviour is causally explicable. Even the adoption of the belief in determinism is the product of some causal chain, and those who advocate determinism have to accept that their own commitment to it is itself causally explicable. Determinism is thus a global doctrine making very strong claims. They are metaphysical since they go far beyond any available empirical evidence. A belief in determinism may even have been an important factor in scientific progress, since one will never discover causal chains unless one is prepared to look for them. For that reason metaphysical determinism is sometimes distinguished from the methodological sort. One can look for causes while not necessarily believing that they must be there to be discovered. Sometimes apparent scientific difficulty may stem from alleged indeterminism in the world. Battles have raged in quantum mechanics because of apparent indeterminism at the sub-atomic level. The problem has been whether quantum mechanical description has to be regarded as incomplete because it still allows for indeterminism.[12] Is that because of our continuing ignorance or because of the nature of the reality being investigated? There is always a difficulty, since saying it is because of the nature of the reality may mean we give up too easily in our scientific investigations. On the other hand, refusing to allow for indeterminism may involve a stubborn refusal to see reality as it is.

These considerations are equally vital when the reality being studied is human rather than merely physical. Does an inability to predict action stem from present ignorance, which the onward march of science will rectify, or does it demonstrate something about human freedom? Since all we are certain of is our failure to make successful predictions, our answer will depend on our metaphysical presuppositions. Any social science which wishes to model itself on the physical sciences is likely to be deterministic (even though modern physics is not), since it wants to produce firm explanations of action. It will not allow for any unpredictability in principle, since it holds a much stronger thesis than the commonplace view that human action can be influenced by all kinds of factors. No one doubts that biological or environmental factors can incline people to some courses of action rather than others. They may argue about which are the most influential, but everyone would agree that human action does not take place in a vacuum. It takes place in a particular social and cultural context and is perhaps constrained by human biology. What is controversial is whether these factors, taken together or severally, are sufficient to explain human behaviour or just illuminate tendencies.

The argument between sociobiologists and their opponents has to some extent cut across the issue of determinism, with one side tracing the springs of human action to genes and the other to our social being. Yet both are happy to talk in terms of causation and to apply scientific categories of explanation to human behaviour. Their disagreement is not so much over determinism but over the kind of causes which should be invoked as explanations in human contexts. We have already come across instances of specialists who are ready to claim omniscience for their discipline, with little left for other disciplines. Social scientists become redundant if biology can explain all human behaviour. Conversely, biology is not needed to illuminate social behaviour if the social sciences can give adequate explanations on their own. It is one of the attractions of the notion of 'gene-culture co-evolution' that it may leave room for both biological and social scientists. The purposes of culture can be a fit topic for biological research, while its independence of direct genetic control could allow the social scientist to study it in its own terms. Yet at the same time a link is established between the physical and human sciences. They can complement each other, without isolating themselves for each other.

Does sociobiology, though, have to be deterministic in its assumptions? At first sight a reductionist programme attempting to explain human behaviour in terms of the evolution of the human brain is thoroughly determinist. It assumes that the physical structure of the brain can provide a satisfactory explanation for what people do. Lumsden and Wilson do seem very ready to slide from the contents of the mind to the structure of the brain. They refer, for instance, to 'the association between symbols in the brain'. In defining 'symbol' they say that 'the physical basis of a symbol in the brain is thought to be a network or cluster of neurons'.[14] Yet symbols are part of the contents of minds and are associated with questions of meaning. Locating them in the brain turns them into something very different. Lumsden and Wilson talk about node-link structures, and it is never clear whether these are part of the content of memory or part of the physical brain. If they have been directly fashioned through evolution, they are going to be the latter, but it is important for a thesis about culture that they are the former. It is very tempting for anyone wanting to make the leap from genes to the meaningful contents of culture to minimize the distinction. The problem is highlighted by the fact that Lumsden and Wilson define 'node' as 'an abstract representation of a symbol, or elementary unit in the brain'. It does matter, however, which it is, since the mental grasp of a symbol is, on many views, utterly distinct from whatever processes occur in the brain. Refusing to notice the distinction is in itself tantamount to reducing the social to the physical sciences.

Nowhere is the reduction of the mental to the physical clearer than when Lumsden and Wilson refer to sex and deny that its main purpose is to give pleasure. Saying the reverse is the case, they remark that 'the feeling of pleasure in the brain makes the performance of sex more likely'.[15] While it is possible to accept their thesis that the pleasurable nature of sex has evolved to encourage reproduction, it is hard not to observe that, wherever pleasure may be felt, it is certainly not in the brain. Once again they confuse the contents of one's mind, in this case felt sensations, with the brain processes which may underlie them. They can be identified only as a result of an explicit materialist theory, and Lumsden and Wilson do refer approvingly to the central-state identity theory of mind, which identifies particular mental events with particular physiological events in the brain.[16] They are thus able to say:

> The mind springs from a machinery of neurons created according to the genetic blueprint, but it grows in an environment created by the pre-existing culture, which is a particular history embedded in the memories and archives of those who transmit it.[17]

Culture is interpreted in a thoroughly individualist manner, existing only in so far as it can be identified with particular brain deposits, or in archives which will then be referred to by individuals. It becomes a matter for psychologists or even neurophysiologists, so that its development and transmission would appear to be totally explicable by physical laws. Their reductionism leaves little room for any notions of culture or of mind which can themselves act on the brain as well as be constrained by the physical characteristics of the brain.

Lumsden and Wilson mention several principles which they believe are inherent in science. They insist first of all that 'all domains of human life, including ethics, have a physical basis in the brain and are part of human biology'.[18] They go on to say that 'none is exempt from analysis in the mode of the natural sciences'. This seems consistent with their reductionist and materialist assumptions, and appears to leave little room for the social sciences. They even describe sociobiology as 'the embattled spearhead of the natural-science advance'. Yet they also wish to emphasize the role of mind and culture in ways which suggest that a crude reductionism is inadequate. One of their other principles, which is supposed to be inherent in human science, is as follows: 'The biases in mental development are only biases: the influence of the genes, even when very strong, does not destroy free will.'[19] They insist that 'the genes create and sustain the capacity for conscious choice and decision'.

Sociobiology and Freedom

It is usual to regard a belief in free will as incompatible with determinism, even though attempts are sometimes made to show their compatibility. There is normally a clear distinction between those who hold that all explanations of human action must ultimately be causal and invoke scientific laws and those who rely on conceptions of rationality, believing that rational action does not have a cause. Arguments certainly rage over whether reasons can be causes, but ultimately it seems that choices and decisions are either themselves at the end of a causal chain or they are not. One's confidence in science to explain human behaviour will stem very largely from how far one views people as in principle predictable in what they do. There may be statistical regularities, but many scientists would hope to explain individual action as well as general trends. Lumsden and Wilson appear to want the advantage of being on both sides of the argument. Whatever they mean by 'free will', their reference to the concept cuts right across their desire to explain culture in terms of the working of the brain. It suggests that culture may be partly the result of free decisions by individuals as well as of the programmed processes of their brains. It certainly does not seem possible easily to talk of choice and will, at the same time as invoking neurophysiological concepts. Certainly a very sophisticated theory would be needed to harmonize the two, even if that were possible.

It is difficult to affirm any form of rigid reductionism with consistency, not least because of the difficulty of applying it to itself. The theory seems to demand a validity which it should not lay claim to if it is itself to be identified with the predictable workings of particular brains. Yet on this issue hangs the fate of the social sciences. If some of the remarks quoted are correct, the neurophysiologist will be able to explain the origin and nature of culture better than any social scientist. If, however, it is accepted that culture may be a powerful force in its own right, acting on brains as well as being produced by them, it is unsatisfactory to identify it with brain processes; it must be studied in its own right. Even if it is accepted that culture can only affect individuals through the functioning of their brains, that does not mean that research into the nature of the brain is a sophisticated form of social science. The fact that the characteristics of the human brain provide a necessary condition for the development of culture, and may predispose humans to some types of culture rather than others, still does not add up to an argument for the identification of the two. Ideas and other contents of the mind may have a more positive role than as mere concomitants of physical processes.

Lumsden and Wilson are quite happy to posit the independence of each other of genes and culture. It would be impossible to talk of them 'co-evolving' if culture could be reduced to genes. The trouble seems to come with the identification of culture with memories laid down physically in brains and with physical 'archives'. Thus when they say that people 'are neither genetically determined nor culturally determined' they continue by claiming 'they are something in between'.[20] They are still able to think in terms of physical determinism, and what is at issue for them is whether the springs of human behaviour lie in genetic programmes or environmental stimuli. Both will be understood in terms of the functioning of the brain.

The role of the social sciences is created through the assumption that such categories as the social and the cultural cannot be adequately studied in the terms appropriate to the natural sciences. The difficulty about attempting to build a bridge between the physical and social sciences is illustrated only too clearly by the work of Lumsden and Wilson. Once it is accepted that biology is relevant to understanding the contours of human society, it seems hard to avoid being dominated by biological and, ultimately, physical categories. The quest for the unity of the physical and social sciences often seems to end in reductionism, and the jettisoning of whatever concepts cannot be dealt with by physical science. The alternative seems to be the total independence of the two types of science. Unless, however, the social sciences are able to develop different methods, they are reduced to being the poor relation, never quite able to live up to the rigorous standards demanded.

Yet the sociobiological concept of 'gene-culture co-evolution' may suggest a way in which the discoveries of the natural sciences can be used to illuminate the social sciences. The recognition that biology puts constraints on the kind of society which can be sustained for long is important, and it is also crucial to realize that human nature does influence the choices made in societies. The biggest single contribution which sociobiology can make to the social sciences is to give some empirical content to the notion of human nature. It has been all too apparent that the study of society can only result in a self-destroying relativism if the concept is not given any substance.

Lumsden and Wilson are themselves full of confidence about the prospects for the scientific study of human nature, claiming that it seems the appropriate way 'to create value-free social sciences': 'When the roots of ethics and motivation are fully exposed, political science, economics and sociobiology can be more easily uncoupled from the genetic and cultural biases of the specialists who originate them.'[21] This is all part of the view that, if we can only discover the forces controlling us, we shall somehow be able to control them. If we only know the values which bias us, we shall be able to shake ourselves free of them. Yet it by no means follows that this is so, if some form of determinism is assumed. Knowledge may be itself a determining factor, but, on the other hand, knowing the evolutionary origin of our taste for sweet things may not stop us wanting them. The point about genetically determined biases is that we have to make the best of them. We may not always give in to them, but we cannot eradicate them at will. The whole message of the doctrine of 'gene-culture co-evolution' is that culture ignores the demands of our genes at its peril. Sociobiology may help us to understand the situation we are in, but it gives us little power to alter it (unless we have sinister plans for genetic engineering). Knowing we are selfish does not of itself give us the power to cure our selfishness. Similarly, mere knowledge of cultural bias may not enable us to alter our culture. We may not want to change it if our desires themselves have been produced by it. If, for instance, sociobiology is a typical product of a capitalist society, accepting this will not necessarily spur sociobiologists to purge their work of prejudice and bias. They may either shrug their shoulders and reflect that they cannot help being what they have been conditioned to be, or they could give up sociobiology completely if they concluded that it was *merely* the expression of a culture and not genuine science.

The opposition between a 'scientific' study of human nature and value-laden social sciences is in any case a false one. We have already seen that the aim should be not to create value-free social sciences, but to ensure that the values inherent in them are appropriate for their subject-matter. The question is how far sociobiology can illuminate human nature, and how far its own assumptions and values result in a misleading picture. The more ambitious it becomes and the less room it allows for the social sciences in their own right, the more suspect it becomes. If, however, it makes modest claims and recognizes that it cannot hope to explain all the quirks of human society, then it can provide a valuable underpinning to the social sciences. They themselves must use the insights of the physical sciences into human nature, because that is the foundation of society.

Social scientists have themselves often made the same kind of global claims that sociobiologists make. Both claim to hold the fundamental insight into the explanation for human behaviour, and as a result each has seen itself in competition with the other. Lumsden and Wilson saw the problem as being one of either genetic determinism or cultural determinism, but their flirtation with the concept of free will reintroduces a further element into the argument. Perhaps human societies cannot ultimately be fully understood by any brand of scientist, since the quest for causal explanations may prove fruitless long before all human behaviour is explained. Since arguing for the reality of human freedom, even of a limited kind, restricts the scope of social science, many social scientists may not take kindly to the possibility. Yet the fact remains that the inability of the social sciences to make exact predictions may not stem from any faults in the techniques being adopted, but have everything to do with the nature of what is being investigated. If we do possess a significant degree of freedom to choose what we do, an increased knowledge of the forces inclining us to one course of action rather than another will give us greater ability to control our fate. Lumsden and Wilson may believe that increased knowledge gives greater independence, but this can only be true if we are free to resist or control the basic tendencies of our nature. Their view of the power of sociobiology to bring enlightenment and an enhanced ability to control our lives itself depends on an assumption concerning human freedom which must limit the scope of that discipline.

Human Freedom

The possibility of human freedom is not just a complication for sociobiology; it haunts the social sciences. Very often the problem is dealt with by being ignored. For example, W. G. Runciman, writing on social theory, says: 'the practising sociologist, anthropologist or historian can safely disregard the suggestion that any behaviour which he has observed, or has been reported to him, is beyond the reach of causal explanation altogether.'[22] He not only remarks that otherwise there would be no point in engaging in research but also flatly asserts that there is no convincing argument that any event 'does not depend on any antecedent condition at all holding true'. Runciman suggests that practising social scientists should sidestep 'old debates' about the freedom of the will 'with all possible speed'.[23] His view is that social science must assume that human decisions *are* 'explicable and not merely justifiable'. In other words, causal explanations can be elicited. He admits that this presupposition itself cannot be conclusively demonstrated, but he is clearly still under the spell of positivist assumptions about the world. He refers to 'the ultimate presupposition of all science, that everything is indeed explicable'.[24] It would follow from this that, to be successful, social science must itself search for causal explanation.

Once, though, it is accepted that human social reality may be different from physical reality, causal explanation seems more dubious as a goal. One point often made is that, whereas attempts at predicting aspects of physical reality do not normally have any effect on that reality, predictions about human behaviour can easily themselves alter the course of events, assuming they become known. Even in the case of sub-atomic particles there is a problem about the way in which the mere act of measuring the state of a system can itself alter the system. There is the added factor of human consciousness, in the case of the social sciences. Humans can take account of predictions in deciding what to do, and can indeed even set out deliberately to falsify them. A candidate in an oral examination is said to have been questioned about free will, and one examiner claimed that they all knew he was not free to walk out of the examination that minute. Whereupon the candidate immediately got up and left, thus proving the point he wished to make. Knowledge of what other people expect us to do can induce us to alter our behaviour, sometimes out of sheer perversity.

Whatever might be said about the constraints on human freedom, human action must be distinguished from merely bodily movements. The former involves choice and decision, whereas the latter, like an involuntary twitch, just happen to us. Many argue that this itself is sufficient to distinguish human action from what can be predicted by the physical sciences. The bank clerk threatened by a gunman may decide there is no reasonable alternative to handing over the money. He is, however, in a significantly different position if a bank robber grabs hold of him and forces him to do what he has been refusing to. In the former case he is an agent, but in the latter his body is no longer under his own control. Many determinist views appear to ignore the distinction.

They might discriminate between different types of causes, but all seem equally compelling. The upshot is that the influences of society can seem as inexorable as the physical force exerted on the bank clerk. It is easy to drift into a position according to which impersonal forces at work in society hold individuals at their mercy. This is not unlike the position attacked by Sir Karl Popper and which he dubs 'historicism':

> I mean by 'historicism' an approach to the social sciences which assumes that *historical prediction* is their principal aim, and which assumes that this aim is attainable by discovering the 'rhythms' or the 'patterns', the 'laws' or the 'trends' that underlie the evolution of history.[25]

Popper, however, is still ready to embrace the notion of sociological laws or hypotheses analogous to those in the natural sciences. While admitting that their existence has often been doubted, he gives examples, claiming that they provide a parallel to physical laws.[26] Antony Flew has commented that Popper's suspicions ought to have been aroused when he found that he was having to provide his own candidates, and certainly the examples do not have the well-known character of physical laws as laid out in a physics textbook.[27] Popper gives as one example: 'You cannot have full employment without inflation.' No doubt belief in this as a law will have significant political consequences, but it is hard to see why it should be a law. Flew himself finds it the 'most persuasive' of Popper's examples, since there will tend to be a measure of wage-push inflation in conditions of full employment, but he comments 'however strong and well-grounded our confidence that we will never in fact suppress our unrelenting desire to better the condition of ourselves and our families, we do nevertheless all know equally well that we could.'

The point is that, although we may be only too ready to exploit economic conditions to our temporary advantage, according this commentary on human short-sightedness the status of a law ignores one simple fact. If we were all ready to sacrifice short-term gain, we might all benefit in the longer term by avoiding the bad consequences of inflation. The tendency of economics to assume the worst about human selfishness makes this state of affairs hard for some economists to comprehend. Yet inflation only accompanies full employment because of people's reluctance to accept less money when they know they could obtain more. This is far from being irrational if the wider consequences of wage-push inflation are taken into account. More to the present point, it is certainly not impossible for anyone to choose less money, rather than more, and it is perfectly intelligible to act with one's eye on the longer term and even on the general good. The situation is not unlike the prisoners' dilemma. It is apparently rational for each wage earner to try to obtain higher wages whenever possible. After all, if you do, I must attempt to keep up, but, if you do not, I have the chance of getting ahead. This kind of reasoning leads to runaway inflation. The paradox is that giving up thinking of one's own interests will not only be in the general interest but may actually prove to be in one's interest too.

It is possible to make generalizations about human nature, relying upon the insights of sociobiology. The issue, however, concerns not what people are likely to do but what they must do. Water does not generally boil at 100 °C at sea level, or have a tendency to do so; it always does. A comparable law about human social behaviour would seem to have to deal with comparable regularities. We are all imprudent and selfish at times, but the opinion we each hold that we could do better and that we are capable of improving need not be mere illusion. Perhaps reference to sea level in the case of the boiling point of water concedes the conditional nature of laws. Other factors such as the purity of the water will also be relevant. A law would maintain that water boils at 100 °C in certain conditions. May not conditions be similarly specified in the case of human action? A law about wage-push inflation will then state among its conditions that people are going to look after their short-term interests. If they do not always behave in this way, the law fails to apply. It is not invalidated. This proposal seems somewhat specious, and may even reduce the law to the truism that people are going to behave selfishly except when they do not. The question is whether humans are normally selfish in the way that water normally boils at 100 °C. Even if laws are interpreted in terms of the constant conjunction of events, as an empiricist such as Hume would have done, it is unduly cynical to assume such widespread selfishness.

Instead of merely correlating phenomena, we may give a different interpretation to laws and think in terms of mechanisms in nature giving rise to the phenomena.[28] In that case sociobiological explanations in terms of human genetic constitution will be relevant, in that an appeal is being made to an apparent cause of much human behaviour. Yet talking in terms of a law would still seem to be claiming too much. The boiling-point of water can be explained in terms of its chemical constitution. Can we explain human selfishness simply in terms of our genetic constitution? That may explain a natural concern for our own interests, but it hardly allows us to make any firm predictions about whether people will act in accordance with those desires or not. We are able to resist selfish impulses, however real they may be.

Some of the other examples Popper gives of putative sociological laws seem curious. One is: 'You cannot introduce agricultural tariffs and at the same time reduce the cost of living.'[29] It may be trivially true that, other things being equal, you cannot reduce the cost of living if you raise tariffs. Presumably, however, Popper means his law to be a substantive one, and it is by no means obvious that a government would not be able to compensate for the raising of tariffs by making reductions in prices of other items. Another of Popper's suggestions is brusquely swept aside by Flew. Popper holds that 'you cannot introduce a political reform without strengthening the opposing forces, to a degree roughly in ratio to the scope of the reform.' Flew says that 'this one is simply not true'.[30] He points out that 'there are plenty of reforms which, once implemented, win the more or less grudging acceptance of those previously opposed'.

To take a final example from Popper's list, it is suggested that 'you cannot in an industrial society organize consumers' pressure groups as effectively as you can organize certain producers' pressure groups'. Since Popper wrote that, the power of consumers' organizations has risen markedly. It may be arguable who possesses the most influence, but it seems questionable that there is anything to prevent consumers' groups being organized as effectively as any other. In this example, as in the others, the proper response always seems to be to go on trying, whatever the obvious obstacles. Human societies are not run according to inexorable laws of nature. The pressures and even the apparent necessities encountered in them are created directly or indirectly by human beings. Because of this they can be influenced and changed by human beings. It is true that people's actions can have unintended and unforeseen consequences, and one function of social science is to show how this fact can affect the nature of society. Popper gives an example of how the liking of some people for mountains and solitude can be explained psychologically. He goes on to point out that 'the fact that, if too many people like the mountains, they cannot enjoy solitude there, is not a psychological fact'.[31] He remarks that this kind of problem is 'at the very root of social theory'. Nevertheless even these unintended consequences do not take on the character of inexorable laws. Popper's attack on historicism should also have led him to be much more suspicious of anything in sociology which appeared to be a law of nature, constraining human freedom.

One reason Popper gave for refusing to accept psychology as the basis of social science was that he believed it was itself 'just one of the social sciences'.[32] He argued that ' "human nature" varies considerably with the social institutions, and its study therefore presupposes an understanding of those institutions.' This brings us back once more to sociobiology, since Popper's assertion is at total variance with the whole basis of that discipline. Anyone who believes that individuals are the creation of their society is bound to be tempted by the notion that social science can discover laws, or at least present hypotheses, which show how society works. Yet, once it is accepted that human nature can sometimes explain the character of social institutions rather than be explained in terms of them, social science can no longer glory in its independence. It must be willing to use the insights of other disciplines, such as sociobiology. More attention has to be given to individuals than to their social context. However powerful an influence the latter may be, the fact remains that the individual's decisions will help to determine the character of the society. While society may not be ignored, the scientific enterprise has to start with the individual. How much human behaviour it can hope to explain depends on the extent of human freedom.

This is perhaps an answer to those who wish to argue against Popper and say that the human and the natural sciences are fundamentally dissimilar. Flew argues this on the basis 'that there could not be any laws of human action as such'.[33] He is right to resist the attempt to construct sociological laws on analogy with physical laws. Yet what if physical science in general, and biological science in particular, can illuminate the springs of human action? In that case, the social sciences would be neither analogous to the physical ones, nor totally dissimilar. Their credibility would depend very largely on their ability to apply the insights of physical science to the functioning of society. To those who fear reductionism, the reply need only be that it is by no means certain that human action can be totally explicable at any level by scientific means.

We seem to be caught between the Scylla of determinism and the Charybdis of being unable to explain anything. On the one hand, every event, including human action, may have a cause, and the job of science seems to be to discover the relevant causal chains, in order to explain past occurrences and predict future ones. On the other hand, if causal

explanation is to be ruled out and prediction thereby becomes impossible, does not that undermine the whole task of the social sciences? The
answer must be that it only does if the social sciences are understood to
be treating the behaviour of humans in the same way as the physical
sciences deal with that of physical objects. It is all too easy to conclude
that they should adopt different techniques and goals, and ignore the
physical sciences completely. The reaction against positivism has too
often meant that social science has felt free not merely to invent its
own methodology but to ignore any advances made by the physical
sciences. Perhaps human sociobiology has pointed out a way of building
the social sciences upon the physical ones without being reduced to
them.

Notes

1 P. Van den Berghe, 'Human Inbreeding Avoidance', *Behavioral and Brain
   Sciences*, 6, 1983, p. 101.
2 See my *The Shaping of Man*, 1982, ch. 9.
3 E. O. Wilson, *On Human Nature*, 1978 p. 175.
4 Ibid., p. 188.
5 Ibid., p. 192.
6 Ibid., p. 184.
7 N. B. Davies, 'Competition for Scarce Resources', in *Current Problems in
   Sociobiology*, 1982, p. 363.
8 See, for example, Alexander Rosenberg, *Sociobiology and the Pre-emption of
   Social Science*, 1981.
9 C. Lumsden and E. Wilson, *Promethean Fire*, 1983, p. 154.
10 Ibid., p. 151.
11 M. Harris, *Cultural Materialism*, 1979, p. ix.
12 See my *Reality at Risk*, 1980, p. 165ff.
13 C. Lumsden and E. Wilson, *Genes, Mind and Culture*, 1981, p. 376.
14 Ibid., p. 383.
15 Lumsden and Wilson, *Promethean Fire*, p. 28.
16 Ibid., p. 76.
17 Ibid., p. 77.
18 Ibid., p. 181.
19 Ibid., p. 182.
20 Ibid., p. 84.
21 Ibid., p. 174.

22 W. G. Runciman, *A Treatise on Social Theory*, 1983, vol. 1, p. 198.

23 Ibid., p. 201.

24 Ibid., p. 183.

25 Karl Popper, *The Poverty of Historicism*, 1957, p. 3.

26 Ibid., p. 62.

27 A. Flew, 'Human Choice and Historical Inevitability', *Journal of Libertarian Studies*, 5, 1981.

28 See, for example, Roy Bhaskar, *A Realist Theory of Science*, 1978.

29 Popper, *Poverty of Historicism*, p. 62.

30 Flew, 'Human Choice', p. 348.

31 Popper, *Poverty of Historicism*, p. 158.

32 Ibid.

33 Flew, 'Human Choice', p. 346.

10

Markets and Social Institutions

Individuals and the Market

As we saw at the end of the last chapter, it is hard to formulate plausible sociological laws. Social scientists may be tempted to assume the truth of determinism in order to justify their search for them. In doing so, they are, they suppose, following the example of the physical sciences in their search for prediction and control. Certainly there was a marked urge through much of the twentieth century to indulge in social planning and 'engineering', whether through architecture and the building of vast housing estates, through the education system and the organization of schools, or through other methods of social control. Yet if one looks at physics as a model for social science, it should become obvious that the assumption that even in the physical world we can really predict and control what goes on is very questionable. It is well known that there is a basic indeterminacy at the quantum level of physical reality that puts limits on how far prediction is in principle possible. Moreover the perils of weather forecasting illustrates that there are other limits to our ability to predict. Chaos theory[1] shows how even great physical upheavals can be sensitive to initial conditions, where differences may be too slight to be measured, but may be catastrophic in their effects. Measurements are of their very nature imperfect, since it may be that precision to one more decimal place might be significant, however seemingly precise a measurement might appear. Indeed it is always going to be impossible in principle for a meteorologist to specify the current weather situation with sufficient exactitude to be sure what will ensue.

All this creates problems in the physical sciences, and arguments can rage in them as to how far everything can be explained in terms of subatomic particles. Might there not be new levels where explanations appropriate to the lower level are inadequate? This applies in physical systems, and we are constantly reminded how similar issues arise about the reduction of the mental to the physical. A strict reductionism will always undermine the social sciences, since, it will be alleged, all the real changes take place at the physical, even the microphysical level. Everything else is mere froth. Social forces, the operation of power in society, social change, all can be explained at the level of individual organisms. Social planners are therefore, it seems, misguided in looking for explanations and causes at the social level. They will plan, and try to control people in the mass, in groups, but, it will be alleged, it is at the individual level that changes occur. Social science becomes a decidedly questionable enterprise, if there are limits on our ability to predict individual behaviour.

These issues have got caught up in wider political debate. The collapse of communism in Eastern Europe was linked to a collapse of faith in central planning. It became clear that it was impossible in principle to have access to sufficient information to be able to plan effectively. It is impossible to oversee the indirect and unintended effect of such planning, even if it is properly directed in the first place. Mistakes in centralized societies become catastrophic. Stories of shoe factories being ordered by mistake to produce shoes for left feet only are no doubt apocryphal, but they illustrate how a single error can infect the whole society. Plans are made because of what the planners deem essential and, unless they are omniscient, they are bound to create some peculiar situations. They do not have the information available to them to plan sensibly. It is partly because the market is regarded as the only reliable source of information of people's choices and preferences that many economists have stressed its central importance. Priorities can be revealed in how much people are prepared to pay, and this is often regarded as a better indicator than the judgement of a central planner about what they need or ought to have, or of a social scientist about the social influences operating.

Once, however, stress is placed on the behaviour of individuals in the marketplace, many will ignore what cannot be given a monetary value or be otherwise quantified. They will concentrate on the preferences of individuals, and pass over the social context in which these preferences may be formed. The preferences are regarded as given, just as each individual is regarded as isolated and not part of a wider group. This approach meshes in with a positivism that is now discredited philosophically, but still has wide influence in the conduct of social science. The concentration on measurable choices and on the interaction of individuals betrays an approach still steeped in the assumptions of a crude empiricism. Yet in so-called 'rational choice theory', with its origins in game theory, the same approach, which we saw gave rise to the prisoners' dilemma, is now applied widely to all the most basic features of society. As one writer puts it, 'the starting point of any rational choice theory of human behaviour is that actors choose options which maximize their benefits as determined by the actors' preferences'.[2]

Religion has always attracted social theorists, but proved recalcitrant to total explanation in terms of social science. It is a fundamental aspect of most, if not all, human societies, and yet makes claims which would go far beyond the nature of human society and even concern a transcendent reality. When the social sciences can get to grips with the fact that religious beliefs are held, it still seems difficult for them to explain their content. That, however, has not prevented rational choice theorists from extending their method of explanation from economics to wider aspects of society, and especially to religion. In this, they provide the polar opposite of an approach such as that of Durkheim who, as we saw in chapter 8, regarded religion as intrinsically social. Rational choice theorists, however, base their analysis on the analogy of the market. They picture religion as a transaction between individuals, with individuals making choices between religions, viewed as commodities. It may seem bizarre that the metaphysical claims enshrined in religions are reduced to questions about the supply of goods, but that basically is what is happening. The idea of individual rational choice is thought to provide a powerful form of explanation which can even underpin social science as such.

We have already seen in chapter 7 some of the problems which a narrow view of rationality, as self-interested action, can produce in economics. The same approach runs into greater problems in a wider context. Yet the ability to generalize from behaviour in a narrow economic context to wider issues about the nature of society demands that individual actions in a real market, buying eggs and potatoes, can be replicated everywhere. They will not just be echoed in the rarefied atmosphere of Wall Street or the London Stock Exchange, but in aspects of human life which may seem totally unrelated to economic concerns. This is why the approach of rational choice theorists to religion is so challenging.

Religion and Rational Choice

One theorist about the character of social interaction in religion, Rodney Stark, makes no apology for using the language of the market. He says that it enables him 'to import some basic insights from economics to help explain religious phenomena'.[3] He goes on to question under what conditions 'religious firms' are able to create a demand. He asks what happens when only 'a few, lazy, religious firms confront the potential religious consumer'. From these questions, he approaches issues about the role of an established church, as compared with the American situation where Christian denominations, and even whole religions, are in competition with each other, in what an economist would judge to be healthy rivalry. The claim indeed is that 'as pluralism grew, levels of the American church membership grew accordingly'.[4] The comparison is drawn between the liveliness of the contemporary American religious scene, and, for instance, the sloth of the established church in eighteenth-century England.

The assumption is that people make rational choices about which religion to adopt and how extensively they will participate in it. Similarly, churches and clergy are viewed as 'making rational responses to the constraints and opportunities found on the religious marketplace'.[5] One aspect of religious commitment that is thereby illuminated is the seemingly paradoxical finding that the more that religions demand of their participants, the more they flourish. The Christian denominations that are declining tend to be those that are liberal and make fewer demands on their members. Rational choice theorists have an explanation for this. According to Iannaccone, 'costly demands mitigate the free rider problems that otherwise undermine a religious group'.[6] In other words, the more a church sets itself apart and asks for particular standards of behaviour, the more are half-hearted members filtered out and wholehearted commitment is encouraged. The more a church merges with the society around it, it is alleged, the less point there will appear to be in belonging to it. The more separate from the rest of society it is, the more its members become involved with its activities to the exclusion of other interests. Cost–benefit analysis thus reveals why strict churches survive and flourish. One either participates with a great deal of commitment or one remains an outsider. There is no room for lukewarm participation or the gaining of social benefits without contributing as well.

There may be some truth in all this, suggesting that the model of rationality as the individual maximizing of utility can be helpful. Yet the concentration on the individual rather than on the existence of any notion of a social reality, coupled with crude measures of what can count as utility, can warp social science. Everything can be seen in terms of the pursuit of individual advantage, or, on the supply side, as the provision of valued goods and services for individuals. Thus Iannaccone can view churches quite seriously on his model as 'profit maximizing firms specialising in the production of religious goods and services'.[7] This is all in stark contrast with a more traditional social theory, which often had a collectivist slant. It saw religion as a social rather than an individual phenomenon, emerging only at a collective level. It cannot then be explained in terms of the supply and demand of goods to individuals. A collectivist in social theory would be unable to see religion as a commodity on analogy with the production and sale of a motor car. Instead the very nature of society would be viewed as entwined with its religion. It would not be a matter of the beliefs of individuals, even when combined. Instead, the society is seen as emerging at a new level, with its own characteristics, outstripping the intentions and understanding of its members. Durkheim would not ask what a believer would get out of religion. Instead, for him, participation in a religion involves participation in the social construction of the reality that is in fact a surrogate for society itself.

Rational choice theory has become vigorous in unexpected spheres even though its natural home would seem to be in the areas of economics and politics. The battle between individualist and collectivist has become carried into areas which previously appeared to be the province of the collectivist. A complicating factor in religion is that any sociological approach at all may appear to leave much that is crucial to religion out of account. Durkheim and many others in classical sociology made no secret of the fact that they considered all religion irrational in its reaching up to the supernatural. They could safely ignore the content, which they took for granted was false in its own terms. What they had to explain was why anyone should come to hold such beliefs. Because they could dismiss the content of all religion, they were able to look to the social underpinning of such belief as the sole explanation for its persistence and importance in society. Thus Durkheim could conclude that no religion was false. 'All', he said, 'are true in their own fashion; all will answer, though in different ways, to the given condition of human existence.'[8] The reasons a religious believer may give could be erroneous, possibly even invoking the supernatural, which Durkheim ruled out. He saw the task of the sociologist as that of revealing the true nature of society and the role its institutions played. Appeals to individual understanding and individual choice would by definition be irrelevant. Genuine social reality, although derived from individuals, need not be, and indeed could not be, explained in terms of their conscious intentions and purposes.

Rational choice theorists need not be so cavalier with notions of the transcendent and supernatural. They do not have to assume that religious beliefs taken at face value are false, since they are happy to remain at the level of an individual conscious motivation. Instead they point out that many of the promised benefits of religion are of their nature risky, with their very existence taken on faith. What has to be explained is not so much why anyone should believe what is false but why anyone should take a great risk in obtaining a commodity whose benefits, though possibly great, may be hard to ascertain at the present. One writer says, in a relentless application of his rational choice model:

> The uncertainty surrounding most religious goods is far greater than that which surrounds used cars. Hence we can predict the emergence of institutions and arrangements designed to increase information (or at least the appearance of information) and reduce fraud.[9]

Nevertheless, rational choice theory itself will obviously be far more effective if it can deal with observable outcomes with measurable costs and benefits. The prospect of eternal life is not something which can easily be dealt with from any scientific point of view. The inevitable reaction of rational choice theorists will be to change the subject to the weight given to its possibility by the individual believer. The issues of risk and paucity of information thus become of central importance. They cannot be resolved, and so there will be a tendency to discount them. Instead there will be a tendency for the theorist to concentrate on factors in the development of religious institutions which can be quantified. In particular, time and money spent as a result of religious commitment will be balanced by the observable 'religious goods and services' acquired. This becomes quite explicit when Iannaccone claims that 'the principle inputs to religious production – time and money – are measurable and indeed are already routinely measured by researchers'.[10] The object of such activity would be to maximize the overall utility derived from 'religious commodities'. Iannaccone does concede that religious products are 'complex and largely unobservable (though possibly no more so than recreational enjoyment)'.[11]

Apart, however, from the intrinsic difficulty in measuring the benefits of religion, the reference to all recreational enjoyment is highly significant. It is apparent that positivist prejudices about the importance of measurement and quantification are coupled with a strong emphasis on the centrality of the individual. The point, it seems, of religious commitment must be seen in terms of the benefits achieved for me, and perhaps my family. Can the inputs of my time and my money be justified in terms of what I get out of it? There are many aspects of human life where this calculation is highly relevant. Is attendance at a professional football match to be justified, when I take into account the time involved in travelling there and the general expense of admission, meals and so on? Is the trouble of getting caught up in vast crowds counterbalanced by the pleasure of seeing the game in person? Everybody makes this kind of calculation, and sponsors of sports events take such calculations seriously when they set the cost of tickets. They have to know their market.

Is religion like this? As with all half-truths, the theory is partially applicable. Aspects of religious life can be subject to such crude cost–benefit calculation. The view, however, that religion is a private, individual matter concerning what is in my interest goes against most understandings of it. Religion has been traditionally seen as an advocate of morality and altruism. Otherwise the origins of self-sacrifice and martyrdom, not to mention more ordinary aspects of morality, would become hard to explain since they then seem irrational. Indeed, altruism never can be explained on this kind of model, unless it is viewed simply as a basic preference to help others. Biology, as we have seen, cannot explain it, and 'society' as been ruled out as a positive influence.

Rational choice theory limits itself to an instrumentalist notion of rationality, as a method of determining whichever ends we happen to want most. It shows us how to find the means to such ends without deciding whether the ends are actually worth pursuing in the first place. It places a premium on measurement. When rationality is seen as the mere optimizing of utility, and when utility is viewed primarily as what can be measured, it becomes impossible to use reason to question the basic worth of any activity. Whereas Durkheim dismissed the alleged contents of religious belief as irrational, and looked for a deeper level of rationality beyond the conscious calculation of individuals, rational choice theorists cannot discuss the rationality of religion as an activity at all. The question becomes one of whether an individual gets enough out of participation, just as whether going to the football match proves worthwhile. Questions about the rationality or otherwise of participating in a particular religion can get as easily lost as the question what is so special about football anyway. An individual's enjoyment or fulfilment is sufficient explanation.

A social scientist may with some justification retort that issues of truth, particularly of a metaphysical kind, must lie outside the ambit of any social science. The latter must investigate why people act as they do. It cannot, within its own terms of reference, start speculating about theological or other kinds of truth. Nevertheless, social theory should not make such speculation impossible. The more that rationality is thought to be merely instrumental, in the pursuit of given preferences, the more any wider view of what it is to be rational is undermined. Wider issues of truth will be ignored if everything is subsumed under a crude form of cost–benefit analysis. In fact, the question of why I choose to believe anything as true can itself be subjected to such analysis. Is it in my interest to believe it? What do I get out of it? How much risk is there in obtaining its benefits, compared with assured costs? As with all types of social theory, rational choice theory can overreach itself. Indeed we can legitimately ask what the costs and benefits are of adopting it as a theory in the first place. Without an ultimate appeal to the way things are, to reality, the remorseless application of one criterion can implode. As we have often seen, any global theory has to be applied to itself.

The Social Context

The individualism espoused by rational choice theory itself raises large questions. The relationship between individual and society is thought by many to be the major problem facing social science, and is a constant theme of this book. The issue has often become explicitly political. Margaret Thatcher, British Prime Minister throughout the 1980s, once

made the controversial remark that there is no such thing as society. She
was widely seen as encouraging the development of a market-based
analysis of society, because of her stress on the centrality of the individual. In her autobiography, she defended her views about the mean-
inglessness of the term 'society'. She said:

> My meaning was that society was not an abstraction, separate from the
> men and women who composed it, but a living structure of individuals,
> families and voluntary associations . . . Society for me was not an excuse, it
> was a source of obligation.[12]

In fact, most social theorists would unite in condemning the 'reification'
of society as something separate from the members who compose it.
Even collectivists such as Marx saw the dialectical relationship between
individual and society. Society was not totally distinct from the activities
of those who may make it up. We may inevitably be formed by a society,
but we go on to contribute to its perpetuation, recreation, or even, at a
time of revolution, its destruction.

   We cannot, however, simply be understood as individuals making a
choice in a vacuum. What makes such choice possible? How are we able
to choose? For a politician such as Lady Thatcher, who wished to stress
the importance of the individual and the centrality of personal responsibility, it may seem as if the acknowledgement of social forces and
influences beyond ourselves will only serve to lessen our own control
over ourselves and society. At the extreme, there are those who maintain
that everything is socially constructed, even the self. It is then, however,
far from clear who or what has constructed the society that then exists. It
is all too easy for a collectivist, or holist, view of society to be opposed to
a strongly individualist one. The result is that the defects of the one
position may seem to show the truth of the other. The collapse of
Marxist societies in Europe makes the worship of the market seem
inevitable. The discrediting of central planning and totalitarian forms
of government has stimulated the idea of the individual as consumer.
This is exemplified in the rational choice models that have gained in
popularity.

   Yet the crude opposition between society and individual choice
cannot tell the whole story. Even Margaret Thatcher's reference to
voluntary associations begins to raise questions. What is the role of social
institutions? They can exist at many levels, from that of local clubs to

national governments. Clearly, though, when people join together in co-operative endeavour, the results cannot always be explained in terms of their individual intentions. Indeed one of the prime motivations of social science is to show how we do not fully understand the results of our combined actions when we act in co-operation with, or alongside, others. It is one thing for a particular family to drive to a beauty spot on a holiday. If thousands of others do the same, most will be spending hours in traffic jams they never envisaged. They will create damage to the countryside, instead of enjoying its peace, cause accidents which provide work for police and hospitals and so on. The fact of unintended consequences can never be ignored. Sometimes they will be the result of a chance combination of activities such as occur when separate families decide to visit the same place, and sometimes the by-product of deliberate co-operation in some corporate scheme. The consequences of what we all do help to create the environment in which subsequent choices can be made.

The intertwined relationship of individual and social setting may tempt some to stress the social context, and ignore the role of the individual. Others may concentrate on the individual's 'rational choice' and ignore the social context. An excessive dose of individualism involves forgetting the crucial importance of that context. It is not merely constituted by the simultaneous choices of my contemporaries, as when we all have unintentionally created a traffic jam. The idea of a society has to take into account the passage of time. My choices may help to create a situation which affects generations to come, just as my choices are made in a context which has been created by the myriad past choices of those to have gone before me. Society can never be seen only in terms of its current members. A community must be more than an accidental conglomeration of individuals, of the kind that, say, the population of an airport concourse at a given moment is likely to be. To be a community, or a society, individuals must be involved in co-operative relationships that extend through time. A common criticism of an excessive concentration on individuals is that it fails to see the enduring importance of institutions. In other words, there are ongoing sets of people who co-operate for various purposes in a way that can continue even when some people drop out, through retirement or death, while others join.

We saw in chapter 3 that an institution can persist, even though its membership gradually changes. The same schools, universities, and churches can serve the same purposes, fulfilling the same functions, in successive generations. There is no radical break in membership, but after a hundred years, none of those associated with such institutions will be the same. Yet the college, or whatever, may very well be identical. This is not just a matter of having the same physical features, although continuity of buildings may help to provide an identity of institution. There need, though, be no contradiction in a school moving to a new site. Institutions can be much more intangible and yet still constrain and influence the choices of those who belong to them. Indeed by excluding others, they may have a further influence on the society of which they are part.

Without the existence of institutions, a society itself can have no real existence. Without common agreement and conventions about how to do things, individuals will be deprived of the contexts in which their choices have any meaning. This is not to deny the importance of individual choice, and the role of personal responsibility. I need to have some idea of what can be chosen and of how I can implement my choices. This information can only come from my surroundings. Even rational choice theory had to assume the existence of churches and religious organizations in order to discuss choice between religions. Institutions, in other words, help to give choice. They can empower us, even if in some situations they may also be seen as limiting and constraining choice. We may not be created by our society, although there are those who believe that the identity is wholly constituted by a social setting. What is unambiguous is that our identity has to be expressed within a particular social context. The times and places in which we find ourselves serve to create some opportunities and limit others. In other words we have to be aware of the network of tacit agreements and conventions that surround us. We have to be aware of the institutions and ways of doing things that are being handed down through time. We must be aware of tradition.

The Nature of Social Institutions

When we talk of social institutions, we must have some idea of whether they are in some sense 'real'. They seem after all to be dependent on human understanding, and could not exist without it. This is a constant conundrum. At one extreme, philosophers such as Richard Rorty make no rigid distinction between physical reality as grasped by our minds, and the social world as constructed by humans. Both are, it appears, merely part of our language. Thus Rorty remarks: 'We can say with Foucault, that both human rights and homosexuality are recent social constructions, but only if we say with Latour, that quarks are too.'[13] Yet this is to make social construction a matter of projection by human minds, perhaps in a collective fashion through language. It is a form of idealism, holding that such disparate ideas as rights, homosexuality and quarks are categories of thought constituting the very reality they refer to. There are then no such entities apart from the way they are spoken of. Rorty's pragmatist, and postmodernist, point is that this is true not just of some of our concepts but applies as well to the entities talked of in science. The latter is merely one form of human practice and can claim no privileged position.

Social institutions, however, cannot be put into this kind of category, if one begins to make realist distinctions. Quarks, unless science is mistaken, have been discovered, not constructed, or so the scientific realist would say. They are part of the fabric of the world, whether humans recognize them as such or not. The possibility that they are not is what gives content to the notion of a mistake in science. At the other extreme, 'human rights' and 'homosexuality' are certainly concepts used in our language, but once we revert to the idea that language is characteristically about the world, there is clearly much room for discussion about their status. Neither are simply social institutions in the way that banks, schools or churches are. If they are called social constructions, it is because they depend on bodies of belief and understanding, and are not deemed to refer to a reality existing independently of the belief. That can clearly be controversial, and it is hardly surprising that those who talk of social construction are reluctant to accept that there is an alternative. If the only reality we live in is the product of common beliefs and concepts, we do not have to worry about what there 'really' is. We can talk of human rights because we want to, without having to worry about whether they are somehow part of the way things are. The other side of this coin, however, is that if we do not wish to talk of human rights, we need not. There is no objective constraint on us to do so.

The immediate issue, though, is whether the operation of social institutions can be seen as just a matter of shared concepts. Human rights, whatever their status, do not appear to exercise any causal power over us, independently of the way we think of them. Yet that is the suggestion about institutions. Their nature and character, and indeed their power, is not a mere reflection of the way we think and talk. Such institutions may be the product of a collective, rather than an individual, construction, but in any case their character can often outstrip everyone's understanding of it. John Searle asks how it is that institutional reality can function causally.[14] After all, as he points out, if money is only money because it is believed to be, how can it have a power of its own? It seems that in the case of institutions, construction must mean more than simply projection. They are not just reflections of our intentions, but have an effect, for good and ill on those who have constructed them, and on their successors. They do not exist apart from humans, and should not be reified, but at the same time they do have a reality that can easily surpass any normal understanding of it. In this sense, human institutions of the kind Searle mentions transcend even collective acceptance. They are not mere categories of thought or understanding. A bank is not like human rights, even though Searle himself assimilates them by analysing each in the same terms. He sees rights as created by collective acceptance in the same way as any institution. Banks, however, are not just powerful ideas, any more than are churches or universities. They embody complex social arrangements which enable us all to do things which would otherwise not be possible. Yet, at least according to some thinkers, social science can uncover facts about the operation of this kind of institution which have little to do with our collective acceptance of their existence and purposes.

John Searle has carried the debate forward by making a firm distinction between what he terms 'brute facts', such as physical objects, and institutional factors, which, he says, are only facts as a result of human agreement. He says that 'in a sense there are things that exist only because we believe them to exist'.[15] He goes on to give as examples the usual ones of money, property, governments and marriages. He makes great play of the role of language in creating and constituting such facts and indeed makes the strong claim 'that language is essentially constitutive of institutional reality'.[16] This might suggest that he is stressing the social aspect of institutions, but the use of language and linguistic rules can possibly be traced back to questions of neural structure in individual brains. If that is done, and Searle would support the project, the theory can then appear much more individualist.

Searle's objective is to make sense of the existence of human institutions in a world that, as he puts it, 'consists entirely of physical particles in fields of force.'[17] Yet this betrays an underlying physicalism, a belief that ultimately the only reality is physical. This is bound to influence, if not actually distort, any account of social reality, since it will not be seen as having any independent causal power except through the physically constituted beliefs and wishes of its participants. The retort may well be that it could not have power in any other way, unless we conceive of social reality somehow floating free of human understanding and control. We would then be redefining it as if it were itself some kind of physical object. Searle himself is certainly at pains to build up a picture of institutions as formed through convention. Influenced, as so many are, by the later Wittgenstein's conception of rule-governed games, he sees institutions as relying on a collective agreement, about, say, somebody's possession over a certain status. Searle says of games that 'the desire to score points has no content independently of a socially accepted system'.[18] He later argues that something similar is true of money, property and other institutional phenomena. As a result, he is able to say that 'a test for the presence of genuine institutional factors is whether or not we could codify the rules explicitly'.[19]

The position Searle wishes to build up is one where our biology and, through neurophysiology, our cognitive capacities, constrain us in building up the rules of our interactions together, and the obligations these engender. Indeed he argues that any divide between biology and culture is as mistaken as that between body and mind. He writes: 'The mental is simply a set of physical features of the brain at a higher level of description than that of neurons: so there is no opposition between culture and biology: culture is the form that biology takes.'[20] He suggests that if there was any opposition between culture and biology, biology would always win. This is however, controversial, as the history of discussions about sociobiology indicates. 'Top-down' causation may be as much a part of both mental and social functioning as 'bottom-up' causation. Emergent levels are not just facts about levels of linguistic description. They may also refer to genuine complexities in the causal framework of the world.

Searle's picture of human agreement constituting institutional reality fits in with his 'bottom-up' approach. It is essentially a view of institutions existing because they are constituted by the agreement of individuals. Searle says that 'the secret of understanding the continued existence of institutional facts is simply that the individuals directly involved, and a sufficient number of members of the relevant community must continue to recognise and accept the existence of such facts'.[21] Institutional power, he maintains, depends on collective agreement. If enough members withhold that agreement, the institution collapses and the power vanishes. Similarly we can create new power relations through the establishment of new institutions by collective agreement. Institutional reality is created through collective acceptance and recognition. When that is withheld, the power vanishes.

The argument is that even the imposition of force involves a system of acceptance. Searle says that police forces and armies are instances of what he terms status functions.[22] In other words, they have the role they do because they have been given a collectively recognized status. Searle's diagnosis of the collapse of Soviet power is that it collapsed when the system of status functions was no longer accepted. He says that 'the fear of Soviet intervention was no longer credible, and the indigenous police and military were unwilling to attempt to maintain the system'.[23]

Is the functioning of systems of power, and of institutions generally, capable of analysis in this quasi-reductionist manner? Can talk of institutions really be translated into the attitudes and actions of individuals? Searle is attempting to explain the role of social institutions by referring to the acceptance of individuals. When enough individuals stop recognizing institutions, they cease to exist. If no one recognizes a piece of paper as legal tender, it is not money even if it once was. There is obviously a great deal of truth in this. Human institutions need human participants. It does, however, suggest that our agreement constitutes an institution, so that the reality and nature of the institution cannot be more than our collective understanding of it. The corollary is that there seems no room for the possibility that an institution could have unintended effects, and thus take on a life of its own beyond our immediate control.

As always, the balance has to be struck between an idea of society somehow existing apart from whatever we all think and do, and one where it is simply the sum total of our individual beliefs. Although Searle's picture takes due account of the public and shared attributes of institutions, there is an idealist flavour in much of what he says, suggesting that institutional arrangements are simple reflections of agreement and negotiations. Social reality is then the shadow cast by a collection of human minds (or brains). The 'bottom-up' analysis pictures society as built up from voluntary situations and agreements. Searle does not consider that we are always conscious of the constitutive rules of human institutions. He admits participants may have false beliefs about them. Nevertheless, although individuals may be simply wrong about the kind of institutions they belong to, just as a player of a game may be mistaken about the rules, or perhaps not be fully aware of them, the institutions depend on enough members recognizing their nature. Games cannot be played if no one knows their rules. Institutions, like games, then become a function of the understanding of those taking part.

The fact of power illustrates the dilemma. Does power have to be recognized as such to function? Searle is surely right in suggesting that a police force that no one recognizes as such cannot act in the way a police force should. It cannot enforce a law no one recognizes, unless, and this is the point, it has more force at its command than its opponents. Everyone would agree that a law depending wholly for its status on the ability of people to enforce it is normally in a shaky position. Power, however, is often thought to undermine some of these calculations. A reign of terror can appear to impose a regime on a country. Searle would retort that that it can only be imposed because it is accepted by enough people. He claims that 'the system of force is itself a system of acceptance'.[24] This is to view everything in terms of what the individual recognizes rather than in terms of what constraints there may be on individual choice. Constraints, it appears, only exist when they are viewed as such. Costs and benefits have to be recognized as such, not just in order to influence people, but before they can have any causal role. It is their perception, rather than any fact of their existence, that matters. Is this all there is to power? Is it what is seen as power, or can it work on people whether or not they acknowledge its validity, agree with its imposition, or even be fully aware of its effects?

Searle remarks that 'in many democratic societies, once the number of lawbreakers reaches critical mass, the police force is largely for show'.[25] The moral he draws is the police have to be recognized as such. Collective authorization has to be given through the agreement of enough people. Yet another conclusion could be that issues of recognition and authorization become irrelevant if sufficient members wish to confront the police. The issue is not one of status. Indeed the lawbreakers could in one sense still recognize them as police, and the agents of the law. They are going to confront them, and then the issue is who has the most power. No doubt in a democratic society, the police may be inhibited in their response, but if they have sufficient weapons and equipment, they may be able to deal with larger numbers. Certainly the recognition offered or withheld by the majority may be irrelevant against a ruthless tyrant. Searle himself admits that the Soviet empire was maintained for over forty years by a system of terror. The question at issue is whether such terror can be analysed in terms of individual responses and agreements, however reluctantly made. Is the imposition of power primarily a matter of how it is acknowledged? Its reality may lie more in its character and its effects. What happens to me may not be just a matter of what I see happening. I can be injured in all kinds of ways without realizing it. Similarly, I can be a victim of social forces of which I am oblivious. So at least it would be claimed.

Collective agreements are certainly important factors in the creation and maintenance of social institutions. They must be, if such institutions are seen as made by humans, and can be reformed or changed. Yet the issue must be finally who has the power, not who is willing to bestow it. If I get killed it is irrelevant whether I, or others, recognize the status and authority of my opponent. I am still dead. Some forms of power and force may help to sustain institutions and their authority in ways that affect their members, whether their members wish or not. They may even be unaware what is happening. Institutions cannot be easily seen as merely constituted by present human agreement, without underestimating the way they can affect us. 'We' may be responsible for our social environment and the sense that humans created it, and we ourselves no doubt help to sustain it. That does not mean, though, that it does not have a causal effect on us. We may be affected by it, just as much as we can affect it. That at least would be the contention.

Many would see Searle's account of institutions as too individualistic. Institutions can enable individuals and they can constrain them, but all this need have little to do with the voluntary acknowledgement or recognition of their members. The baleful effects of one institution may have little to do with the reasons people participate in it. The benefits of another institution may be very different from those intended by its creators. The effects of institutions can change over time, so that what was beneficial once is now so no longer. The causal role played by various sets of social arrangements may be of increasing importance, despite the fact that those who originally made the arrangements, and those who continue them, may be oblivious of it. To take a contemporary example, new forms of social interaction are coming into being daily through the greater use of computer technology in the construction of the Internet. Yet although this all depends on the shared agreement of participants, it would be rash to predict what the social consequences may be or how all will be affected. It will no doubt create unlooked-for opportunities and also levy unknown costs. We are in the process of creating something with consequences that must be hidden from us. Our contemporaries have created it, and we share in its use, but that does not mean that its social role is only constituted by our understanding or acceptance.

Notes

1   See my *Rationality and Science*, 1993, pp. 189ff.
2   Darren E. Sherket, 'Embedding Religious Choices', in Lawrence A. Young (ed.), *Rational Choice Theory and Religion*, 1997, p. 69.
3   Rodney Stark, 'Bringing Theory Back In', in Young, *Rational Choice Theory*, p. 17.
4   Stark, 'Bringing Theory Back In', p. 36.
5   Laurence A. Iannaccone, 'Rational Choice', in Young, *Rational Choice Theory*, p. 27.
6   Ibid., p. 36.
7   Ibid., p. 40.
8   Emile Durkheim, *The Elementary Forms of the Religious Life*, 1971, p. 3.
9   Iannaccone, 'Rational Choice', p. 34.
10   Ibid., p. 30.
11   Ibid.
12   Margaret Thatcher, *The Downing Street Years*, 1993, p. 626.
13   R. Rorty, *Truth and Progress*, vol. 3, 1998, p. 8.
14   John Searle, *Mind, Language and Society*, 1999, p. 114.
15   John Searle, *The Construction of Social Reality*, 1995, p. 1.
16   Ibid., p. 59.
17   Ibid., p. xi.
18   Ibid., p. 67.
19   Ibid., p. 87.
20   Ibid., p. 227.
21   Ibid., p. 117.
22   Ibid., p. 91.
23   Ibid., p. 92.
24   Ibid., p. 91.
25   Ibid.

11

Tradition and Reason

Tradition

Institutions persist through time and are passed on down the generations. Some, indeed, may be venerated by many people, just because they are ancient. The role of tradition is intimately connected with the nature of institutions. The social world we inhabit is created in large part by what has been handed down to us. However 'modern', or even revolutionary, we may wish to be, our starting-point must be a society we entered, and did not create ourselves. Indeed we were probably born into it. We have been surrounded by the consequences of tradition. What, then, is the function of tradition? Mere awareness that tradition can have a significant role does little to guide us. Social theorists themselves diverge in their attitudes to it.

The Marxist emphasis on revolution rested on the assumption that traditions had been framed in the interests of some to the detriment of others. Marxism concentrated on the class structure in society, which was held to be based on economic interests. Marx argued that many were not even aware of how their judgements were warped by the interests of their class. As a result, for they were embroiled in a false consciousness, which had to be exposed. The world was not really as the bourgeoisie had been brought up to believe. What seemed quite natural was a carefully constructed social fabric, designed for the benefits of some but not others. Even the proletariat did not see how they were being exploited. The future lay in the revolutionary overturning of the class society. Capitalism, the source of these ills, would be destroyed through the pressure of its own internal contradictions, and socialism would triumph. The communist society would enable humans to flourish.

Whatever the faults of capitalism, as an economic system (and communists were always ready to criticize its emphasis on the individual and the way it appeared to encourage human selfishness), one thing is clear. As a historical forecast, Marxism proved hopelessly wrong. Socialist societies, and not capitalist ones, collapsed from 1989 onwards. The result has inevitably been a downgrading of interest in Marxist theory and its search for revolution. Yet the pattern of explanation, invoked by Marxism, cannot so easily be put aside. Some would argue that Marxism, seen as an economic theory, has been shown to be false. The analysis of society, however, in terms of false consciousness produced by tradition, remains attractive to many. Once it is thought that the interests of the few can govern the consciousness of the many, a deep suspicion of tradition can be raised. The post-Marxist accusations of false consciousness are not so much preoccupied with the alleged pursuit of class and financial advantage. They tend to have a different focus, although perhaps we should remain alive to the possibility of economic exploitation through social structures.

Accusations are centred on areas such as relations between the sexes. Tradition can be viewed with what the French philosopher, Paul Ricoeur, has memorably called the 'hermeneutics of suspicion'. Much of it has been constructed, it will be said, over the centuries by males in the interests of males. It is the product of a patriarchal society. What we all been brought up to consider 'natural' is in fact just a view that has been imposed for the interests of some, but not of others, in society. It is easy to see the role of women as being essentially that of nurturing and rearing children. Major consequences for the way societies are organized follow from that view, not least in the way that marriage is regarded. Once, though, such practices are seen, rightly or wrongly as a result of a patriarchal tradition, which can and should be changed, people's understanding will be changed. The structures of society, the agreed ways of doing things, will be changed too.

Similar analyses can be given of the way in which other institutions in society can be questioned and altered. The fact that we are brought up to believe that certain things are proper and right, may mean nothing more than that that is the prevailing assumption in our society. Our ideas of human rights, which appear to make a claim for universal application, can be culturally formed. We can be in the grip of a local convention, which we mistake for the way things are. A leader of a British bakers' union was once heard in a broadcast, in defence of rights to holidays, to exclaim that it is a basic human right for bakers to have a Bank Holiday Monday off. He was confusing local institutions with universal truths and it is often the task of social science to point out that we must not confuse the two.

The attribution of false consciousness does of course presuppose that there is a standard of truth and falsity available. What we believe and what we ought to believe can then be distinguished. We shall see in the final chapter how some argue that any social science worth its name has to be able to grasp social reality and even be prepared to show people that they do not always fully comprehend what is actually happening around them. Social currents may be flowing, and carrying us along, without our being aware of what is happening. If social science can only tell us what we already know, or speak to us on the terms that we are already using, it would appear to have a diminished role.

We must, however, beware of assuming uncritically that tradition is always going to warp our judgements, and that social science must be subversive, if not revolutionary. This is no doubt a view that can often be held. There is, however, another way of looking at the traditions we are inevitably born into. Traditions constrain, hinder and create obstacles. They can and do, however, also enable us. The work of Kuhn showed how important traditions can be even in the development of science, where scientists allegedly depend on the passing on of 'paradigms', which may have eventually to be overthrown. Scientists need a paradigm in the first place. Unlike the empiricists, Kuhn believes that they cannot confront the world without any theory to guide them. Scientific tradition has to show them what to look for. Yet tradition alone is an uncertain guide at moments of crisis. Kuhn himself found great difficulty in showing how to choose rationally between alternative paradigms. Tradition, it seems, cannot be a simple substitute for reason.

Yet none of us starts without tradition, and language itself encapsulates much of it. We should perhaps be wary of Wittgenstein's preoccupation with language. The emphasis on language rather than thought immediately places a focus on the social rather than the individual. We learn language in a social setting, and if public language is thought prior to private thought, the role of the individual is thereby lessened. The German philosopher H.-G. Gadamer has put a great deal of emphasis on the priority of language in tradition. Coming from the tradition of hermeneutical philosophy, he has been particularly concerned with the importance of meaning. Unlike the phenomenologists who locate meaning in individual consciousness, others, such as Gadamer, typically locate it in tradition. The role of language is stressed in such a way that subjects are held to be what they are because of the linguistic world they inhabit. Interpreters themselves cannot claim to be in a privileged position, because they themselves are located in a tradition and must acknowledge that their interpretation is dependent on the context in which it is made. Hermeneutics began as a discipline which concentrated on the interpretation of biblical and legal texts. Now, however, it has been given a much wider application, so the problem of interpretation is seen by many as being of central importance in social science. It has, in fact, given rise to the whole movement of postmodernism, which believes that the historical situation of the interpreter is as important as that of those being interpreted.

Hermeneutics

The main emphasis in hermeneutics has been on understanding and communication. It is opposed to a more scientific view of society that looks for general laws and regularities. The paradigm for hermeneutics, as for its unruly heir postmodernism, is the interpretation of the text. In the case of hermeneutics, the text would be traditional, and the problem will be how we can come to understand in our own context something written in a radically different situation. A proper interpretation has to allow for the interplay of the two contexts. Gadamer refers to this as the 'fusion of horizons'. The problem is that the doctrine of the historical nature of understanding seems to imprison us within our in our own tradition while the text recedes into its own. Hermeneutics, it seems, has to show how this gap can be bridged. Yet this illustrates the dangers of elevating tradition to a dominant role. It can provide us with opportunities, as well as constraining us. If, however, it is regarded as a prison, which holds us captive, the problem will be how those outside the prison can communicate with those inside. Indeed, the problem is worse than that. It is a question of how people in different prisons can possibly communicate. Gadamer has elevated the initial strangeness of an ancient text into an argument about the separateness of traditions. The attempt to fuse horizons becomes necessary because he has split traditions apart, largely because of his insistence on the priority of language. He refers to the 'indissoluble unity of thought and language' and concludes that linguistic tradition forms us and our thoughts. He says:

> The interpreter does not know that he is bringing himself and his own concepts into the interpretation. The linguistic formulation is so much part of the interpreter's mind that he never becomes aware of it as an object.[1]

According to the doctrine of the Enlightenment, reason can lay claim to universality. Languages, on the other hand, must be particular and distinctive. When language creates the categories with which we think, any attempt to understand the thinking of those writing at a different time in a different language, is fraught with difficulty. Their thought must be conditioned by their historical situation, just as ours is by ours. Again and again, Gadamer emphasizes the primacy of language. Tradition is, he says, 'linguistic in character',[2] and he stresses, in a manner reminiscent of Wittgenstein, that 'all forms of human community of life are forms of linguistic community.'[3] Because language creates our world, there will in a sense be a succession of different worlds as human society and language alter. He says:

> The historical 'worlds' that succeed one another in the course of history are different from one another and from the world of today, but it is always, in whatever tradition we consider it, a human, i.e. a linguistically constructed, world that presents itself to us.[4]

The 'world' is then part of language, rather than its basis. Gadamer denies any realist idea of a 'world in itself' against which different views of the world can be set. We can never escape the presuppositions and prejudices of our own tradition. The most that we can hope for is the inclusion of another version of 'the world' within our own. Gadamer writes:

> The criterion for the continuing expansion of our own world picture is not given by a 'world in itself' that lies beyond all language. Rather, the infinite perfectibility of the human experience of the world means that, whatever language we use, we never achieve anything but an ever more extended aspect, a 'view' of the world.[5]

The loss of grip on the notion of an objective world can easily result in the world as we comprehend it appearing to be merely the product of our own viewing. It seems that we are simply trapped in our own linguistic world, or we must base our interpretations on concepts that are bound to render them inappropriate. This is an ongoing dilemma for social science, and it is exacerbated by undue emphasis on the governing role of tradition. Without an ability to appeal to a reason that can transcend our immediate situation, and even stand in judgement on the tradition that nurtured it, social science becomes a mere social commentary, and moreover a commentary that is governed by the prejudices of our own time and place. Even Gadamer's 'fusion of horizons' runs the risk of being far from a genuine meeting of two points of view. It is bound to be the appropriation of one set of understandings in the terms of another. Gadamer's stress on the linguistic character of our world may free language from the constraints of reality. It also removes it from any foundation in human nature. He dismisses any idea of similarity between different human beings in different historical contexts. No such 'connaturality', he believes, unites the creator and interpreter of the text.[6]

The result of all this is that we are conditioned by society and become what we are through its agency. Our reasoning is not so much the outcome of our own efforts, as a reflection, even if unintended, of our own historical situation. A sociologist of knowledge could not have expressed the matter better. The result is that any Cartesian notion of the self, or indeed any Kantian notion of contextless rationality, is squeezed out. Instead of the individual, we are presented with the tradition of a society in a holist manner. Reason has in fact been replaced by tradition, instead of being envisaged as empowered by it. Gadamer paved the way for the subsequent concentration on our historical situation. There can be no possibility of any dispassionate or disinterested reason, transcending local circumstances. Even our understanding of other traditions will be circumscribed by our own presuppositions. Real dialogue or conversation can never take place, since everything is seen from our own particular historical standpoint. As so often in the philosophy of the social sciences, this somewhat banal point is made to appear an important insight.

The Reaction against the Enlightenment

The Enlightenment project is much derided by many philosophers nowadays, and is seen as constituting the modernity against which postmodernism has rebelled. The writings of Kant exemplify the Enlightenment hope that a pure reason, held universally by all rational beings, could be employed to bring 'improvement' to human society. Reason was seen as an antidote to tradition and to any authority, such as that of the Catholic Church or of an absolute monarch. Humans could be set free by this systematic application of rationality. They could become autonomous. Kant tried to construct a morality for individuals who had broken free of the shackles of tradition. Rationality was seen as the possession of individuals, who were thus able to exercise it prior to their entry into social relations. One grave problem remains, despite the optimism that saw all rationality as the cure of all human ills. Even with the growth of modern science, which has been largely seen as the instrument of the pure rationality of the Enlightenment, agreement between societies and individuals about what precisely all rational persons should believe has not been forthcoming. This is particularly noticeable in the sphere of morality, in which Kant tried to demonstrate what every rational being should hold. The temptation, which is now all too evident, is to react to the Enlightenment contempt for tradition by reverting to a view that everything is dictated by tradition. This in turn becomes a battle between individualism, based on belief in the rationality of the individual, and a holism that concentrates on how a tradition, or society, governs the way we think.

It is perhaps significant that a Kantian stress on the centrality of rationality, and the historicist stress on the formative role of tradition in forming us, both neglect reality and the concept of human nature. Without holding to a realist conception of the world, to which we all have access, and without a substantial belief in human nature, it becomes miraculous that the members of one culture, or historical epoch, should understand those of another. Kant made the world seem inaccessible,[7] with his doctrine of 'things in-themselves', and he laid the way for his successors to concentrate on the mere fact of different conceptual schemes. With his 'Copernican revolution', he gave priority to our viewpoint, instead of what is being viewed. He drew the parallel between Copernicus' discovery that the spectator revolved around heavenly bodies, rather than the other way round, and his own understanding of the relationship between concepts and reality. He wished to see how objects had to conform to our knowledge, rather than the reverse. He believed there was only one possible conceptual scheme available to all rational beings but he gave a hostage to fortune by making concepts rather than reality the centre of attention.

Some of his successors, particularly as a result of empirical investigation, could not ignore the continuing variation in belief and understanding. It then became a small step to stress the difference between traditions. Human understanding can appear to be formed not according to some universal canon of rationality, but by the particular, and local, circumstances of a place and time. Reality has dropped out, and any human nature, bridging different societies, can be discarded. Both are constructed, it might appear, in significantly different ways in different circumstances. Our very identity derives, it might be concluded, not from a common humanity, but from the particular circumstances of a local tradition.

One major repository for ideas of such identity is the concept of a nation. Marxism can be seen as an application of the Enlightenment drive to improvement through knowledge. It has not always, however, been an expression of the Enlightenment desire for individual autonomy. Even in that respect, however, Marx showed leanings to the idea of a romantic 'self-realization'.[8] In the place of avowedly Marxist societies, however, old nationalisms have reasserted themselves, sometimes with catastrophic effects. The result has been a splintering of political units. The nation has been thought to be of central importance, to the detriment of any idea of a common humanity. This process has not just taken place in the political world. The philosophical underpinning of appeals to common humanity are being called into question. This becomes a burning issue, when many want to prevent the depredation of one nation by another with an appeal to human rights. If tradition is prior, and the source of identity, perhaps we should seek to preserve our own traditions at all costs without regard to those who belong to others. Indeed we may wish to destroy them precisely because they threaten our own position.

Postmodernism typically distrusts appeals to a universal reason, drawing attention to the way they are likely to be historically conditioned. Even 'rationality' can be portrayed as the product of a particular historical period. It is in fact, it will be said, Enlightenment rationality. Yet at the same time, many still wish to appeal to the Enlightenment conception of human rights which were typically invoked at the foundation of the United States and in the French Revolution. Yet one cannot have it both ways. Either rationality transcends local circumstances, and identity is not determined wholly by our historical context, or we are creatures of time and place. If the latter, the concept of human rights can have no application. If the former, reason can be understood as the property of individuals who may be influenced and constrained by their circumstances, but whose nature is not fully explicable in terms of them.

What then of nations? The concept of a nation is much contested. Language, a common history, or race are only some of the myriad factors that can be appealed to. Major problems arise when alleged nations do not coincide with the boundaries of the organization of the state, or when territory is disputed. The difficulty in giving clear definitions, suggests that whatever background is being appealed to itself often depends on local circumstances. Differences that do not seem to matter in one generation may suddenly become significant in the next. Similarities that have been honoured at one time may become irrelevant later. Differences between nations are not imaginary, but the weight given to them may vary in different epochs. There is, in other words, a large element of so-called social construction in the decision about what to count as a nation. At one point in the eighteenth century most Americans saw themselves as British. Later they did not. Issues about what makes someone Scottish or Welsh, as well as, or instead of, being British are much contested.

The concept of social reality returns again. Traditions are important, and are very often bound up with perceived national identity. We are who we are because of where we collectively have come from. The language we speak, the anniversaries we celebrate, the heroes we have, depend on our origins. Anything that ignores this and pretends that we are all equally rational and devoid of presuppositions and prejudices, must be ignoring an important part of human social life. Yet the danger is to imagine that, just because we have been brought up in one particular society and inculcated in one tradition, we are unable to extract ourselves from that background and make reasoned judgements about it. The choice should not be between tradition and reason, or between holism and individualism. We are not puppets mouthing sentiments produced by our social tradition. We are not the vehicles for mere prejudice. We have certainly all been born into a social reality that can have a partial influence on us. If we are not careful, it can dictate our preferences and our choices.

The Enlightenment vision of an individual using rationality in an autonomous way was not itself free from criticism. In many ways, the market-orientated view of the consumer as an atomic individual derives from it, and perhaps suffers some of the defects of the vision. Both tend to view rationality in an instrumentalist manner, as a matter primarily of devising means to ends. Both are uncomfortable about reasoning about the worth of ends. The market, it seems, is there to provide people with what they happen to want. Little effort is given to enquiry about whether they ought to want it. Indeed, in true Enlightenment fashion it might be thought a challenge to the autonomy of the individual even to ask the question. One result of this is to make the central issue simply how much someone wants something, and hence how much he or she is prepared to pay for it. The kind of society being produced as a result of such choices is regarded as irrelevant.

We are not isolated individuals operating without any formative influences on us, and we cannot afford to ignore the social consequences of our actions. In the same way, we are not mere carriers of tradition. Traditions are passed on and can be a great source of good and harm. A conservative will respect them as the repositories of the accumulated experience and judgement of past generations. Others will be suspicious of them, thinking that they were serving the interests of some or other powerful grouping. Nevertheless, none of us can escape their influence since they form the social context in which our present decisions have to be taken. At the same time, we are not the prisoners of tradition. Those who have preached human autonomy are right to the extent that we can decide whether to hold to traditions and pass them on. Whilst the Enlightenment may have been too optimistic about the ability of reason alone, unguided by the past, to map out a better future, those who attack the very idea of reason are adopting a self-destructive policy. All social science, and all social criticism, must be rationally based. A social science that repudiates the possibility of any detached reasoning is undermining itself in a spectacular way.

Even social science may be more constrained by its own traditions, or 'paradigms', than it likes to imagine. That does not mean that it can never have access to the way society actually operates, as opposed to the way a group of social scientists may be predisposed to imagine it does. The notion of social reality, like other forms of reality, demands an ability on our part to reason in a detached and dispassionate way. We may not always achieve this goal, but to suppose it is impossible is to deny the possibility of a social science. It is to deny our ability to stand back from a reality that has been constructed and to see its character. If we are always so bound up with it that we can never understand it or compare it with other societies, social science itself becomes yet another product of the Enlightenment that must be discarded as illusory.

Richard Rorty is merely a representative of many who deny that reality can be investigated or truth sought. He denies that truth can be a goal of enquiry and asserts: 'The purpose of inquiry is to achieve agreement among human beings about what to do, to bring about consensus on the ends to be achieved and the means to be used to achieve those ends.'[9] He thus in true American pragmatist fashion wishes to substitute agreement for reality and consensus for truth. It seems almost as if it does not matter what agreement is reached as long as people agree. Politics is everything. Yet the notion of a reality to be investigated has always been one which can explain why agreement might be forthcoming. There is an objective world constraining our choices. What we believe is not arbitrary, and this is as true in the conduct of social science as anywhere. We are individuals who can transcend our society, but we cannot ignore the social reality which surrounds us. It is the task of a social science to tell us something about the nature of society.

Social science studies a reality that is of its nature constituted by human understanding in some sense. Yet that reality is not constituted by a social science. What is being studied should be separated from our study of it. Nevertheless, just because we are examining what is in the end the product of the human mind, we can assume that social science should find society intelligible. It may be very complicated, and at times outstrip our understanding, but we are not going to discover that the reality in which we live our lives is in principle incomprehensible to humans. It is our home, or that of humans who are fundamentally like us. This may seem obvious, but there is a major philosophical problem about why we are able to find the physical world comprehensible. Does it possess an inherent order, or must we be pushed to a Kantian view of the priority of our conceptual framework in order to understand it? If it possesses an underlying order, why is it there? Basic metaphysical questions like these, which are anathema to empiricists, need not arise in social science. There should be no mystery why the human mind can grasp what is being produced by the human mind. That is why a realist separation of the object being investigated from the investigator can accompany a more anthropocentric understanding of the nature of society. Society does not exist as something alien and apart from us as humans, but is bound in some sense to reflect our nature. If we have not formed it ourselves, it has been formed over time by people like us, and depends for its continuation on our own contribution, both as individuals and in co-operation with others.

A Middle Way?

The argument about the relation of individual to society is crucial for any political view. A 'neo-liberal' individualism stresses the role of markets, particularly as sources of information about the wishes of consumers, while old-style collectivism has been swept aside in the general reaction against Marxism. Yet these are too extremes, each only gaining credibility because of the faults of the other. One says that individuals in combination in societies are no different than individuals apart, while the other exaggerates the role of the structures of society, while ignoring the role of its members. It is hardly surprising that many thinkers have looked for a third way, which avoids the pitfalls of extremes. This is a theoretical issue, even a philosophical one, but it has major implications for how our societies are organized and governed. A Thatcherite neo-liberal may dislike an old-style socialist who stresses the collective, but both may be uneasy about political proposals which agree with neither.

Anthony Giddens is a sociologist who has been much concerned with the relationship between 'structure' and 'agency' in society. What is the relationship between the so-called social structures, which may govern our behaviour, and our individual choices as agents? Can the two be properly distinguished? Clearly individualists will deny that there are structures, separate from the understanding of individuals, or constraining their choices in a way they do not realize. Collectivists will, on the other hand, stress the fact of structure at the expense of any reference to the power of individual agency. We must always, too, be wary of what is being meant by 'structure' in any given context. A Marxist would always see structures in economic terms, while others might think more readily in terms of visible institutions. Although social aspects are clearly being stressed there is an elasticity about the term which can encourage vagueness about how precisely it is being used on any given occasion.

This all forms the background to arguments in social theory in which Giddens has played a major part, but it is also important in modern political debate. Indeed Giddens himself advocates a third way, and asserts that 'having abandoned collectivism, third way politics looks for a new relationship between the individual and the community, a real definition of rights and obligations.'[10] Yet it should be obvious that there may well be many 'third ways' between the two extreme positions, one of individuals acting with each other in a social vacuum, with ready formed preferences, and one that totally denies the role of individual freedom and responsibility. Giddens writes as a social democrat, but a conservative respect for tradition and custom could also act as a counterbalance to the worship of the marketplace. Individuals live in a context formed by ongoing institutions which a conservative may be inclined to trust, just as a radical will be inclined to suspect them. Some, who allow that our choices are focused and constrained by the existence of social institutions, can also accept that we are free to change them or overthrow them. We can respect the inherited experience contained in the traditions of institutions whilst still accepting individual freedom. This is no doubt a conservative, rather than a neo-liberal position. Yet it will certainly distrust markets, where everything has its price and is to be quantified, just as it would regard the collectivist assault on the individual with horror. It is, from a theoretical point of view, another third way between polar opposites.

Names and slogans matter little, but the point is that it is sometimes easier to identify the faults in extreme positions, than chart a proper middle course. Yet whatever is advocated will have a major political effect. Theories about the constitution of society must go to the heart of politics. The way in which we envisage ourselves as being organized will ultimately affect the way we are organized. Our vision of what society is will eventually change society. This itself gives the lie to a rigid collectivism that refuses to accept that the beliefs of the participants in a society do affect the society of the time. It should not give comfort to extreme individualists because it is being suggested that there is such a thing as society, into which we are born and which will affect us. Our beliefs and actions may change the circumstances and social context in which future generations are born. It would, however, seem naïve to suggest that political and economic arrangements have no effect on individuals. Those who participate in politics do assume that they can actually change social arrangements in a way that is beneficial to the members of society. Different views of society may result in different estimates of how possible this is. If human agency is of little effect, change in structure may achieve a lot. Yet those politicians who have such ambitions may feel that their own personal agency can achieve a great deal, and thus be contradicting their basic assumptions. They may not accept that they themselves are a reflection of a pre-existing society. Similarly those who deny the existence of structures, and assume the utter priority of agency, should not underestimate their own role in exercising responsibility to create conditions in which individuals can flourish. This, however, reintroduces the question as to what those conditions are, and it may be that the climate and atmosphere of society can stifle or encourage individual responsibility. In other words, we may still be dependent on circumstances, however free and responsible we may wish to be.

These matters are closely tied up with the most basic issues in philosophy. There is, for example, the ongoing issue of the role of human nature, since there is no doubt that an ability to 'improve' society, as philosophers of the eighteenth-century Enlightenment wished to do, is dependent on an ability to mould human nature to our liking. The only alternative would be the optimistic assumption that humans are not basically selfish or likely to resist genuine co-operation in the interest of others. It is often said that left-wing thinkers tend to deny the existence of a recalcitrant human nature, or to be optimistic of an ability to direct it, while right-wing thinkers despair of going against the grain of human nature, and tend to accept the way things are. Indeed, market economics takes as its starting-point the final, fixed nature of human preferences, while collectivists would stress the way in which they have been constituted by particular societies.

We are pushed back from a consideration of the nature of human society to an assessment of the ability of social science to come to grips with its nature. Margaret Archer, in putting forward what she terms a realist social theory, tries to show how social science has to pick its way carefully between two extremes, one of betrayal, the other of delusion. She writes:

> We would betray ourselves, as well as our readers, by offering any form of scientism with 'laws' which are held to be unaffected by the uses and abuses we make of our freedoms, for this renders moral responsibility meaningless, political action worthless and self-reflection pointless. Equally, we delude one another by the pretence that society is simply what we choose to make it, and make of it, now or in any generation.[11]

Society can be gradually transformed, but even then it resists both our individual and collective efforts. It changes, but cannot be changed in a way anyone wants. It is too complicated, and whatever we do, the fact of unintended consequences will always haunt us. As a result, there are both ontological and methodological implications. We have to face the question as to whether there is such a thing as social reality apart from the understanding of agents. We must also show what kind of social science is then necessary, since social science must depend on a prior philosophical understanding of its nature. This may not always be explicit, but the fact remains that no social science can operate without philosophical assumptions about the nature of society, its relationship to its constituent members, and how we can set about investigating those factors.

The mutual interplay of structure and agency marks one element of this. As Archer remarks, 'the core notion of structure as the simultaneous medium and outcome of action is central to Giddens' structuration theory.'[12] Yet once the element of time is introduced, it must be apparent that things are not so straightforward. The structures of society are part of its inheritance from previous generations. They can be reinforced or transformed through what we do, but running the two elements together, as Archer says, 'precludes examination of their inter-play, or of the effects of one upon the other, and of any statement about their relative contribution to stability and change at any given time.'[13] We may only be able to act in a social context, but our actions do not thereby create the context, any more than the context causes our actions. Conditions are created which render what we do possible, or make it very difficult. The conditions themselves, however, may be outside our control, and even our proper understanding, just as our actions may affect the future choices of other people. A realist social theory holds that social reality is in fact an emergent level, which cannot be analysed out of existence by reducing it to its constituents. We have not given a true account of society when we have described the activities of each of its members, however crucial they may be to its continuance. Their action cannot explain the context in which they occur.

Group Selection

Many will be uneasy about talking of a reality that emerges at a level above that of individuals. They will be concerned that the value of the individual is somehow thereby lessened, because the absolute autonomy of the individual is being questioned. Yet this is to suppose that indi-vidual freedom is of an absolute kind, so that we either have it or do not.

We are all of us constrained by our physical circumstances in some way or other, and all that is being suggested is that our social environment influences our choices, and gives them a context in which they make sense. Just because the various groups to which we belong have a role in forming our lives, it does not follow that we are any the less responsible for our actions. Attention is merely being drawn to an important dimension of our lives, namely the way in which living in communities has as much effect on us as we do on the community.

There is, too, a general suspicion of identifying people through their membership of a group. There is a justified fear of somehow defining individual worth in terms of the way in which people are classified. Racist theories are rightly attacked for doing precisely this. It is, however, surprising how often individuals, sometimes in pursuit of political interests, are eager to be defined in terms of their membership of some group or other. This may itself, paradoxically, even be a racial group, which perhaps wishes to redress a grievance. Often, however, it can be a grouping of a somewhat amorphous kind. The challenge for social science will always be to distinguish between an arbitrary classification of a collection of individuals, and the recognition of a group, which functions in a socially significant manner.

Mention of groups, however, raises again the biological question of group selection. We saw in chapter 8 how it is usually taken for granted in contemporary biology that selection takes place at the individual level. Indeed, one powerful source of extreme individualism in recent years has come from the emphasis on the 'selfish gene' in sociobiology and its allies. Just as sociobiology and evolutionary psychology have been influenced by game theory and the same patterns of thought that lay behind rational choice theory, so they too have had an influence on social science. The reductionism of many biologists, such as E. O. Wilson, has been very marked, but the problem with reductionism is precisely that it is no respecter of levels. In other words, it may emphasize the individual at the expense of society, but its concentration on the replication of individual genes means that it even tends to lose sight of the individual except as some vague vehicle for genes. Once, though, it is recognized that genes must co-operate for an individual to flourish, it will be seen that concentration on the lowest level cannot always explain what is going on. An insistence, for instance, on selection at the level of the individual rather than the group begs the question as to why it does not rather operate at the lower level of particular genes.

Matters have been further complicated in recent years by the way in which some see units of culture as themselves replicators on analogy with genes. These units have been called 'memes', following the lead given by Richard Dawkins. The idea is that memetic selection drives the evolution of ideas in the interests of replicating memes. This is supposed to happen in a way analogous with the biological mechanisms of selection. It is plausible to view genes as real parts of our DNA. It is much less so to split culture into recognizable and stable units, which can be transmitted separately across societies and generations. The idea treats culture in an overtly mechanistic way, in which reason and individual choice can have no place. Humans certainly imitate each other and are swayed by the pressure of their peer groups, but that does not mean that everything can be seen in terms of the impersonal spread of memes. The latter, which are human creations by definition, are being reified, and given an autonomous life of their own. Our cultural environment can provide a context in which genes can succeed or fail in being passed on. It is unhelpful, however, to break that environment up into arbitrary packages which are then thought to drive human behaviour. Susan Blackmore says that in 'memetics' 'we should expect to find behaviour that is in the interests of the memes, as well as behaviour serving the genes'.[14] Yet this is to separate us from the contents of our culture in a totally illegitimate way. We may well be influenced by our cultural context, just as we each contribute to it. It does not have an existence so apart from us that it can mould us to its advantage.

Because memes can be shared, they could be seen as contributing to the fitness of a group and in fact increasing differences between groups. This might then help to provide a renewed case for group selection. Other arguments have also, however, been put forward to make a renewed case for what had been a discredited position in biology. Genes can compete against each other in the same individual, in a way that does not contribute to the benefit of the organism as a whole. Sober and Wilson maintain that 'if gene-level selection is stronger than individual level selection, then genes will evolve that make individuals less fit'.[15] This raises the question as to whether such genes can be successfully passed on, and reinforces the case for seeing the importance of the individual as vehicle. Sober and Wilson suggest that adaptation at the individual level may then be explained,[16] but the door is opened to the idea of groups as adaptive units. They ask: 'If individuals can be vehicles of selection, then why can't groups?' They proceed to argue for the importance of seeing groups as relevant to the process of selection, suggesting, for instance, that 'altruism can evolve to the extent that altruists and non-altruists become concentrated in different groups'.[17] They would then expect that the altruistic group would do significantly better than its competitor. They argue that 'the fact that individuals are such good vehicles of selection, managing to suppress evolution within themselves as well as they do, suggests that the population structure can itself evolve'.[18] Selection can occur, they argue, at different levels. Just as the individual is as important as the gene, so the existence of the group can explain characteristics that an appeal to individuals leaves on one side. Some traits, such as altruism, can increase the relative fitness of groups, and that is what is meant by group selection. It is not intended to be an alternative to individual selection, but an addition to it.

Arguments rage about some of the legitimacy of the idea of such group selection, but its relevance to social science is clear. If biologists can accept that the idea of a social grouping is not only relevant to biology, but can be used to explain basic biological mechanisms, the strongly individual slant given by concentration on genes and their vehicles is put into question. The point is not that we should replace an emphasis on individuals with one on groups, but that sometimes appeals to the existence of a group can explain some behaviour, and indeed put constraints on it. Even some biologists envisage that there might be such a thing as social reality. The perennial problem is how to divide humans into groups in a way that may not be quite arbitrary. It is always tempting to explain fundamental social differences by an appeal to membership of different groups. Yet if the differences define the groups, the argument becomes circular.

The fundamental issue remains, however, as to whether everything must be explained in terms of individual behaviour, or whether that behaviour is itself constrained by the communal context in which it takes place. Even if society cannot be blamed for our behaviour, it may place limits on what can be done, as well as providing its own opportunities, which individuals could not produce individually. The mere organization of society, and the apparatus of social control and law enforcement, can explain some human behaviour. As Sober and Wilson point out 'Human groups are like single genomes, which achieve their unity by being organised to prevent subversion from within as much as possible.'[19] They conclude that 'group selection has not been the only force in human evolution but in all likelihood it has been a tremendously powerful force.'[20] It seems that even in biology the remorseless drive to explain everything only in terms of the individual can now be questioned.

Notes

1   H.-G. Gadamer, *Truth and Method*, 1975, p. 364.
2   Ibid., p. 351.
3   Ibid., p. 404.
4   Ibid., p. 405.
5   Ibid.
6   Ibid., p. 277. Also see my *The Shaping of Man*, 1982, p. 55ff.
7   See the chapter on Kant in my *Ideas of Human Nature*, 2nd edn, 1999.
8   Ibid., p. 131.
9   R. Rorty, *Philosophy and Social Hope*, 1999, p. xxv.
10 A. Giddens, *The Third Way*, 1998, p. 65.
11 M. Archer, *Realist Social Theory*, 1995, p. 2.
12 Ibid., p. 13.
13 Ibid., p. 14.
14 S. Blackmore, *The Meme Machine*, 1999, p. 154.
15 Elliott Sober and David Sloan Wilson, *Unto Others: The Evolution and Psychology of Unselfish Behaviour*, 1998, p. 90.
16 Ibid., p. 88.
17 Ibid., p. 26.
18 Ibid., p. 97.
19 Ibid., p. 332.
20 Ibid., p. 333.

12

The Philosophical Basis of Social Science

Critical Realism

Social science cannot ignore philosophical assumptions, since they will help to govern the focus of its attention. A realist social theory, for example, holds that the social world comes previously structured. It does not wholly depend for its character on the present agreement, acceptance, or even understanding of present participants in it. An analysis of society in terms of individuals negotiating in a market is bound then to be deficient. That is the why the notion of social groups is relevant. As Roy Bhaskar himself puts it, agents 'are always acting in a world of structural constraints and possibility that they did not produce'.[1] Bhaskar's work has been influential in giving rise to a whole movement in social theory, calling itself 'critical realism', and his analysis of the nature of society is closely connected with the methodology he believes social science should adopt. There will, he says, inevitably be an 'analytical dualism', which recognizes that the conditions under which action takes place, and the actions themselves, should be kept separate. Society is not the same thing as the individuals who make it up, any more than the behaviour of individuals can explain on its own the working of international finance. Bhaskar writes:

> Social structure, then, is both the ever-present condition and the continually reproduced outcome of intentional human agency. Thus people do not marry to reproduce the nuclear family, or work to sustain the capitalist economy. Yet it is the unintended consequence (and an inexorable result) of, as it is the necessary condition for, their activity.[2]

As we have seen in earlier chapters, people cannot marry unless there is a society with an institution of marriage, which is recognized as such. At the same time, marriage will not continue as an institution unless people do marry. It will wither, as more and more live together without seeing the need for any formalized public recognition of the fact. It would not be passed on to future generations, as it has been passed on in previous generations. Some people may welcome this, others may be indifferent and others again may fear the social consequences. Thus individual choice does matter, even though it is constrained by external circumstances. The choices I make have to be made against a pre-existing social background. Crime flourishes more in some social contexts than others, but it is facile to say that the context causes the crime. Some actions are made easier and others more difficult in some situations. Similarly, it is easier to get a good education if one comes from some social backgrounds rather than others. That does not mean that some people are not prepared to pay the cost (not necessarily financial) of being educated in spite of the social obstacles placed in their path. 'Society' does not cause behaviour, but it can make some behaviour easier or more costly. Then it becomes a matter of personal determination and responsibility as to whether the opportunities are seized and obstacles surmounted. The structures of society are very often real, but so is the fact of individual choice. The challenge to social science, both in its practice and its philosophy, is to take both aspects seriously, without over-emphasizing the one at the expense of the other. That, at least, is the message of critical realism.

The emphasis on the fact that we are born into pre-existing structures, which we can reproduce or transform, stems from the recognition of emergent features in social systems. It gives social science a real function. Human conceptions and understanding form the starting-point for society, but as Bhaskar puts it, 'actors' accounts are both corrigible and limited by the existence of unacknowledged conditions, tacit skills and unconscious motivations'.[3] Social science is thus in a position, it is alleged, to stand back from all this and discover what is really going on. The suggestion is that because they are investigating the nature of an independently existing reality, 'the social sciences can be "sciences" in exactly the same sense as natural ones, but in ways that are as different (and specific) as their objects'.[4]

Realism in the social sciences is rather different, in one respect, from realism in the physical sciences. Social reality is anthropocentric in a way that physical reality could never be. Even if present social reality was not wholly created wholly by us ourselves, it was certainly produced by humans. Its mechanisms are not alien to us, and are not likely therefore to be ultimately beyond our control. Yet that does not mean that social scientists are inventing its nature rather than discovering it. Because of its complicated nature, stretching through the generations, it is perfectly possible that those who bring a scientific, and detached understanding to social questions should be able to identify mechanisms which particip-ants in ongoing social processes may not be fully aware of. It is not surprising that economists can identify patterns in the activity of financial markets that particular dealers, caught up in everyday transactions, may not see or understand.

Roy Bhaskar and some of those who espouse critical realism have a further aim in view. Just as Marxists have looked to the possibility of the liberation and freedom through the removal of oppressive social arrange-ments, there is a strand in critical realism whose wish is to identify the constraints upon our actions precisely in order that they can be removed. The idea of critical realism indeed suggests that it is not enough to note the actual state of affairs in society. This has within it the seeds of emancipa-tion. Knowledge, it is hoped, can bring freedom. This is particularly so since our increasing knowledge of social structure would include, as Margaret Archer puts it, the detection of 'the causal efficacy of properties which do not depend upon consciousness of them'.[5] In other words there are conditions in society which exert their influence but which go far beyond the construction of the human mind. We have seen how the brute exercise of power in a material form can control the forming and working of constitutions. The existence of a large armoury goes far beyond issues of understanding or social negotiation. Crude threats, depending on over-whelming military might, are rooted in issues of power and wealth, which constrain society in ways that philosophical idealists talking of 'social construction' cannot deal with. As Archer says, 'there is no warrant for confining social causes to the mental or to meanings'.[6]

The emancipatory potential of critical realism sometimes has a rather Marxist tinge. Yet it must be true that understanding what produces a situation may give us the ability to do something about it. Indeed there is little point in furthering social science if it is useless in helping to deal with the human world in which we are situated. If, though, themes of emancipation and liberation are stressed too much, the question is bound to be raised as to how 'scientific' social science is. Are 'values' entering into it too much? Can it become a weapon in a war of ideologies, while remaining the detached, objective judge of reality that critical realism seems to suggest it should be? There does seem at times to be a strong Enlightenment flavour about what critical realists say. In addition, does simply knowing about something give us the power to intervene? We can know the cause of a disease, without being able to cure it. We can perhaps be set on a path that might one day produce a cure, whereas total ignorance would not even have got us that far. Knowledge on its own, however, will not necessarily be liberating. Hungarians, Poles, and others, no doubt knew in the forty years after the Second World War that their actions were constrained by the threat of Russian force, but that of itself did not give them power to do anything.

Emancipation, through knowledge, is essentially a process that takes place through the medium of human consciousness. Bhaskar, however, looks to a causal order in reality, with mechanisms at work that outstrip human consciousness. That is the whole point of critical realism. The social is, he believes, a precondition for any intentional human act, and, he argues, the pre-existence of social forms 'establishes their autonomy as possible objects of scientific investigation' while 'their causal power establishes their reality'.[7] Society acts as an independent variable, creating the background against which we can act, and constraining our actions. The reality of such social structures, however, has to predate our consciousness, if it is to have a causal impact on it. It cannot be the product of the understanding, our knowledge or our language. Denying the ontology of society and making its processes logically dependent on our knowledge is for Bhaskar an instance of what he terms the 'epistemic fallacy'. Indeed no realist, in any sphere, will countenance the running together of the reality that can be known with our knowledge of it. Otherwise 'our world', limited as it is, will become synonymous with 'the world'. No distinction can then be made between reality and our conceptions of it (whoever 'we' may be). We suddenly by definition become suspiciously omniscient, without the ability to distinguish what there is and what we know.

All such blurring of knowledge and reality is clearly based on an idealist philosophy, and many will recognize that the physical world cannot be made to depend on minds or language in this way. Yet it is much less clear-cut in the philosophy of social science that social reality somehow lies beyond the understanding and control of those participating in it. Critical realism refuses to allow that even at this level reality and knowledge, structure and consciousness, can somehow be conflated. Yet the fact remains that social reality must be a human creation in a way that sticks and stones are not.

The existence of power, and other material constraints, suggest that human institutions and social arrangements are themselves the result of factors that can lie beyond mere human intentions. They have an effect on us, but are themselves constrained by external circumstances including human biology and environmental factors such as climate. The factors that help create a viable society come from many quarters, and human design and purpose may be only one of them. That is why they can come to have something of an independent existence and autonomy. Their continuance through time is a subtle matter, having a major influence on the participants, and explicable in terms that social science will hope to elucidate. Yet all this makes the urge for emancipation or liberation hard to implement. It could be that some structures seem to be oppressive, and we judge that we would be better off if they could be radically altered or removed. We may become more conscious of the constraints upon us. Yet the very emphasis on the autonomy of social structure and its comparative independence from our individual consciousness suggests that our growing knowledge of the influences on us is not necessarily enough to gain control of them. Once it is accepted, as a critical realist must acknowledge, that this reality of structure gives it a certain autonomy and causal power, we must recognize that it is not necessarily within our control at all times. We may endeavour to reform, and improve it. We may turn to revolutionary change. The doctrine, however, itself implies that all this may not be enough, even though we must always remember that such structures do not exist apart from the practices that instantiate them.

The more that knowledge is seen as a social product, the more it will appear that structure governs knowledge, rather than the other way round. That is why too great an emphasis on social context can be self-defeating. It is important for critical realism that social scientists can be detached from their surroundings, and are not seen to be merely vehicles of particular social arrangements. They may be enabled by their background. A particular kind of society with a certain level of wealth is necessary for social science to be possible on the first place. In the end, science cannot be the knee-jerk reaction of people embedded in a social context. Social science, like physical science, needs an ability to use a reason that might be influenced by its background, but that can rise above it.

Reason and Realism

Once the role of reason is stressed, some will complain we are back with an Enlightenment conception of reason, which does not pay sufficient attention to the historical and social conditioning of our understanding. Yet we cannot escape relativism, if our judgements are not just constrained, but strongly determined, by our social circumstances. Bhaskar says that 'critical realism claims to be able to combine and reconcile ontological realism, epistemological relativism and judgmental rationality'.[8] He is treading a slippery tightrope here, and courts disaster with his acceptance of the relativity of our knowledge. In one sense, this is a truism, in that our knowledge is always constrained by circumstances. There are always limits on what we can find out, and how we can find it out. Suggesting, however, that what counts as knowledge is dictated by the criteria and standards of our society is to return us to a sociology of knowledge. We must all have sufficient rationality to recognize reality when it confronts us. The more that an independent causal order is stressed, the more it is incumbent on us to be able to recognize it. If we cannot, all science is impossible.

No scientific enterprise can be an automatic response to stimuli, whether physical or social. Scientists have to make reasoned judgements, and that in turn suggests that the possibility of science demands the idea of a rational self, able to assess the evidence and recognize truth. Such an idea is mocked in many quarters, and can be dismissed by postmodernists as yet another Enlightenment illusion, an idea that is the product of a particular time and place. Yet even such a dismissal is itself presumably not mere rhetoric. It is intended as a reasoned argument put forward by those who do not regard themselves as simply repeating the prejudices of their age. The fact that such people enter supposedly rational argument suggests that they think they can see reality for what it is. Without the possibility of rational subjects, who are more than the mere outcome of various solitary causal chains, there can be no rationality.

As Thomas Nagel says, 'Whoever appeals to reason purports to discover the source of authority within himself that is not merely personal, or societal, but universal – and that should also persuade others who are willing to listen to it'.[9] He believes that 'the objectivity of any form of thought must lie in some unqualified thought about how things are'.[10] This places the issue of the role of reason firmly with that of realism.

There need be no suggestion that we are infallible or even usually right. The point is that our reasoning has to purport to be grounded in reality. To echo Nagel again, there are some thoughts which we cannot get outside of.[11] We hold them because we believe that is what the world is like. We do not hold them because of our membership of a group, community or form of life. The issue must in the end be the nature of the world (including the social world) and not just the character of people's beliefs about it. Nagel says: 'We begin from the idea that there is some way the world is, and this, I believe, is an idea to which there is no intelligible alternative.'[12]

Critical realism would have to accept all this, since no realist view could afford to undermine itself by casting doubt on our ability to extract ourselves from our particular social context. A phrase like relativity of knowledge must be used with great care. It must be a fundamental realist tenet that if we obtain knowledge, it is knowledge for everyone. If it is only what passes for knowledge for one society, it is not genuine knowledge. Yet realism must hold, if it is not to be an empty theory, that knowledge is attainable, that reason is not merely historically situated. Historicist attacks on the possibility of a rationality that can transcend context are inevitably attacks on the idea of reality.

The idea of a realist philosophy of science is intended to attack remaining positivist pretensions and to face developments in the understanding of social science from the hermeneutical wing. It thus faces two enemies, which between them have over the years occupied most of the ground in the philosophy of social science. They are still active. The legacy of positivism can be seen throughout social science, particularly in its more unreflective corners. An unremitting emphasis on measurement, and quantification, may have its uses, but inevitably it can imply that if something cannot be measured it is not real. The converse is that, if it is real, it must be measurable here and now. This is pure positivism, reducing reality to the way we are currently able to check it. No realist, at any level, could countenance such an approach. Social structures, such as institutions, will be defined out of existence, since the only grip on them that we might have can occur when we measure and quantify individual behaviour. Positivism must be individualist, and it will also be reductionist, breaking complex webs of relationships and interactions into their component parts.

The other form of opposition to realism stemmed from the arch opponent of positivism, hermeneutics, together with its successors.

The stress on meaning rather than cause, on the whole community rather than the individual agent without any appeal to an objective reality as a constraint, has inexorably led to the emphasis that postmodernism makes on the historically situated nature of our understanding. Instead of seeing rationality as the indispensable medium and presupposition of all thought and language, it sees reason as merely the vehicle of the prejudices of a particular age. It is no wonder that if we are deemed no longer to share those prejudices, it becomes unclear how far we can enter into the thought processes of previous generations. Indeed, the past is made as alien as any remote, 'primitive' tribe appeared to Victorian explorers.

Realism can intervene in the battle between the positivism that looks unreservedly to science, and a postmodernist holism that emphasizes the fact of different traditions. A concentration on science as a method and body of belief without any corresponding stress on what science is investigating inevitably leads to an anthropocentric view of the nature of the world. Those who stress interpretation, and then go on to point out its roots in the passing presuppositions of successive ages do something very similar. They focus on the fact of people's judgements rather than on the content. They show how people's understanding changes over time. We are left with a multiplicity of traditions, perhaps overlapping, which explain who we are and what we understand and believe. Yet even this presupposes that we can somehow abstract ourselves sufficiently from our own context to be able to say that there are different traditions. Postmodernism, at least in some of its moods, implicitly treats changing traditions as social structures which must be as real as any critical realist would hold.

The God's eye view, much disparaged by some thinkers, reappears when it is suggested that we can know enough of different contexts and additions to say that we and our beliefs are constructed by them. We can abstract ourselves sufficiently from our presuppositions to see them for what they are. We know enough of other traditions to see that they are different from ours. Indeed if none of this is possible, any pretence to social science has to be given up. It is tempting to apply the arguments of postmodernism to itself, and to see it as merely the outworking of a particular phase of contemporary thought. One might enumerate the conditions in society, such as the breakdown of religious faith in many quarters, which could give rise to the nihilistic despair that is all too evident in the more extreme versions of postmodernism. Yet this kind of sociology of knowledge, and analysis of the social construction of ideas, is itself scientific in origin and intent. It suggests that theorists can stand back from their own context, and look dispassionately either at it or at other people's. This kind of science is light years away from the intent of much postmodernism.

Neo-positivism

Like many other kinds of opponents, positivism and postmodernism each gain credence because of the perceived shortcomings of the other. E. O. Wilson, the founder of sociobiology, has entered the debate forcibly on the side of science. Indeed, he shows the different extremes of Enlightenment and of postmodernist thinking by saying that 'Enlightenment thinkers believe we can know everything and radical postmodernists believe we can know nothing.'[13] Since he believes that 'science was the engine of the Enlightenment',[14] and he is a champion of science, with its search for testable laws and principles, he is on the side of the Enlightenment. He pursues this project remorselessly, and accepts the reductionism flowing from it, defining it as the breaking apart of nature into its natural constituents. His aim is what he calls 'total consilience', which, he says, 'holds that nature is organised by simple universal laws of physics to which all other laws and principles can eventually be reduced'.[15] This is the goal of 'scientific materialism', which regards the existence of different levels of organization as a mere challenge to science, so as eventually to obtain predictions of complexity from the most fundamental levels.

All this must pose a challenge to social science, and it is not surprising that Wilson is quick to draw conclusions about it. Like the Vienna Circle, he is looking for a basic unity in science, and, like the Vienna Circle, that means for him the dominance of physics, the science of what he regards as the fundamental level. He writes that 'units and processes of a discipline that conform with solidly verified knowledge in other disciplines have proved consistently superior in theory and practice to units and processes that do not conform'.[16] That means that he has little room for the social sciences as presently constituted. He can complains that 'never – I do not think that too strong a word – have social scientists been able to embed their narratives in the physical realities of human biology and psychology, even though it is surely there and not some astral plane from which culture has arisen.'[17] He then assumes that the fact that human genes have enabled us to build cultures and societies means that everything of significance that can be said about those constructions must be explained in terms of our genes. Exactly the same mode of reasoning takes it for granted that because minds arise from brains, and brains are physical, every belief and mental content can be explained wholly in terms of fundamental physical processes. This in fact is not so much consilience between disciplines as the demolition of every putative science in favour of physics. Wilson despairs of the lack of progress he sees evident in the social sciences, and compares this with advances in medical research. His explanation is that medical scientists 'build upon a coherent foundation of molecular and cell biology'.[18] Social science takes little notice, he maintains, of scientific psychology and biology. The result 'is the debilitating failure of the social sciences to communicate with the natural sciences and even with one another'.[19]

Wilson is a good example of someone who believes that the social sciences should be in the business of prediction and control. He says 'People expect from the social sciences . . . the knowledge to understand their lives and control their future. They want the power to predict . . . what will happen if society selects one course of action over another.'[20] He is contemptuous of what he sees as the present inadequacy of social science even to foresee such major events as the breakdown of communism and the rise of nationalism. His solution is to link social science explicitly to natural science, since he believes even the workings of social institutions are reducible to the laws of physics. As he says, 'The main thrust of the consilience world view, and hence the unique qualities of the human species, will make complete sense only when linked in causal explanation to the material sciences.'[21] Culture and and society are profoundly affected, he holds, by our hereditary human nature.

The danger in all this is that society is then seen as ruled by a biological determinism, denying the fact of genuine choice. Wilson, in fact, wants to have it both ways. He advocates an Enlightenment view of reasoned choice, at the same time as he extols the role of science in understanding everything. He advocates what he terms 'a powerful conservation ethic'[22] while suggesting that human behaviour is scientifically predictable. Yet either we are free to choose or reject a particular ethics, or we are determined by forces very often beyond our knowledge and control. Bringing them within the ambit of our knowledge, through science, does not guarantee an ability to control them. Wilson writes: 'The legacy of the Enlightenment is the belief that entirely on our own we can know, and in knowing, understand, and in understanding, choose wisely.'[23] That is the credo of someone who in true Enlightenment fashion equates the growth of knowledge with the use of scientific methodology, and both with a faith in progress and even moral improvement. Yet such a programme has always had its internal contradictions, most strikingly that between the determinism espoused by science, and the freedom that appears necessary for moral choice. Since the days of Kant, that has often appeared an insoluble conundrum. Wilson seems to imply that he is only talking of constraints, such as biological ones stemming from our human nature, rather than causes. In that case, his tough reductionist programme must be much less ambitious in what it can hope to achieve. The fact of human freedom and unpredictability may mean that human society, as the product of unpredictable choices, may not be itself so predictable. On the other hand, if our choices are determined, the Enlightenment vision of a rational pursuit of truth, and of responsible moral choice, must itself be undetermined. Our rational assessments would then be seen as conditioned by circumstances that may be beyond our knowledge. This Enlightenment programme of wisdom through scientific understanding demands reasoning that is not itself wholly within the ambit of causal explanation. Science itself must be the expression of human rationality, and has to presuppose it. It cannot explain it away.

Postmodernism, as its name suggests, is perhaps more sure of what it is against than what it is for. It is against the idea of sure foundations for knowledge, and in fact is opposed to the idea of a separation of the subject and object of knowledge. In thus supposing Enlightenment ideas of the cumulative growth of knowledge, it also stresses, as Gadamer and Wittgenstein have, the way in which we are all caught up in language. Michel Foucault was influenced by French structuralist thought, but is known for his repudiation of any distinction between subject and object. The knower and the known run together in one historical situation. He has argued that what he terms the modern 'episteme' or framework of knowledge, which has existed for the last two hundred years or so, has been bound up with the emphasis on objectivity rather than on language as an end in itself. Now that the role of language is stressed, he asks whether language should not be given priority even over the idea of humanity. He asks:

> Ought we not rather to give up thinking of man, or, to be more strict, to think of this disappearance – and the ground of possibility of all the sciences of man – as closely as possible in correlation with our concern for language?[24]

Foucault, with his concentration on language, and the different historical forms of what he terms discursive practices, is not searching for any universal theory of language. He will have nothing to do with any realistic understanding of the world, or with any notion of a conscious subject existing prior to language. We must all be trapped in the assumptions of our own society. Foucault explains that his purpose 'has been to create a history of the different modes by which, in our culture, human beings are made subjects'.[25] He further asserts that conceptualization 'should not be founded on a theory of the object', but that 'we have to know the historical conditions which have to motivate our conceptualisations'.[26] Thus the notion of a subject, according to Foucault, is very much the product of a particular society, and for this reason he investigates the forms of power that can apparently impose their categories on individuals. He is drawn back from our reasoning to analyse the power relations in society which lead us to reason as we do and to make the distinctions we do. We are no longer to be seen as autonomous agents trying to understand an objective world. Instead, we must be viewed as in the grip of domination through power. Foucault, though, has seen that the most successful forms of imposition of power are not those that depend on threats and tanks. They are those that govern our ways of thought, and the very categories we use. We can then be made into a people that sees certain things as natural and right because that is the way we have been taught to speak. The demolition of the distinction between the subject and object of knowledge, coupled with the stress on the use of power, forms a formidable challenge to the optimistic belief in human autonomy that was the bedrock of Enlightenment thinking. In this, Foucault was much influenced by Nietzsche, operating with his hermeneutics of suspicion.

Postmodernism

Foucault was an early example of a whole wave of contemporary thinking, which espouses a relativism that stresses the priority of social context. He draws attention to the pervasive exercise of power in a social setting. Yet how can Foucault himself be immune to these practices? The more it is shown how our own culture has constructed a world composed of subjects and objects, the more the problem of reflexivity appears. If reality is defined by culture in a particular way, how can individual members of that culture distance themselves from its effects? Foucault must himself do this in order to theorize about it. Once the practices of our culture are laid bare, and we see objectification and subjectification for what they are, we must already have abstracted ourselves from the culture. It seems that we are able to withdraw from the very practices that apparently made us what we are. All forms of social enquiry demand that we can reflect on features of our society without being conditioned by them. Foucault himself remarks that 'maybe the target nowadays is not to discover who we are, but to refuse what we are'.[27] It is banal, but perhaps appropriate, to add that it must be we who refuse what we are. The distinction between ourselves and the way things are, in this case in society, is still crucial.

Like Wilson's faith in science, which depends on a rational autonomy science cannot explain, Foucault's project is inherently unstable. He needs to assume what he wishes to repudiate. He has to suggest that one can understand the way society works, and the way people are historically conditioned. Yet that understanding cannot itself be historically conditioned, if it is to have any general validity. Foucault's whole enterprise presupposes the distinction between subject and object which he wishes to supersede. We cannot understand our own society, let alone reject its influence, without discriminating between ourselves as the possessors of knowledge, and the culture we come to know in a way we did not before. As soon as we stop taking the presuppositions of our society for granted, and can no longer accept as real what we were previously conditioned to accept, we thereby reaffirm our allegiance to a distinction between how things are and how we can see them to be. We may realize that our unquestioning acceptance of certain categories, our 'objectification', is merely the outcome of a particular set of power relations. If this is to be a reason for rejecting what we are, it must be because we realize that reality, even social reality, may not be as we have been conditioned to view it. Indeed if the concept of an objective reality is rejected, there can be no reason to take exception to whatever way we have been conditioned to think. There is nothing to measure it against. It is just an arbitrary fact. The whole manner of Foucault's unmasking of the use of power can only make sense given a commitment to realism rather than the relativism which he appears to encourage. Otherwise, he must be seen as the mere mouthpiece of a particular kind of society, subject to domination by various forms of power. There is then no more need to take his views seriously than those of anyone else. They can lay no claim to truth, and we can be given no reasons for believing them. Foucault would presumably wish to distinguish the historical facts he purveys about, say, prisons or sexuality, from his own views about them. He was attempting to write a form of history, not autobiography. Once reality and conceptions of it collapsed into one another, we must be involved in a mire of contradictions.

Similar arguments apply to the writings of Richard Rorty, who flirts with postmodernism from the standpoint of American pragmatism. He says of pragmatists that 'we hope to replace the reality–appearance distinction with the distinction between the more useful and the less useful'.[28] Yet it is an argument as old as Plato that this relativist move, favoured once by Protagoras, cannot escape the distinction between appearance and reality. It is not a matter of opinion whether something is or is not useful. It may appear useful for certain purposes, but really be deleterious to them.

Rorty places himself firmly on the side of those would attack the Enlightenment, which he says, replaced the idea of some kind of supernatural guidance 'with the idea of a quasi-divine faculty called "reason"'.[29] The suggestion that such reason is a mirage, together with the stress on historical context, continues the secularism of the Enlightenment, and perhaps takes it to its logical conclusion. The minute that human judgement rather than reality is made the arbiter of truth, the way is open to those who to point out its historically varying nature. Any distinction between social constructions and reality is lost, and we cannot separate our beliefs from what they are about. Rorty's philosophy joins with much postmodernism in stressing that the purpose of language is not the representation of reality. It is a tool for our various purposes, and not a mirror. He says, 'Once we give up the idea that the point of discourse is to represent reality accurately, we will have no interest in distinguishing social constructs from other things.'[30] Instead, he maintains that we should merely debate the utility of alternative constructs. Everything is apparently a social construct since all that matters are our purposes. Indeed, since the notion of humanity is itself a construct, it becomes very unclear who we are.

The idea of a social construct is a slippery one, since the whole of society must be constructed. 'Social constructionism' is usually a much more full-blooded thesis, not just pointing to the dependency of society on humans, but suggesting that our whole picture of the world, and indeed 'the world' itself, is a product of social construction. The boldness of the claim that atoms are social constructions should not blind us to the fact that by definition many features of society are socially constructed. The construction of social reality should not be assimilated to the very different claim that reality as such is socially constructed. The postmodernist stress on social construction assimilates different kinds and levels of reality. It not only regards everything as a social construction, in the sense of being an artefact of our minds, but it sees the social scientist as constructing the social reality as it is investigated. The attack on reason can become an attack on the possibility of all scholarship or science. The categories inspired by the social theorist, whether as broad as 'religion' or as specialized as a particular economic theory, can never illuminate reality, since all representation is regarded as impossible. In the end, we have to take it for granted that our ideas are best, since there is no external standard against which they can be judged. Rorty himself betrays this kind of complacency with an explicit assumption of the superiority of American ways. In referring to possible alternatives to a Platonic respect for the fixed and eternal, he says, 'Of these, contemporary America, warts and all, is the best so far discovered.'[31] His criteria for this judgement cannot, by definition, have any universal application, but presumably arise from American pragmatism. His remark is essentially circular. Judged by American standards, America is best.

Conclusion

It would seem axiomatic that we should avoid ethnocentricity. Social science should encourage the dispassionate study of, and comparison between, different societies, if it is to be possible at all. Yet this must involve philosophical presuppositions about the possibility of rationality and the nature of reality. It involves a careful discrimination between levels of reality. Once everything is classified as a social construction, even the conduct of social science itself, every discussion becomes a political negotiation rather than a detached investigation into the nature of reality. This is particularly so when the notion of social construction is such a vague term. It fails to differentiate between an idealist idea of projection by the understanding of participants in a society, and the more robust idea of actually setting up an institution which has the momentum to continue through the generations. There is also an ambiguity about the term 'social' in that it can mean a construction in society or a construction by society. The former aids a realistic interpretation, while the latter veers back to idealism. Whatever defects there may have been in the Enlightenment conception of reason, we can only discover them with the use of reason. Distrust of the Enlightenment cannot be translated into a distrust of all reasoning. A full assault on the possibility of rationality undermines the possibility of all science, including social science. Positivism may have been too optimistic in equating reality with what is accessible to us. It deliberately confused reality with knowledge. Postmodernism has reacted to it by removing the possibility of any knowledge.

One of the difficulties of social science is that the issue of the constitution of social reality is itself hotly contested. Even postmodernists have to live in the physical world, and to depend on its regularity, however much they wish to talk of its social construction. The most rabid postmodernists trust that the aircraft they are travelling on will actually take them to their destination. There is a far deeper problem with social reality. The argument is not just over its philosophical status, but reaches back into the question as to whether the whole notion is ill-conceived. Some have used the contested nature of social reality to suggest that sociology in particular, and social science in general, are not proper intellectual disciplines. This is couched in the allegation that they are not sciences, but the suggestion is that they have nothing to study. At issue is the whole context in which we live our lives. The dispute is not just between those who see science as a narrow search for prediction and control and those who argue for the importance of meaning and interpretation. That is the traditional divide between positivism and hermeneutics. There is also the dispute about whether society means anything more than the conglomeration of individual action.

For the individualist, the role of social reality is suspect from the beginning, in that it constrains the individual. Yet for those who want to improve society, particularly by legislation, this dispute is of the utmost importance. How far can individuals be influenced by changes in social context? How far do institutions or 'structures' matter? Do they have to be fostered in ways other than through individuals and their commitment to them? Can a level called 'society' have a top-down influence on individuals, even if it is also granted that they must have a bottom-up influence as well? This is the stuff of philosophical argument about social science, but it is also central to political controversy. It is vital in the arguments between socialists, liberals and conservatives. The primacy of the community over the individual is a view that can lead to communism. The exaltation of the individual and of the centrality of individual choice and freedom leads straight to liberalism, and even so-called libertarianism. A more cautious respect for individual responsibility, coupled with a recognition of the value of tradition and continuing institutions, leads to conservatism. All operate with a philosophy of social science, and not just a political philosophy. Their view of the functioning of society directly governs the way they think they can intervene in it. Politics not only needs a philosophy of social science. It always operates with one. In fact, the philosophy is often at its most dangerous when it is not recognized and not explicitly defended.

The same is, of course, true of social science itself. It is remarkable how different views of society and the role of the individual can govern whole research programmes. It is vitally important that we see society as it is, and not as we might wish it were. This very notion of society 'as it is' itself betrays a realist emphasis. Yet the whole argument about the existence and composition of social reality is an argument about what there is. Even the idea of social construction leaves open the possibility that collectively we and our predecessors have produced something that can affect us, just as we can influence it. The postmodernist view of construction, tending to the view that constructions are mere projections of our society, goes so far as to imply that they are 'fictions', which are merely ideas guiding us. The controversy about social reality is not about whether it is constructed. It is about how far it is a mere reflection of our minds, and how far it generates its own effects, just as a tall building can affect the weather and wind speeds in its immediate vicinity. This indeed can happen in spite of the best of intentions of the architect and builders. Postmodernists may see us as the creatures of a tradition, but they are not willing to think in terms of the operation of cause and effect, independently of human understanding. Positivists are, on the other hand, happy to do just that, but tend to analyse the situation on the basis of the influence of one individual on another. To make sense of the operating of 'social reality', they have to reduce it to individual, and then to physical, terms. Critical realism, on the other hand, takes the idea of human construction seriously, but is willing to concede that social structures can and do have an effect on us, as well as being affected by us. It can itself run the risk, though, of stressing social structures at the expense of any substantial notion of the self. However much society inhibits us, we are not its creation.

It matters which view we adopt. If one sees the basic purpose of social science as prediction and control of the workings of society, this itself will alter people's expectations of what is possible. Assumptions about the function of social science inevitably involve a commitment to one picture or another of human society. We cannot study anything, society included, without making up our minds about what it is we are studying. Because we are ourselves human, we will find that our most basic conceptions about human needs and interests are involved. We cannot look at human society without some conception of human nature, and if we try it, we will find it impossible to make comparisons between societies, or even to understand one society from the standpoint of another. I cannot become a social scientist without facing the question who 'I' am. This constitutes a radical difference from physical science. I can normally study the behaviour of material objects without being constantly brought face-to-face with myself, and with what I think important and valuable in human life.

Social science is riddled with controversies that are difficult to resolve. The illusion that it could investigate 'facts' was an attempt to avoid this unpalatable conclusion. Yet once we recognize that the practice of social science cannot be detached from philosophical assumptions about people's nature and the way that society is formed and changed, we should not despise it for this. Far from being an inadequate copy of 'proper' science, it is wrestling with some of the most important questions facing humanity. Empirical social science must itself start from a properly articulated philosophical base if it is to be successful. Quantitative analysis, and measurement, of whatever kind, is of little use without an understanding of what is being measured and why it matters. The philosophy of the social sciences cannot be an optional activity, indulged in by those reluctant to get on with the real empirical work. It is the indispensable starting-point for all social science.

Notes

1   Roy Bhaskar, 'General Introduction', in *Critical Realism: Essential Readings*, ed. Margaret Archer, Roy Bhaskar, Andrew Collier, Tony Lawson and Alan Norrie, 1998, p. xvi.

2   Ibid., p. xvi.

3   Ibid.

4   Ibid., p. xvii.

5   Margaret Archer, 'Introduction to Part II', in *Critical Realism*, p. 199.

6   Ibid.

7   R. Bhaskar, *The Possibility of Naturalism*, 1979, p. 31.

8   Bhaskar, 'General Introduction', in *Critical Realism*, p. xi.

9   Thomas Nagel, *The Last Word*, 1997, pp. 3–4.

10   Ibid., p. vii.

11   Ibid., p. 13ff.

12   Ibid., p. 81.

13   Edward O. Wilson, *Consilience: The Unity of Knowledge*, 1998, p. 40.

14   Ibid., p. 22.

15   Ibid., p. 54.

16   Ibid., p. 198.

17   Ibid., p. 183.

18   Ibid., p. 182.

19   Ibid., p. 191.

20   Ibid., p. 181.

21   Ibid., p. 267.

22   Ibid., p. 292.

23   Ibid., p. 297.

24   M. Foucault, *The Order of Things*, 1970, p. 386.

25   Foucault, 'The Subject and Power,' in *Michel Foucault: Beyond Structuralism and Hermeneutics*, ed. H. Dreyfus and P. Rabinow, 1982, p. 208.

26   Ibid., p. 209.

27   Ibid., p. 217.

28   R. Rorty, *Philosophy and Social Hope*, 1999, p. xxii.

29   Ibid., p. xxvii.

30   Ibid., p. 85.

31   Ibid., p. 85.

Glossary

The definitions are not intended to be exhaustive, but merely indicate how the terms are used in this book.

adaptation Any physical structure, or behaviour, that aids an organism's ability to survive and reproduce.

alienation A term used in Marx's early writing to denote the dehumanization of people confronting the products of their social activity. Their labour becomes a commodity, apparently independent of the producer.

altruism Serving the interests of others, without any regard to the cost to the agent.

anti-realist Any position which denies the realist claim concerning the logical independence of reality from human minds and concepts.

atomistic Any view holding that persons or events must be understood separately rather than merely as part of a wider whole. Opposed to holism.

behaviourism The analysis of apparently private mental phenomena, such as pain, in terms of publicly observable behaviour.

causal law The correlation of two independent types of events so that the occurrence of one is explained by the occurrence of the other.

causation The process whereby an event is produced by another independent one.

collectivist Anyone treating people in groups and not as individuals.

concept The way we think of something and pick it out. Concepts can be shared and are sometimes identified with words in a language.

conceptual relativism The view that the nature of our concepts depends on the particular society we belong to. The concepts of one society cannot be translated into those of another.

conceptual scheme The whole set of our concepts. Arguments rage over whether humans can have different schemes, or must all share the same one.

consciousness The private awareness of the world, directly accessible to the person possessing it in a way that is not available to others.

contextualist Someone who emphasizes the social background of any practice as the source of its meaning.

counterfactuals They posit what would have occurred if circumstances had been different in some significant way. They are relevant for the establishment of causal laws.

critical realism The view that agents act in a social world that is already structured, but which they can in turn transform.

culture Whatever is passed by teaching from one generation to the next and is not inherited.

cultural determinism The view that culture is the sole influence on humans.

cultural materialism The grounding of culture in a material base, so that its features can be explained in terms of, say, economic factors.

cultural relativism The stress that everything can be judged only by the standards of its own culture. An African culture, for example, should not be judged by European standards.

deduction The logical derivation of a conclusion from premisses. One would not be able to assert the premisses and deny the conclusion without self-contradiction.

determinism The view that every event has a cause.

dualism The view that the physical and the mental are distinct kinds of events, so that one cannot be reduced to the other.

egoism The evaluation of everything solely in terms of one's own interests.

emergent properties Characteristics that are possessed by an entity or collection of entities, but not by the parts which compose it.

empirical Pertaining to human experience. An empirical science produces knowledge from experience such as observation and experiment.

empiricism The view that all knowledge is obtained from human experience.

the Enlightenment A movement extolling the central importance, and the autonomy of, human reason, in the place of authority and tradition. It is widely seen as a phenomenon of the eighteenth century, inspiring the American Declaration of Independence, and the French Revolution. Its roots lie, however, in the seventeenth century with such thinkers as the Cambridge Platonists.

epiphenomenon An experience or feature of one which has no causal influence.

epistemology The philosophical study of the basis of our knowledge.

ethnomethodology An attempt to examine empirically the ways in which meanings are produced in social practice. It holds that all knowledge is a social creation, even itself.

ethology The study of animal behaviour.

eugenics A science, later discredited, which stressed the importance of biological inheritance, and wished to improve human genetic constitution.

evaluation A term often distinguished by empiricists from description, so that whatever is evaluative is non-factual. It implies the making of a value-judgement.

evolution The process by which different species acquire their characteristics through natural selection.

existentialism A philosophical position which emphasizes the central importance of the individual subject or self as the source of meaning and values. All understanding has to derive from experience of one's own self and situation.

expressive Revealing an attitude to the world as opposed to saying anything about the world.

fact Something that is the case. Often opposed to value on the grounds that facts are part of the fabric of the world, and values are not.

false consciousness The misapprehension of features of a society, so that one does not perceive social reality as it is.

falsificationist The stress on the importance of being able to refute a theory rather than conclusively verify it.

fitness A biological term referring to an organism's capability to survive and reproduce. The kinds with greatest fitness become more prevalent in a population.

form of life Wittgenstein's term for the way in which words are embedded in particular practices and cannot be understood apart from them.

foundationalist An epistemological position resting knowledge on an incorrigible and certain basis.

free-rider Anyone who receives the benefits of a collective policy while avoiding the costs of contribution.

free will The ability to make uncaused, but rational choices.

functionalism The explanation of human institutions in terms of their contribution to the good of society as a whole.

gene The basic unit of heredity, composed of DNA.

gene–culture co-evolution The thesis that genes and culture can act on each other.

genetic determinism The view that important features of society can be explained solely by reference to genes.

group selection The controversial alternative to individual selection. It is the biological process by which one group of individuals leaves more descendants than another group. Kin selection is one accepted form of group selection.

hermeneutics The attempt to elucidate meaning, first in ancient texts and, by analogy, in all human activity.

holism The insistence that societies must be understood as wholes and not in terms of their parts. Thus individuals, and particular events, can be understood only in their social context.

humanist Someone opposed to naturalism, who stresses the separate nature of the human.

hypothesis In science, a possibility which is entertained and put to empirical test.

idealism The view that existence depends logically on perception by a mind.

ideology A system of ideas justifying the vested interests of a group. The term normally assumes their falsity, but it can be used, more generally, to refer to any definition of reality.

incommensurability The inability to compare, or interchange, the terms of one theory with those of another.

individualism The stress on the individual rather than society as a whole, so that the latter must be understood in terms of its members.

individual selection The biological process whereby an individual and its direct descendants are favoured through evolution.

infrastructure Whatever underlies and causes the manifest features of society.

kin selection The biological process whereby relatives, who probably share the same genes, are favoured by the behaviour of an individual. Thus even self-sacrifice can encourage the spread of one's genes, if relatives are thereby kept from harm.

language-game Wittgenstein's term for the manifold, rule-governed ways in which language is embedded in human activity.

legitimation A social process whereby institutions are explained and justified.

materialism The doctrine that everything, even the apparently mental, is composed of matter or totally dependent on it.

metaphysical Anything beyond the scope of physical science which is accessible to reason. Positivists would deny the possibility of metaphysics.

memes Alleged units of culture which can be replicated, by analogy with genes.

methodology The theory of the aims and procedures of a discipline.

natural selection The biological process whereby different genetic types produce more or less offspring, and the fittest come to predominate.

naturalist In the context of social science, someone who believes that society can be studied in the same way as the physical world. Often, but not necessarily, linked with positivism.

nihilism The possibly incoherent view that nothing matters and that there is no such thing as truth. It is therefore a matter of indifference what one believes or does.

objectivity The property of being the case whatever human conceptions of the matter may be. Also used to signify detachment from all particular points of view.

ontology The theory of what there is.

paradigm Used by Kuhn to signify examples of scientific practice in 'normal science' that provide the starting-point for traditions of research.

phenomenology The analysis of human consciousness or subjective experience, 'bracketing-off' questions of truth.

phylogeny The evolutionary history of a group of organisms or species, contrasted with 'ontogeny', referring to the development of a single organism in its lifetime.

physicalism The doctrine that everything can be explained in terms of physical laws.

pluralism The view that different theories and ways of life have to be accepted as they are, and one should not seek supremacy or domination.

positivism The view which considers scientific method the only path to truth. Opposed to any form of metaphysics.

postmodernism A reaction to the Enlightenment conception of rationality. It is opposed to the idea of foundations for human knowledge, or of an independent reality. All judgements have to be made from a particular perspective or tradition.

private language A language which can only be understood by one person. The possibility was attacked by Wittgenstein, who stressed the social character of language.

public good A benefit available to more than one person (such as street-lighting).

rational choice theory An analysis of human behaviour in terms of the maximizing of benefits, and minimizing of costs, as measured by individual preference.

rationality The ability to reason to what one considers true conclusions. Mere ignorance is not a sign of irrationality, but inconsistency is.

realism The view that reality is objective and logically independent of all beliefs and conceptions of it.

reciprocal altruism The performance of acts beneficial to others so that similar benefits may be received in return.

reductio ad absurdum An argument which refutes a position by demonstrating the absurd consequences necessarily following from it.

reductionism The attempt to demonstrate that statements about one kind of entity are in reality about a different kind – for example, that statements about minds are really about bodies.

reflexivity The application of a statement, or theory, to itself. If all beliefs are socially conditioned, then so must be the belief that they are.

reification The viewing of human products as if they were entities independent of human beings.

relativism The view that there are different, possibly self-contained, traditions and ways of life, each to be judged only in accordance with its own standards.

ritual A practice performed for its own sake, regardless of any beliefs accompanying it.

scepticism Doubt about whether we can obtain knowledge.

science In general, any form of knowledge, but more particularly that body of empirical knowledge obtained through observation and experiment.

scientific revolution Kuhn's term for a major change in scientific outlook as one theory is discarded in favour of another.

sense–data The basic elements of sense-experience, according to many empiricists. They were supposed to be neutral in respect of differing theories and interpretations and to form the foundation of empirical knowledge.

social construction The forming of institutions, concepts and perhaps even reality, through collective rather than individual agency.

social reality The humanly constructed environment, formed by beliefs and expectations, and contrasted with physical reality.

social structure A sometimes vague term used to denote constraints and influences exerted by society and individuals, in economic and other forms.

society A group of individuals co-operating with each other. Arguments rage over whether emergent properties can be attributed to it.

sociobiology The biological study of the development of social behaviour in all organisms including humans.

sociology of knowledge A discipline which attempts to uncover the social origins of belief.

solipsism The denial of any reality beyond myself and my experiences.

subjective Used in opposition to 'objective', and referring to what is accessible to only one person or has validity for only one person.

symbolist In anthropology, a stress on what is expressed by behaviour such as a rain-dance, as an alternative to viewing it as a means to the achievement of a desired end.

tabula rasa 'A blank slate'. Refers to the empiricist belief that we are born without any inherited tendencies.

theory In science, a system of laws and hypotheses which attempts to explain and predict observable phenomena.

theory-laden Any word or concept which can only be understood within the context of a particular theory. It could not normally be used within another theory without a significant change of meaning.

underdetermination A term used, particularly by Quine, pointing out that a theory may not be deducible from empirical evidence but may go far beyond it.

universal A property attributed to all the individuals of a certain kind. The universal, redness, is thus predicated of all red objects.

utility maximizing A procedure to achieve the best possible outcome in a situation. Utilities (namely, whatever is preferred) are estimated, together with the probability of obtaining them. The rational action is considered the one with the maximum expected utility.

values Often thought to be matters of personal choice and preference, and contrasted with 'facts' about which agreement can be obtained.

value-freedom The ideal of making judgements about facts without the intrusion of values.

verificationism The adoption of the positivist view of the link between verification and meaning.

verification theory of meaning The doctrine that the meaning of a statement consists in our knowledge of the way its truth can be ascertained.

Verstehen Term used by Weber to denote what he considered to be the practice of social science, namely the interpretative understanding of human agents and of the meaning they themselves attached to their actions.

Bibliography

Alexander, R. D., 'The Search for a General Theory of Behavior', *Behavioral Science*, 20, 1975.

Archer, M., *Realist Social Theory: The Morphogenetic Approach*, Cambridge, 1995.

Archer, M., Bhaskar, R., Collier, A., Lawson, T. and Norrie L. (eds), *Critical Realism: Essential Readings*, London, 1998.

Barnes, B., *T. S. Kuhn and Social Science*, London, 1982.

Beattie, J., *Other Cultures*, London, 1964.

Berger, P. and Berger, B., *The War over the Family*, London, 1983.

Berger, P. and Kellner, H., *Sociology Reinterpreted*, London, 1982.

Berger, P. and Luckmann, T., *The Social Construction of Reality*, London, 1967.

Bhaskar, R., *A Realist Theory of Science*, Hassocks, Sussex, 1978.

—— *The Possibility of Naturalism*, Brighton, 1979.

Blackmore, S., *The Meme Machine*, Oxford, 1999.

Bloor, D., *Knowledge and Social Imagery*, London, 1976.

—— *Wittgenstein: A Social Theory of Knowledge*, London, 1983.

—— 'A Sociological Theory of Objectivity', in S. C. Brown (ed.), *Objectivity and Cultural Divergence*, Cambridge, 1984.

Bloor, D. and Barnes, B., 'Relativism, Rationalism and the Sociology of Knowledge', in M. Hollis and S. Lukes (eds), *Rationality and Relativism*, Oxford, 1982.

Braithwaite, R. B., 'An Empiricist's View of the Nature of Religious Belief', in I. T. Ramsey (ed.), *Christian Ethics and Contemporary Philosophy*, London, 1966.

Buchanan, A., 'Revolutionary Motivation and Rationality', *Philosophy and Public Affairs*, 9, 1979–80.

Cohen, R. S. and Wartofsky, M. W. (eds), *Epistemology, Methodology and the Social Sciences*, Dordrecht, 1983.

Cupitt, D., *Taking Leave of God*, London, 1980.

Cupitt, D., *The World to Come*, London, 1982.

Davies, N. B., 'Competition for Scarce Resources', in *Current Problems in Sociobiology*, King's College Sociobiology Group, Cambridge, 1982.

Dore, R. P., 'Function and Cause', in A. Ryan (ed.), *The Philosophy of Social Explanation*, Oxford, 1973.

Durkheim, E., *The Elementary Forms of the Religious Life*, London [1915] 1971.

—— *The Rules of Sociological Method*, ed. S. Lukes, London, 1982.

Evans-Pritchard, E., *Witchcraft, Oracles and Magic among the Azande*, Oxford, 1937.

Fay, B. and Moon, J. D., 'What Would an Adequate Philosophy of Social Science Look Like?', *Philosophy of the Social Sciences*, 7, 1977.

Feyerabend, P., *Science in a Free Society*, London, 1978.

—— *Philosophical Papers*, vol. I, *Realism, Rationalism and Scientific Method*, Cambridge, 1981.

—— *Philosophical Papers*, vol. II, *Problems of Empiricism*, Cambridge, 1981.

Flew, A., 'Human Choice and Historical Inevitability', *Journal of Libertarian Studies*, 5, 1981.

Foucault, M., *The Order of Things*, London, 1970.

—— 'The Subject and Power', in *Michel Foucault: Beyond Structuralism and Hermeneutics*, ed. H. Dreyfus and P. Rabinow, Brighton, 1982.

Frazer, J., *The Golden Bough*, London, 1922.

Freeman, D., *Margaret Mead and Samoa: The Making and Unmaking of an Anthropological Myth*, Harvard, 1983.

Gadamer, H.-G., *Truth and Method*, London, 1975.

Garfinkel, H. and Sachs, H., 'On Formal Structures of Practical Actions', in J. C. McKinney and E. A. Tiryakin (eds), *Theoretical Sociology*, New York, 1970.

Giddens, A., *The Third Way*, Oxford, 1998.

Graham, L., *Between Science and Values*, New York, 1981.

Grandy, R., 'Reference, Meaning and Belief', *Journal of Philosophy*, 70, 1973.

Grene, M., 'Dogmas of Empiricism', in R. S. Cohen and M. W. Wartofsky (eds), *Epistemology, Methodology and the Social Sciences*, Dordrecht, 1983.

Haan, N., Bellah, R., Rabinow, P. and Sullivan, W. M. (eds), *Social Science as Moral Inquiry*, New York, 1983.

Habermas, J., *Knowledge and Human Interests*, London, 1972.

—— 'Interpretative Social Science vs. Hermeneuticism', in N. Haan et al. (eds), *Social Science as Moral Inquiry*, New York, 1983.

Harris, M., *Cultural Materialism*, New York, 1979.

Hempel, C., *Philosophy of Natural Science*, Englewood Cliffs, NJ, 1968.

Hesse, M., *Revolutions and Reconstructions in the Philosophy of Science*, Brighton, 1980.

Hirsch, F. and Goldthorpe, J. H., *Political Economy of Inflation*, London, 1978.

Hollis, M. and Lukes, S. (eds), *Rationality and Relativism*, Oxford, 1982.

Holmstrom, N., 'Rationality and Revolution', *Canadian Journal of Philosophy*, 13, 1983.

Homans, G. C., 'Bringing Men Back In', in A. Ryan (ed.), *The Philosophy of Social Explanation*, Oxford, 1973.

Hume, D. *Hume's Ethical Writings*, ed. A. MacIntyre, New York, 1965.

Kahn, V. Saifullah, 'Pakistanis in Britain: Perceptions of a Population', *New Community*, 5, 1976.

Kuhn, T. S., *The Structure of Scientific Revolutions*, Chicago, 1962.

―― *The Essential Tension*, Chicago, 1977.

Lévi-Strauss, C., *Structural Anthropology*, New York, 1963.

―― *The Savage Mind*, London, 1966.

―― *Structural Anthropology*, vol. II, London, 1977.

Luckmann, T., *Life-World and Social Realities*, London, 1983.

Lukács, G., *History and Class Consciousness*, London, 1971.

Lumsden, C. and Wilson, E., *Genes, Mind and Culture: The Co-evolutionary Process*, Cambridge, Mass., 1981.

―― *Promethean Fire: Reflections on the Origin of Mind*, Cambridge, Mass., 1983.

MacDonald, G. and Pettit, P. *Semantics and Social Science*, London, 1981.

McPherson, M. S., 'Want Formation, Morality, and Some Interpretive Aspects of Economic Inquiry', in N. Haan et al. (eds), *Social Science as Moral Inquiry*, New York, 1983.

Malinowski, B., *A Scientific Theory of Culture*, Chapel Hill, NC, 1944.

Mannheim, K., *Ideology and Utopia*, London, 1936.

Marx, K., *Capital*, New York, 1967.

―― *A Contribution to the Critique of Political Economy*, New York, 1970.

―― *Early Texts*, ed. D. McLellan, Oxford, 1971.

―― *Grundrisse*, ed. M. Nicolaus, Harmondsworth, 1973.

Mead, M., *Coming of Age in Samoa*, 1928, reprinted London, 1943.

Mehan, H. and Wood, H., *The Reality of Ethnomethodology*, London, 1975.

Meltzer, B. N., Petras, J. W. and Reynolds, L. T., *Symbolic Interactionism, Genesis, Varieties, Criticism*, London, 1975.

Merton, R., *Social Theory and Social Structure*, New York, 1968.

Nagel, T., *The Last Word*, Oxford and New York, 1997.

Neurath, M. and Cohen, R. S. (eds), *Otto Neurath: Empiricism and Sociology*, Dordrecht, 1973.

Passingham, R., *The Human Primate*, Oxford, 1982.

Phillips, D. Z., 'Primitive Reactions and the Reactions of Primitives', Marett Lecture, Exeter College, Oxford, 1983.

Popper, K., *The Poverty of Historicism*, London, 1957.

Quine, W. V., *Word and Object*, Cambridge, Mass., 1964.

Rawls, J., *A Theory of Justice*, Oxford, 1972.

Reynolds, V. and Tanner, R., *The Biology of Religion*, London, 1983.

Rorty, R., 'Method and Morality', in N. Haan et al. (eds), *Social Science as Moral Inquiry*, New York, 1983.

—— *Philosophy and the Mirror of Nature*, Oxford, 1980.

—— *Truth and Progress: Philosophical Papers*, vol. 3, Cambridge, 1998.

—— *Philosophy and Social Hope*, Harmondsworth, 1999.

Rosenberg, A., *Sociobiology and the Pre-emption of Social Science*, Oxford, 1981.

Rubinstein, D., *Marx and Wittgenstein: Social Praxis and Social Explanation*, London, 1981.

Runciman, W. G., *A Treatise on Social Theory*, vol. I, Cambridge, 1983.

Ryan, A. (ed.), *The Philosophy of Social Explanation*, Oxford, 1973.

Saussure, F. de, *Course in General Linguistics*, London, 1974.

Schutz, A. *Collected Papers*, vol. I, *The Problem of Social Reality*, and vol. II, *Studies in Social Theory*, The Hague, 1962.

Searle, J., *The Construction of Social Reality*, Harmondsworth, 1995.

—— *Mind, Language and Society*, London, 1999.

Sen, A., 'Rational Fools', *Philosophy and Public Affairs*, 6, 1977.

—— *Choice, Welfare and Measurement*, Oxford, 1982.

Sober, E. and Wilson, D. S., *Unto Others: The Evolution and Psychology of Unselfish Behavior*, Cambridge, Mass., 1998.

Stigler, G. and Becker, G., 'De Gustibus non est Disputandum', *American Economics Review*, 67, 1977.

Taylor, C., 'Rationality', in M. Hollis and S. Lukes (eds), *Rationality and Relativism*, Oxford, 1982.

Thatcher, M., *The Downing Street Years*, London, 1993.

Trigg, R. *Pain and Emotion*, Oxford, 1970.

—— *Reason and Commitment*, Cambridge, 1973.

—— 'Thought and Language', *Proceedings of the Aristotelian Society*, 79, 1978–9.

—— *Reality at Risk: A Defence of Realism in Philosophy and the Sciences*, Brighton and Totowa, NJ, 1980.

—— *The Shaping of Man: Philosophical Aspects of Sociobiology*, Oxford, 1982, and New York, 1983.

—— 'The Limits of Science', in H. P. Duerr (ed.), *Science and the Irrational*, New York, 1984 (also in H. P. Duerr (ed.), *Der Wissenschaftler und das Irrationale*, Frankfurt, 1981).

—— 'The Sociobiological View of Man' in S. C. Brown (ed.), *Objectivity and Cultural Divergence*, Cambridge, 1984.

—— *Rationality and Science*, Oxford, 1993.

—— *Rationality and Religion*, Oxford, 1998.

—— *Ideas of Human Nature*, 2nd edn, Oxford, 1999.

Turner, D., *Marxism and Christianity*, Oxford, 1983.

Van den Berghe, P., 'Human Inbreeding Avoidance: Culture in Nature', *Behavioral and Brain Sciences*, 6, 1983.

Weber, M., *Theory of Social and Economic Organization*, trans. A. Henderson and T. Parsons, London, 1947.

—— *Selections*, ed. W. G. Runciman, Cambridge, 1978.

Wilson, E. O., *Sociobiology: The New Synthesis*, Cambridge, Mass., 1975.

—— *On Human Nature*, Cambridge, Mass., 1978.

—— *Consilience: The Unity of Knowledge*, New York, 1998.

Winch, P., *The Idea of a Social Science*, London, 1958.

—— 'Understanding a Primitive Society', in *Ethics and Action*, London, 1972.

Wittgenstein, L., *Philosophical Investigations*, Oxford, 1958.

—— *On Certainty*, Oxford, 1969.

—— *Remarks on Frazer's Golden Bough*, ed. Rush Rhees, Retford, 1979.

Young, L. A. (ed.), *Rational Choice Theory and Religion*, New York, 1997.

Index

action, 47
adolescence, 85–6
agreement, 31, 211, 212, 214, 226
alienation, 65
altruism, 144, 152, 170–4, 179, 204, 233
Archer, M., 229–30, 237
arms race, 141
astrology, 24, 90
atomism, 25, 57
autonomy of individual, 225
Azande, the (African tribe), 89, 92, 104

Barnes, B., 35, 37
Beattie, J., 103
Becker, G., 137–8
behaviourism, 44, 49, 122, 124
Berger, B., 160–1
Berger, P., 40–2, 52–4, 57, 58, 128, 160–1
Bhaskar, R., 235–8, 240
birth control, 81, 165–6
Blackmore, S., 232
Bloor, D., 31, 32, 33–8
Boas, F., 84, 86
Braithwaite, R., 99

capitalism, 181, 216–17
caste system, 77–9, 151, 182
causal explanation, 190, 191
causation, 8
    top–down, 211, 251
causes, and constraints, 245
central planning, 199, 206
chaos theory, 198
classes, 56
coherence theory of truth, 117
collectivism, 151
communism, 199
community, 207, 231
concepts, 26, 70, 73–4, 222
conceptual relativism, 82, 114
consciousness, 44–5, 53, 55, 59, 64, 65, 161, 162, 191, 238, 239
conservatism, 32, 159, 225, 251
consilience, 243
contextualism, 26
convention, 211, 217
co-operation, 136, 144, 171
Copernican revolution, 222
cost–benefit analysis, 202, 205, 213
critical realism, 237–8, 241, 252
cultural determinism, 86
cultural materialism, 155
cultural relativism, 100, 177

culture, 155, 156, 157, 167–70, 173,
176–9, 182, 185, 211
Cupitt, D., 99

Darwin, C., 164
Davidson, D., 109
Dawkins, R., 232
desire, 135, 137
determinism, 115, 119, 143, 165,
183–5, 190, 195, 198, 244, 245
disagreement, in economics, 133
in science, 121
dualism, 50, 58, 68
duck-rabbit drawing, 6, 14
Durkheim, E., 57, 60–2, 158, 177,
200, 202–3, 205

economics, 4, 51, 125, 133, 135, 137,
138, 139, 143, 180, 200, 229
egoism, 139, 140, 144, 146, 171, 179
emancipation, 237, 238
emergent levels, 55, 211, 230
empiricism, 3–7, 13, 25, 34, 50, 112,
114, 132
Enlightenment, 220, 221–5, 229, 240,
243, 245, 248, 250
epistemic fallacy, 238
epistemology, 13, 94
foundationalist, 5, 12, 95
and ontology, 24
ethnomethodology, 91–3, 95
eugenics, 84
Evans-Pritchard, E., 104
evolution, 164, 176
evolutionary psychology, 231
explanation, 'deductive-nomological',
8

facts, 7
contrasted with values, 112–15
false consciousness, 40, 56, 66, 160,
216, 217, 218

falsificationism, 117
family, 62, 157, 160–1, 170
feminism, 118, 160–1
Feyerabend, P., 17–20, 24, 120
Flew, A., 192, 194–5
form of life, 19, 29, 70, 73, 74, 82, 92,
99
Foucault, M., 209, 245–8
Frazer, J., 96
freedom, 143, 144, 187, 190, 191,
195, 230, 237, 245
Freeman, D., 85–7
free-rider, 145–6, 152, 179
functionalism, 157–9, 177
functions, manifest and latent, 158
fusion of horizons, 221

Gadamer, H.-G., 218–22, 245
gene culture: co-evolution, 167, 173,
182, 183, 188
genes, 164–6, 173, 182, 231–3,
244
Giddens, A., 227–8
Graham, L., 121
Grandy, R., 109
Grene, M., 25
group selection, 172, 230–4

Habermas, J., 122
Hare, R. M., 6
Harris, M., 151, 155–6, 162, 168,
183
Hempel, C., 7–8
hermeneutics, 3, 94, 124, 219, 241,
250
of suspicion, 217
Hesse, M., 114–15, 123
historicism, 192
history, 1, 4
Hobbes, T., 140, 144
holism, 57, 105, 181, 206, 222, 242
Homans, G. C., 159

humanist approach, 3
human nature, 54, 60, 61–2, 87, 110,
 124, 137, 155, 188–9, 193, 221,
 223, 229, 245, 252
human rights, 209, 217
Hume, D., 6, 7, 9, 112, 113, 132, 142
Husserl, E., 48

Iannaccone, L. A., 201–2, 204
idealism, 52, 55, 65, 162, 250
ideology, 115, 126–9, 147, 148, 153,
 181
imperialism, 78
incest, 54, 167–8
incommensurability, 15, 19, 82
individualism, 5, 147–50, 163, 181,
 205, 222, 227, 231
individuals and society, 50, 55, 66,
 148–9, 206–7
infinite regress, 36–7
inflation, 193
infrastructure, 156, 162, 168
institutional facts, 211
institutions, 207–15, 228, 236, 250
Internet, 214–15

justice, 143

Kant, I., 222
Kellner, H., 40–1, 128–9
kin selection, 170
Kuhn, T. S., 13–17, 20, 28, 30, 33,
 36, 71, 82, 95, 114, 218

language, 210, 220, 248
 learning, 74, 82
 private, 26
language-game, 19, 27, 29, 33
law, of nature, 193, 243
 of non-contradiction, 35
 sociological, 194, 198
leash principle, 165–6, 176–7, 182

liberalism, 144, 251
libertarianism, 251
logic, 35
London Missionary Society, 85
Lukács, G., 41
Luckmann, T., 52–4, 57, 58
Lumsden, C., 165, 166–7, 170, 173,
 176, 182, 185–6, 188–9, 190

MacDonald, G., 100, 110
Mcpherson, M., 138–9
magic, 90, 96, 100, 102–3
Malinowski, B., 122, 157
Mannheim, K., 126–7
markets, 200, 206, 225, 228, 236
 and information 199, 227
marriage 52, 58, 66, 75, 81, 157, 210
Marx, K., 10, 64–6, 126, 147–9, 153,
 206, 216, 223
Marxism, 150–4, 216–17
meaning, 42
 and use, 26
measurement, 198
Mehan, H., 91–2
'memes', 232
memetics, 232
metaphysics, 98, 183
modernity, 221
monogamy, 75

Nagel, T., 240–1
nations, 223–4
naturalism, 3
nihilism, 90

objective reality, 11, 20, 37–8, 95
objectivity, 34, 122, 123
original sin, 150

pain, 26, 73–4, 122
paradigm, 13–16, 30, 218, 225
Passingham, R., 46

Pettit., P., 100, 110
phenomenology, 50, 59, 161
Phillips, D. Z., 105–6
philosophy, 13, 25
    of science, 4, 7, 16–17, 23, 114
phobias, 170
physicalism, 211
physics, 198, 244
Plato, 248
pluralism, 201
politics, 226, 228, 251
Popper, K., 117, 192, 194–5
positivism, 3, 23, 44–5, 48, 90, 97, 99,
    112, 117, 119, 122, 196, 200,
    241, 243, 246, 250
postmodernism, 209, 219, 222, 223,
    242, 243, 245, 246–9, 250
power, 199, 212, 213, 239, 247
pragmatism, 248–9
prayer, 101–2, 108
prediction, 117,123, 125, 135, 184,
    191, 196, 198
preferences, 136–7, 143–4, 199–200
'primitive' societies, 89, 96, 112
'prisoners' dilemma', 139–40, 200
projection, 210
Protagoras, 248
psychology, 1, 195
public goods, 136, 145–6

quantum mechanics, 4, 13, 184
Quine, W. V., 10–12, 14

rational choice theory, 200, 201–5
rationality, 89–90, 92, 94–5, 98, 104,
    109, 112, 143, 146, 147, 204–5,
    221, 222, 224, 225, 240, 245,
    249
Rawls, J., 143–4
realism, 24–5, 118, 148, 236, 240,
    241, 248
    critical, 237–8, 241, 252

realities, 92
reality, 222, 223, 225, 238, 247, 248,
    249
reason, and realism, 240–1, 248
    and tradition, 221, 222, 224
    detached, 225
    universal, 223
reciprocal altruism, 171, 179
reductionism, 64, 122, 163, 178,
    185–6, 187, 199, 231, 243
reflexivity, 36, 37, 40, 92, 119
reification, 54, 57, 206
relationism, 126
relativism, 18, 21, 24, 28, 29, 76, 82,
    93, 126, 148, 188, 240, 246, 248
religion, 30, 39, 62, 99–100, 106–7,
    156, 160, 177, 200, 201–5
responsibility, 206, 208
revolution, 152
Reynolds, V., 77
Ricoeur, P., 217
ritual, 98, 105–8
roles, 57
Rorty, R., 94–6, 124, 208–9, 226,
    248–9
Rubinstein, D., 51, 58–9
rules of a society, 26–9, 59, 66
Runciman, W. G., 190–1

Samoa, 83–7
scepticism, 50
Schutz, A., 48–9, 55–6, 92
science, and objectivity, 24, 45
    and rationality, 90, 97
    and truth, 117
scientific revolutions, 13–14
Searle, J., 210–14
self, 206, 221
self-evidence, 35
selfishness, 134–5, 172
Sen, A., 135, 137, 142
sense data, 4–6, 10, 50

simplicity, 117
Sober, E., 232–3
social anthropology, 1, 26, 75–7, 83, 87, 93, 99, 105, 108
social construction, 209, 248, 249–50, 251
social engineer, 125
social psychology, 1, 51
social reality, 41, 48, 57, 64, 125, 191, 203, 211, 225, 230, 233, 236–7, 239, 249, 251, 252
socialism, 216
society, 50, 69, 156, 202, 206, 207, 212, 235, 236, 238
  and time 207, 239
sociobiology, 118, 156, 163–74, 177–83, 185–6, 188–90, 193, 231
sociology, 1, 40, 51, 56, 125, 138–9
  of knowledge, 28, 33–8, 127, 139, 243
solipsism, 59–60, 70
Stark, R., 201
Stigler, G., 137–8
structures, and agency, 227–8, 230
  of society, 217, 227, 228, 235, 236, 239, 250
subject and object, 245–6
subjective meaning, 48
subjectivism, 59, 70
subjectivity, 48, 122
suttee, 79
symbol, 101, 108, 185
symbolic interactionism, 60
symbolist, 103, 105, 107

taboos, 169
tabula rasa, 167
Tanner, R., 77–8
Taylor, C., 101
Teresa, Mother, 172
Thatcher, M., 205–6

theology, 1
theoretical entities, 4, 11
theory, choice of, 114, 117
  priority of, 9, 114
tradition, 46, 208, 216–19, 224, 225, 228, 242
translation, 12, 82–3, 109
truth, 38, 94, 99, 101, 117, 118

underdetermination of theory, 11–12, 114
unintended consequences, 207, 212
utility maximizing, 136–7, 145, 152, 202, 204–5

value freedom, in physical science, 120–1
  in social science, 7, 121, 125, 129, 132, 189
values, contrasted with facts, 7, 112–15, 130, 134, 189
Van den Berghe, P., 168, 169, 176
verificationism, 50, 98
Verstehen, 19, 20, 48, 50, 67, 73
Vienna Circle, 3–4, 9, 10, 27, 243
virginity, 85
voting, 142

Weber, M., 48, 49, 55–6, 72, 132–3
Wilson, D. S., 232–3
Wilson, E. O., 165, 166, 167, 170–1, 172, 173, 176–8, 182, 185–6, 187–90, 231, 243–5, 247
Winch, P., 30, 67, 72, 74, 80–1, 104, 105
witchcraft, 24, 89, 104
Wittgenstein, L., 6, 19, 26–30, 32, 33, 34, 50, 58, 62, 66, 69, 70, 73, 92, 95, 96, 105, 147, 211, 218, 220, 245
Wood, H., 91–2